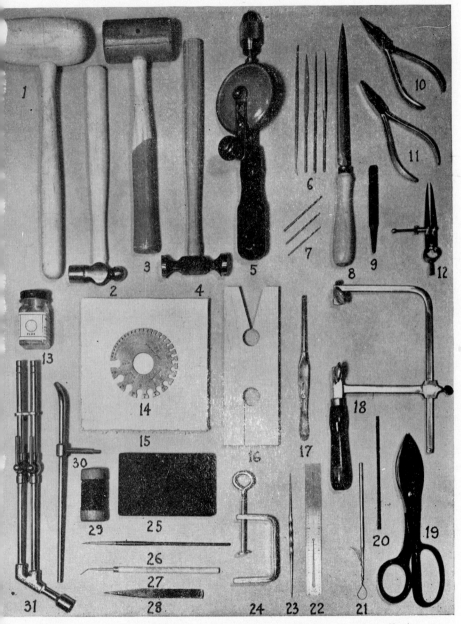

1. *Wood Mallet*; 2. *Ballpeen Hammer*; 3. *Rawhide Mallet*; 4. *Planishing Hammer*; 5. *Hand Drill*; 6. *Needle Files*; 7. *Twist Drills*; 8. *Half Round File*; 9. *Center Punch*; 10. *Round Nose Pliers*; 11. *Flat Nose Pliers*; 12. *Dividers*; 13. *Soldering Flux*; 14. *B&S Wire Gauge*; 15. *Asbestos Block*; 16. *Bench Pin*; 17. *Soldering Tweezers*; 18. *Jeweler's Saw Frame*; 19. *Jeweler's Shears*; 20. *Jeweler's Saw Blades*; 21. *Dentimetre*; 22. *Steel Rule*; 23. *Scratch Awl*; 24. *Bench Pin*; 25. *Charcoal Block*; 26. *Soldering Brush*; 27. *Spatula*; 28. *Tweezers*; 29. *Binding Wire*; 30. *Mouth Blow Torch*; 31. *Gas & Air Blow Torch*

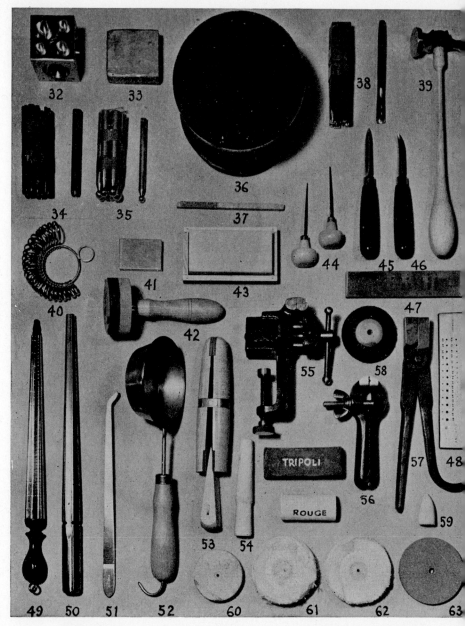

32. *Dapping Die*; 33. *Lead Dapping Block*; 34. *Dapping Die Cutters*; 35. *Dapping Die Punches*; 36. *Pitch Bowl*; 37. *Scotch Stone*; 38. *Chasing, Repousse, Tools*; 39. *Chasing Hammer*; 40. *Ring Sizes*; 41. *Steel Surface Plate*; 42. *Shellac Stick*; 43. *Oil Stone*; 44. *Gravers*; 45. *Scraper*; 46. *Burnisher*; 47. *Square Hole Draw Plate*; 48. *Round Hole Draw Plate*; 49. *Ring Gauge*; 50. *Ring Mandrel*; 51. *Copper Tongs*; 52. *Pickle Pan*; 53. *Ring Clamps*; 54. *Felt Ring Buff*; 55. *Table Vise*; 56. *Hand Vise*; 57. *Draw Tongs*; 58. *Bristle Buffing Wheel*; 59. *Felt Cone*; 60. *Felt Buffing Wheel*; 61. *Muslin Buffing Wheel*; 62. *Chamois Buffing Wheel*; 63. *Emery Grinding Wheel*

JEWELRY & ENAMELING

BY

GRETA PACK

SECOND EDITION

D. VAN NOSTRAND COMPANY, INC.

TORONTO   NEW YORK   LONDON

NEW YORK
D. Van Nostrand Company, Inc., 250 Fourth Avenue

TORONTO
D. Van Nostrand Company (Canada), Ltd., 25 Hollinger Road

LONDON
Macmillan & Company, Ltd., St. Martin's Street, W.C. 2

Library of Congress Catalogue Card No. 53-8772

06552b25
PRINTED IN THE UNITED STATES OF AMERICA

To CLEO MURTLAND, *Associate Professor, University of Michigan,* in appreciation for generous assistance which went into the making of this book.

PREFACE

This book is a work manual as well as a source of technical information for instructors and pupils interested in the art and technique of jewelry making. Since work procedures, techniques, and their sequence are the same for the instructor as for the learner, whether taught in the class room or self taught, no sections are directed specifically to one or the other.

Sections one through three deal with the basic processes of jewelry making with the techniques for each process specified in the order in which they are to be carried through. Jewelry construction in section four is presented in the same way.

Throughout the book, emphasis is given to the application of the principles of design which must be used as consistently with metal as they are used with other working mediums. The beginner finds it necessary to pay strict attention to proportion, mass, balance, unity of line and form because the medium and the processes with which he is engaged are influenced by the weight, solidity, and texture of the material. If these things are observed systematically the effect of processes will become apparent as the work progresses, and by the same token, as he gains experience he will learn to select processes which give weight, lightness, or strength to the article under construction and thus to the design. Design and technique must balance if the jewelry produced is to have art value.

The author wishes to acknowledge with appreciation the encouragement given by Louise L. Green, Head of the Art Department of Cass Technical High School, during the preparation of this book. Thanks are due also to members of the Jewelry classes who have lent jewelry for illustrations; to Laurine Muethel, a student in the Commercial Art class, who made the drawings, and to Richard G. Askew, and Elmer L. Astleford who did the photographic work. Acknowledgment is made also to Camp Hanoum for the photograph of the camp workshop, and to the Cleveland Dental Manufacturing Company for permission to use the photograph and drawing of the casting machine.

Detroit, Mich.,   G. P.
  January, 1941.

CONTENTS

THE SAMPLER

A working knowledge of the techniques and processes used in jewelry making should be learned as soon as possible. In order to accomplish this, the first piece of work should be a simple article which involves a number of processes and the use of various tools.

For beginners in the day school where pupils work in the jewelry room daily and with the same purpose that dominates other class work, the sampler is a most effective way of establishing fundamentals of work techniques at the very beginning of work with metals and metal tools. A well made sampler is a profitable and interesting piece of work and, when the design is good, the finished article is attractive and useful. However, the most important feature is that it is a constant reminder of methods and techniques which are to be applied over and over again in other articles the jewelry worker creates. Since the foundation of techniques and workmanship is begun in this article, the student should incorporate in his design as many materials as possible and include in his plan processes which require the tools most commonly used. The samplers on page 4 show a wide range of processes.

These designs are pictorial. A figure or an animal depicting action is usually more effective for a sampler than an abstract design, because the units brought together to show the whole demonstrate the unity of the design more effectively for the beginner than the assembly of the units of an abstract design the relationship of which may not be so evident.

Since the purpose of the sampler is to introduce beginners to processes, tools, and materials mainly, but with good design a close second, it is important to keep the design simple enough to demonstrate the relation between techniques and design. Rhythm and movement shown in the flat twist used for the costumes of the skaters, and the waved wire line of the floor, the choice of round and flat coils for hair style contribute to the sense of design which the beginner needs to develop early in work with metals.

3

Sampler—The Circus

Sampler—The Skaters

These samplers illustrate ways of developing a simple idea into a working design. The beginner is expected to work out a similar plan for a sampler to be executed in metals with metal tools. This is done after the instructor has demonstrated the various processes and explained the essential points to be kept in mind when creating a well designed sampler.

As the work progresses it is also important to acquire the ability to follow the instructor's demonstration and to understand oral explanations and written directions since these three methods are used throughout the beginning stages of this form of craft work.

When the demonstration has been completed, the student is ready to make his design. Two items must be kept in mind: (a) the design must be created around the processes to be used, and (b) the jewelry methods used for the sampler must be consistent with good design and jewelry technique. One of the samplers selected for analysis includes practically all the elements to be used in creating the first metal piece.

Processes, tools, and materials are listed below in the order in which they are to be used.

PROCESSES

Gauging the metal	Drawing wire
Transferring the design	Twisting wire
Sawing	Coiling wire
Filing	Cutting disks
Annealing	Doming
Pickling	Stamping
Chasing	Bezel making
Repoussé	Ball making
Soldering	Coloring
Cleaning	Finishing
Polishing	Stone setting
Carving	Drilling
	Mounting

TOOLS

Metal gauge (Brown and
Sharpe)
Soft pencil
Gas plate
Burnisher
Scratch awl
Bench pin
Jeweler's saw frame
Jeweler's saw blade #1/0
Needle files
Jeweler's hand vise
File card or brush
Blow torch
Earthenware pitcher
Copper pickle pan
Copper tongs
Pitch bowl and holder
Chasing tools
Repoussé tools
Chasing hammer
Pliers
Borax slate or saucer
Jeweler's shears
Camel's hair brush
Steel tweezers
Polishing motor
Felt, bristle buffing wheels
Granite pan
Scrub brush
Shellac mounting stick
Steel surface plate
Gravers
Oil stone

Bench (secured to the floor
or wall)
Bench vise
Round hole draw plate
Draw tongs
Hand drill
Steel or iron hook about ½
inch
Rolling mill
Small round mandrel
C clamp
Two boards (Fig. 23)
Mallet
Small wire nails
Wire cutters
Dapping cutters
Lead dapping block
Dapping punches
Dapping die
Stamping tools
Wax stick stone lifter
Dentimetre
Dividers
Burnisher
Tin snips
Fine muslin, cotton, or cham-
ois buffing wheels
Center punch
Twist drill
Steel wire buffing wheel

MATERIALS

Sterling silver sheet 24-gauge

Silver solder sheet medium 28-gauge
Sterling silver wire 14-gauge
Sterling silver sheet 28-gauge
Fine silver wire 18-gauge
Copper sheet 18- or 20-gauge
Sketch pad
Tracing paper
Fine pumice powder
White bees wax
Soft cloth
Chalk
Fine emery cloth
Charcoal block
Pickle (sulphuric acid solution)
Prepared pitch
Light oil
Kerosene cloth
Prepared borax or prepared flux for hard solder

Boric acid and alcohol solution
Powdered rouge
Gum tragacanth
Binding wire 26- and 18-gauge
Scotch stone
Tripoli cake
Rouge stick
Soda, ammonia, and water solution
Yellow flake shellac
Alcohol
Yellow bees wax
Potassium sulphide solution
Whiting
Floor wax
Wool cloth
Tin wire 30-gauge

SAMPLER DESIGN

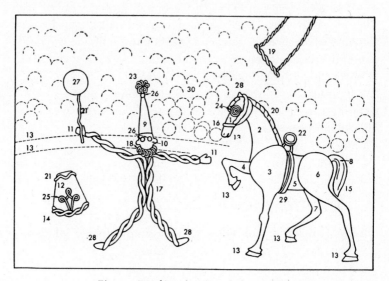

Fig. 1.—*Working drawing of the sampler*

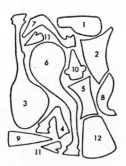

Fig. 2.—*Pattern for cutting*

PROCESSES	NUMBERED
Saw out parts	1 through 12
Chase lines	13 and 30
Repoussé	1 through 12
Solder pieces	1 through 12
	14, 17 through 29
Carve lines	15 and 16
Draw wire	14, 18 through 21
	and 23 through 29
Twisted wire	17 and 19
Incised wire	20
Flat open twist . . .	14

DIRECTIONS FOR EXECUTING THE SAMPLER

As the student selects processes he should be able to determine their suitability to the design he wishes to develop. A sampler design is created as follows:

1. Draw the design on paper as shown in Fig. 1.
2. Analyze the design and divide it into parts.
3. Determine the processes to be used.
4. Indicate and list the processes with numbers on the drawing.
5. Make the layout as shown in Fig. 2.
6. Execute the design in metal.

When the design and the processes to be used are determined, the student is ready to proceed with the construction of the piece he has planned, according to the following work plan.

PROCESSES	CENTRAL FIGURES
Gauging p. 346	Gauge the sheet, sterling silver 24-gauge.
Transferring the Design p. 33	Transfer the layout on the silver. Use the wax method.
Sawing p. 31	Saw out the parts numbered 1 through 12.
Filing p. 25	File all sawed edges smooth.
Annealing p. 18	Anneal the silver to make it pliable.
Pickling p. 22	Pickle the silver after annealing.
Chasing and Repoussé p. 77	Chase the lines numbered 13 on 3, 4, 6, 7. Repoussé the pieces numbered 1 through 12.
Soldering p. 38	Solder together the parts numbered 1 through 8. Solder together the parts numbered 9 and 10.
Pickling	Clean in pickle after soldering.
Cleaning p. 70	Remove excess solder and scratches from the surface of the silver.
Polishing p. 71	Polish the silver.
Carving p. 87	Carve the lines numbered 15 and 16.

WIRE WORK

Gauging	Gauge the wire, sterling silver 14-gauge.
Annealing	Anneal the wire.

PROCESSES

Wire Drawing p. 96	Draw the wire to the sizes required 14, 18 through 21 and 23 through 25. (Fig. 22)
Cutting	Cut the wire in required lengths.
Twisting p. 101	Twist wire for 17. (Fig. 27) Make an incised wire for 20. (Fig. 29) Make a flat open twist wire for 14. (Fig. 30) Make a flat smooth waved wire for 21. (Fig. 31)
Coiling p. 106	Make a band of overlapping rings for 18. (Fig. 38) Coil the wire into a knob of rings for 23. (Fig. 39) Coil the wire to form a flat coil for 24. (Fig 42) Coil the wire unit for 25. (Fig. 46)

SOLID ORNAMENTS

Gauging *Cutting* *and* *Doming* p. 120	Gauge the sheet, sterling silver 28-gauge. Cut a disk for 27. Dome the disk.
Stamping p. 123	Stamp three forms for 28.
Bezel *Making* p. 153	Make the bezel and bearing for the stone 22. (Fig. 56) Solder a ring on the back.
Gauging *Ball Making* p. 122	Gauge the wire, fine silver 18-gauge. Make three balls of equal size for 26.

JOINING THE CENTRAL FIGURES
WIRES AND SOLID ORNAMENTS

PROCESSES

Soldering

Solder

Two lengths of 17 in the center 28, 11, 18 to 17.

18 to 10.

26 to 9 and 23.

21 to 27 and 11.

21, 25, 14 to 12.

1 through 8 together.

24, 28, 20 to 1 and 2.

20 to 2.

22 and 29 to 5.

19 together.

FINISHING

Pickling   Clean in pickle.

Cleaning   Remove excess solder with file, or scotch stone.

Polishing   Buff all surfaces. Use tripoli cake with felt or bristle buffing wheel to remove marks of the file or scotch stone.

Wash in a warm solution of soda, ammonia, and water to remove oil.

Polish with rouge stick and muslin buffing wheel.

Wash in solution of soda, ammonia, and water.

Coloring   Color with potassium sulphide solution.

p. 72   Remove excess color with whiting.

Polish with chamois buffing wheel.

Stone setting   Set the stone.

p. 165

PROCESSES   MOUNTING PLATE

Gauging   Gauge the sheet, copper 18- or 20-gauge.
                     Cut the copper the desired size.
Chasing   Chase the lines numbered 13 and 30.
Coloring   Color the copper with potassium sulphide so-
p. 72   lution.
                     Remove excess color with whiting if desired.
Polishing   Polish with a steel wire buffing wheel.
Finishing   Wax the surface with floor wax and polish.

MOUNTING THE DESIGN

Drilling   Lay all parts on the copper plate and balance.
p. 35   Locate points to connect the design to the plate.
                     Mark and center punch these points.
                     Drill holes at punch marks with a #70 drill.
Carving   Carve lines 16 in the mounting plate.
Mounting   Loop the 30-gauge tinned wire over parts of
                     the sampler.
                     Insert the ends of the wire through the holes
                     in the copper background.
                     Twist these wires together to hold the design
                     firmly and cut off loose ends.

Work may be begun on any one of the first three sections
of this sampler. The order of processes may vary but each section should be carried through before taking up another in order
to make each experience contribute to a sense of accomplish-
ment. If all parts are constructed, finished, and mounted in an
orderly, well-planned fashion, this experience will give a beginner the sense of workmanship so essential in handwork of this

nature. Consistent planning, systematic procedure, and careful attention to techniques enable the beginner to focus attention upon manipulative processes the mastery of which is craftsmanship.

These principles of workmanship apply also to camp beginners and evening school pupils although, because of limited time and available equipment, their first work may be a simple article, as a ring of wire and balls, or a twisted wire bracelet rather than a sampler. In any case the beginning project must be kept within the range of basic processes, simple substantial construction, and satisfactory design.

II. JEWELRY MAKING PROCESSES

Working Processes
   Annealing
   Pickling
   Filing
Construction Processes
   Sawing
   Piercing
   Soldering
      Soldering with Hard Solder
      Soldering with Soft Solder
      Special Soldering
      Binding Wire—Its Use in Soldering
   Casting
      Metal Casting in Cuttle-bone
      Metal Casting in Dental Investment
Finishing Processes
   Cleaning
   Polishing
   Coloring

JEWELRY MAKING PROCESSES

Processes used in jewelry making are grouped according to the purposes they serve. Annealing, pickling, and filing are termed working processes because they are used to keep the metal in working condition, that is, clean and malleable, as the work on it progresses. Annealing, pickling, and filing do not contribute directly to construction but keep the metal in condition for sawing, soldering, and casting which are construction processes, and for chasing, carving, and repoussé which are decorative processes. Cleaning, polishing, and coloring are finishing processes which bring out the techniques of construction and, if well done, enhance the beauty of the article. If construction and work techniques are poor, finishing processes reveal crudeness of workmanship.

Construction processes in jewelry work must be treated frankly and decoration and ornamentation used for this type of craft work should be consistent with them. A stone set on a curved surface without apparent support is out of keeping with jewelry technique and good design. An article rugged in construction adorned by a dainty stone or delicate wire ornaments loses all the values of good construction that might have been maintained by ornamentation of comparable weight and texture.

It is well to remember that form itself often constitutes the design. When the form is the design, good workmanship becomes the ornamentation. Conversely, poor workmanship may detract measurably from any design values the form may have.

A piece of jewelry may be satisfactory structurally but lack beauty of form. Its decorations may be interesting or beautiful in themselves but deficient in the sense of harmony which is necessary to make them an integral part of a satisfying design. The processes used for jewelry making are the hall marks of good design in this form of craft work.

17

Fig. 3.—Annealing the metal with the blow torch flame.

ANNEALING

Annealing is heating metal to soften it and to render it more pliable. The number of times the article has to be annealed depends upon the amount of rolling, hammering, twisting, bending, and drawing to be done. These processes invariably harden metal in the course of construction and, in order to keep it sufficiently pliable to be worked, annealing may have to be done frequently. The amount and intensity of the heat to be used depends upon the area and the thickness of the piece to be annealed and to the heat retaining qualities of the surface upon which the metal rests when heat is applied as shown in Fig. 3. The distribution of the heat is important in annealing and the worker must learn how to keep the flame spread evenly until the whole piece turns a glowing red. It is the heat which renders the metal pliable.

Tools   Charcoal block
and   Asbestos pad
Working   Annealing pan and charcoal
Materials   Gas and air blow torch
                Iron binding wire 22-gauge
                Snub nose pliers
                Jeweler's shears
                Sheet iron 26-gauge, 2 pieces about 4 inches square

PROCESSES   ANNEALING

Annealing   Lay the metal to be annealed on the charcoal
Sheet   block. If the piece is large use an asbestos pad
Metal   or annealing pan and charcoal.

Light the gas. Start with a loose flame, the size depending upon the gauge and size of the piece to be annealed.

Turn on the air to make the flame blue.

Keep the flame moving.

Remove the flame when every section of the metal has become a glowing red.

Cooling   Cool silver by immersing in water or pickle or
Metal   let stand until cold enough to handle. Gold 14k or under should not be immersed. See Question 7.

Annealing   Coil lengths of wire into a compact circle about
Wire   three inches in diameter to anneal.
Heavier   Bind with iron binding wire as shown in Fig. 4.
Than   Be sure the ends of the coiled wire do not
24 Gauge   protrude.
Which Can   Anneal as described for sheet metal.
Be Coiled

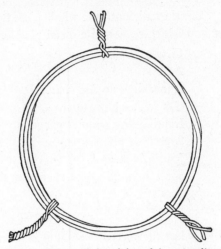

Fig. 4.—*Wire coiled and bound for annealing*

Annealing
Wire
Lighter
Than
24 Gauge

Coil the wire and bind as above.

Place the coil between two pieces of 26-gauge sheet iron.

Bind the iron sheets together with iron binding wire 22-gauge.

Place upon the charcoal block or asbestos pad or in the annealing pan.

Heat the iron sheet with the blow torch until the top piece of iron is red hot.

Turn the iron sheets over and heat the other sheet until it is red hot.

Cut the binding wire from the iron sheets.

Remove and cool the annealed wire.

Annealing
Heavy
Wire
or
Rod

Use a large flame for heavy wire or rod which cannot be coiled.

Lay the piece on the asbestos pad or in the annealing pan.

Commence annealing at one end. Continue slowly until the entire length is annealed.

1. *What hardens metal?*
   Metal hardens when it has been rolled, twisted, hammered, bent, or drawn.

2. *What methods of annealing are used in making jewelry?*
   Metal can be annealed with any heat which is sufficiently intense to produce the red glow required; the gas blow-torch, the gasoline torch, the Bunsen burner, or the alcohol torch are commonly used.

3. *What merit is there in the charcoal block?*
   When charcoal becomes hot it retains heat and reflects it back on the metal.

4. *Why is the asbestos block used?*
   The asbestos block is used to anneal larger work, also to place under the charcoal block to protect the bench from the flame.

5. *What is the annealing pan?*
   The annealing pan is made of sheet iron which rotates on a base. The pan is usually filled with charcoal, which retains and spreads the heat.

6. *When is the annealing pan used?*
   It is used when it is more convenient to rotate the pan than to move the flame.

7. *Can silver, copper, and gold be cooled immediately?*
   Silver or copper may be cooled immediately by plunging it in water or acid while it is still hot. Gold under 14-K, which becomes brittle if cooled too quickly, should be laid aside to cool.

8. *Should metal hammered on lead be cleaned before it is heated?*
   Clean the metal with emery cloth; lead particles eat into the metal when heated.

PICKLING

Pickling is the most satisfactory way to clean a working surface. Silver oxidizes when it is exposed to the air and during all processes which require much heat. The coat of oxide must be removed as a clean surface is essential, especially for soldering. Boiling the metal in pickle is the most effective method for cleaning silver although plunging hot metal in pickle is also effective and simpler, particularly when metal is being annealed.

Pickling is used frequently during the construction of an article. It is also used before buffing and finishing. Sulphuric and nitric acids are commonly used for the pickles.

Tools
and
Working
Materials

Sulphuric acid pickle for silver, gold, or copper
Earthenware pitcher
Copper pickle pan for sulphuric acid
Gas plate
Copper tongs
Soda, ammonia, and water solution
Nitric acid pickle for gold
Porcelain pan for nitric acid
Granite pan

PROCESSES
Preparing
the
Pickle

PREPARATION OF THE PICKLE

For silver, copper, and gold

Sulphuric formula—1 sulphuric acid to 8 or 10 water.

Prepare in a deep earthenware pitcher to avoid splashing.

Pour the acid into the water; sulphuric acid burns.

Heat in a copper pickle pan.

For gold 14-K and over

Nitric Formula—1 nitric acid to 8 water.

Heat in a porcelain pan.

PROCESSES

PICKLING

Pickling
Silver,
Gold
and
Copper

Remove all binding wires.
Place the article of silver, gold, or copper to be cleaned in a copper pan.
Pour enough pickle in the pan to cover the article.
Place the pan on the burner.
Boil the article in pickle until pure white if silver; even coral if copper; self color if gold.

Removing
from
the
Pickle

Remove the article from the pickle with copper tongs.
Rinse thoroughly in cold water.
Wash thoroughly in hot water.
Boil in soda, ammonia, and water solution if there are recessed parts.

Pickling
Gold
14-K
or over

Place the article of gold in a porcelain pan.
Pour enough pickle in the pan to cover the article.
Boil in pickle until a pure gold color appears.
Remove from the pickle as described above.
Rinse thoroughly.

QUESTIONS

1. *Does the pickle have to be used immediately?*
   The pickle may be kept for future use in porcelain or earthenware.

2. *Why should the binding wire be removed from the article before pickling?*
   Pickle reacts on binding wire and discolors silver and gold.

3. *Does this discoloration ruin the article?*
   The discoloration may be removed by buffing as the film of discoloration is thin.

4. *How can the borax glaze be removed from the metal after the soldering process?*
   The article should be boiled in the pickle to remove the borax glaze.

5. *How is scale removed?*
   Remove the scale with fine emery cloth.

FILING

Filing is cutting away metal with a file. It is used to remove rough edges and irregular surfaces. The types of files most commonly used in jewelry making are needle, half round, triangular knife, and rat tail. Other files, four or six inches in length, second, and smooth cut, half round, triangular, flat, riffle, and barrette are also used for jewelry construction and finishing.

The technique to be used in filing depends upon the condition of the metal, the type of surfaces or edges to be produced, and the file selected for the filing to be done.

Any sawed or cut edge or clean surface can be filed without being pickled. An annealed or soldered surface to be filed for construction practically always requires cleaning in the pickle to remove the oxidation or the borax glaze. The latter is difficult, and sometimes impossible, to remove with the file.

Tools	Pickle
and	Copper pickle pan
Working	Gas plate
Materials	Copper tongs
	Steel surface plate
	Wooden mallet
	Table, hand, or ring vise
	File to suit the work and metal
	Emery cloth or scraper
	Chalk
	File card or brush

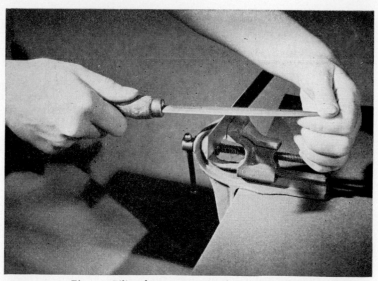

Fig. 5.—*Filing heavy gauge metal using two hands*

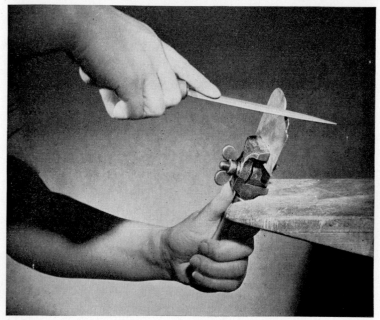

Fig. 6.—*Filing light gauge metal using one hand*

26

PREPARATION FOR FILING THE METAL

PROCESSES

Pickling
p. 22

Pickle the work to be filed to clean and remove any scale which has formed during any heating process.

Straightening

Place the sheet metal on a steel surface plate. Hammer with a mallet to straighten, if necessary.

*Holding
the
Metal*

Hold the article to be filed rigid in a table or hand vise, with pliers, on a shellac stick, or by hand. The selection depends largely upon the size and the shape of the article to be filed.

*Large
Work*

Large work is held in the jaws of the table vise about even with the elbow.

*Small
Work*

Small work may be held higher than the elbow as only arm and wrist movements are necessary for filing.

HOLDING THE FILE

*Grasping
the
File
with
Two Hands
For
Heavy
Work*

Place the handle of the file in the palm of the hand.
Grasp the handle so that the ends of the fingers point upward toward the worker and the thumb lengthwise along the handle.
Hold the point of the file with the thumb and two fingers of the other hand as shown in Fig. 5. The thumb rests on the top of the file for the greatest pressure, changing to the edge when the pressure has to be lessened.

PROCESSES

Holding
the
File
With
One Hand
For Light
Work

Grasp the handle in the way described above. Turn the hand so that the forefinger lies in the direction of the point, and the thumb lengthwise on the side of the handle as shown in Fig. 6.

Chalking

Rub the file with chalk to keep the teeth of the file free from metal filings.

FILING

Filing

Place the pressure on the forward stroke of the file.

Remove the pressure on the return stroke; pressure on the back stroke wears off the points of the teeth.

Remove the burr which remains on the metal after the filing process with a file, scraper, or emery cloth.

Cleaning
the
File

Clean the file at intervals with a file card or brush.

Rub finer files over the rough surface of cloth.

QUESTIONS

1. *What is meant by kind or name of file?*
   The kind has reference to the shape or style of the file such as: flat, half round.

2.. *What is meant by cut?*
   The cut refers to the teeth whether single, double, or rasp cut. It also refers to the fineness of the teeth.

3. *What files are usually used for jewelry work?*
   Needle files in assorted shapes: half round, flat taper, knife,

barrette, round, square and riffle, half round files 4 or 6 inches long, single cut, and smooth.

4. *How should irregular shapes and curved lines be filed?*
   The strokes should blend with and keep the contour or the shape of the line or form.

5. *How often should a file be cleaned?*
   The file should be cleaned at intervals during the filing process depending upon the nature of the material being filed and the readiness with which the file becomes clogged. Files should be always cleaned before being put away.

6. *How can oil be removed from new files?*
   Rub chalk on new files to remove the oil.

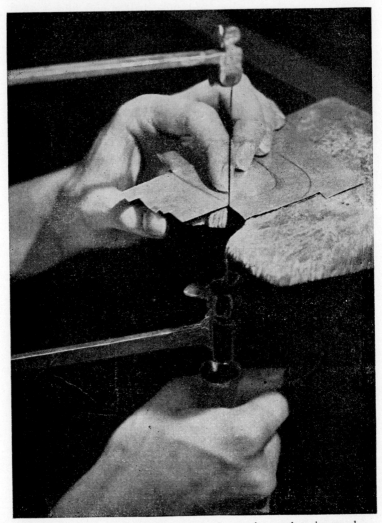

Fig. 7.—Sawing. The saw perpendicular to the metal to be sawed

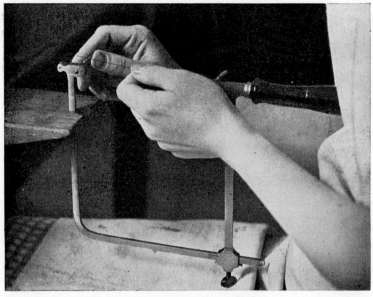

Fig. 8.—Setting the saw blade

SAWING

Sawing is cutting metal to a line. The jeweler's saw consists of an adjustable metal frame into which fine saw blades are fitted. Blades used for gold and silver 18-gauge and lighter are numbered 1/0 through 8/0. Heavier blades used for heavier gauges are numbered 1, 2, etc.

Sawed lines which may be straight, curved, or angular frequently form the outline or shape of a solid design. When the design is cut out or pierced, the background is cut out and the design remains in the metal.

Since the lines of sawing have a close relationship to the design of the article to be fashioned, it is important that the sawing follow the lines as accurately as possible. Filing may remedy irregular sawing if breaks occur outside the traced line of the design, but if they occur inside the traced outline, filing cuts away and alters the shape.

When open work is made by piercing, the regularity of a line is quite important because of the difficulty of filing inside edges and maintaining adequate points of contact which keep the pierced pattern in place and give it strength.

Tools	Soft pointed pencil—thin tracing paper—pum-
and	ice powder
Working	Gas plate, electric plate, Bunsen burner, blow
Materials	torch
	White beeswax
	Burnisher or any small tool with a smooth pol-
	ished surface
	Scratch awl
	Soft cloth
	Jeweler's saw frame
	Bench pin with V cut out
	Jeweler's saw blades
	Hammer or mallet
	Center punch
	Twist drill
	Hand drill
	Files
	Shellac, alcohol, dye solution
	Carbon paper
	Glue

PROCESSES   PREPARATION FOR SAWING THE
                              PATTERN

Tracing   Trace the design on thin tracing paper with a
                 soft, sharp pointed pencil.

PROCESSES
Cleaning
Waxing

Rub the metal to be used for the article with dry pumice powder.

Warm the metal and melt a small amount of beeswax on the surface; only a thin film of wax should remain on the surface.

Let the metal cool until the wax sets.

Transferring
the
Pattern
to the
Metal

Place the tracing so the pencil lines of the traced design touch the waxed surface.

Hold the tracing paper firmly.

Rub the tracing paper with a burnisher or any small tool with a smooth surface.

Remove the tracing paper; an exact pattern should be transferred on the surface of the wax.

Scratch the transferred design with a scratch awl through the wax into the metal.

Warm the metal and remove the wax from the metal with a soft cloth.

Setting
the Blade
in the
Frame

The position of the worker for sawing should be as follows: the shoulder about three inches above the bench pin and the right arm in line with the V of the bench pin.

Place the upper arm of the saw frame in the V of the bench pin.

Hold the handle of the frame against the body as shown in Fig. 8.

Fasten the blade in the jaw of the saw frame nearest the handle; the teeth must point away from the saw frame and down toward the handle.

Press the saw frame thus held to shorten the span about one-fourth inch.

Place the loose end of the saw blade in the upper jaw of the saw frame; tighten the thumb screw.

PROCESSES

Remove the pressure; the saw blade thus inserted should be taut. Rub a small amount of wax on the blade to make it run easily.

*Holding
the
Metal*

The worker sits in the same position as described above. Place the metal flat, the part to be sawed over the V of the bench pin.

Hold the metal tight against the bench pin with the fingers of the left hand.

Place the thumb on the underside of the bench pin.

*Holding
the
Saw Frame*

Grasp the handle of the saw frame firmly with tue little finger and thumb and hold the other three fingers loosely on the handle.

Place the saw blade at right angles to the edge to be sawed as shown in Fig. 7.

SAWING

Sawing

Saw away from the worker; make each stroke the length of the saw blade; the blade should not be pressed too firmly against the metal.

Move the forearm up and down while sawing.

*Straight
Lines*

Keep the back of the saw frame in a vertical position.

*Curved
Lines*

Move the saw frame slowly from right to left as the saw blade follows the curve of the line.

Angles

Move the saw with short quick strokes about the center of the blade without going forward, turn the metal or saw frame to allow the saw to turn the angle.

Filing
p. 25

File the edge smooth and even.

PREPARATION FOR PIERCING

PROCESSES

Transferring
p. 33

Transfer the design to the metal as described above.

Center Punching

Depressions are made in the metal with the center punch and hammer to guide the drill while boring holes in all the sections to be sawed out. The drilled holes must not interfere with the traced outline of the design.

Drilling

Place the twist drill in the chuck of the hand drill.
Drill holes in the metal as marked with the center punch; the metal must be supported from below and held firmly.

Setting the Blade in the Frame
p. 33

Set the blade in the lower jaw of the saw frame as described above.
Thread the loose end of the blade through one of the drilled holes nearest the center of the design.
Hold the metal to be pierced against the lower jaw of the saw frame.
Fasten the loose end of the blade in the upper jaw as described above.

PIERCING

Sawing
p. 31

Saw out the parts nearest the center first, those nearest the outside border last. Follow the directions under sawing.

OTHER METHODS OF TRANSFERRING THE DESIGN

Painted Method

The following mixtures may be used to paint the metal before transferring the pattern.

Formula—1 part liquid shellac
3 parts alcohol
Enough methol violet dye to color solution deep violet.

Paint the above mixture on the metal surface and allow to dry.

Place the pattern on the painted surface.

Scratch the pattern on the metal.

Carbon Method

Carbon paper may be used for large surfaces to transfer the pattern onto the metal.

Rub the surface of the metal with pumice powder.

Place the carbon paper with the glossy side on the metal.

Place the traced design on top of the carbon paper.

Hold firmly to the metal.

Follow the outline of the pattern with a hard pencil.

Remove the tracing and the carbon paper. The design should be transferred on the surface of the metal.

Scratch the design into the metal with a scratch awl.

Wash off carbon lines.

Pricked Method

Trace the design on thin tracing paper.

Clean the metal with pumice powder.

Spread a thin film of glue over the surface of the metal.

Place the traced design on the metal.

With a pointed tool prick the design through the tracing paper into the metal. The pricks should be very close together.

Remove the tracing paper and glue with warm water.

Scratch the design into the metal following the pricked marks.

QUESTIONS

1. *What size saw blade is usually used by beginning classes?*

   Size 1/0 or 2/0 for light gauge, size 1 for 14-gauge or heavier.

2. *What should be done if the saw blade becomes stuck during the sawing process?*

   Do not force the blade. Remove the pressure and the blade should adjust itself.

3. *Can the saw blade be backed out on a sawed line after the sawing process has been started?*

   The saw blade can be backed out by keeping the saw frame in the sawing position, moving it up and down while draw-it out toward the worker.

4. *If a rough edge of metal is left on the sawed line, how should this be removed?*

   This rough edge of metal is called a burr and should be removed by a file, scraper, or emery cloth to smooth the edges.

SOLDERING

The purpose of soldering is to hold pieces of metal together. In all soldering, flux, solder, and heat are necessary. Binding is often essential to insure a close fit as illustrated in Figs. 12 and 13.

Hard solder is used to solder gold and silver jewelry and larger pieces of silverware. Either hard or soft solder is used to solder copper and brass. Soft solder is used to solder pewter and tin and other metals but is not practical for jewelry because it lacks strength and its color is different from that of silver or gold. Sometimes soft solder is used for jewelry repair.

Different qualities of solder used for jewelry melt at different temperatures depending upon the kind and amount of alloy used. Hard solders contain alloys different from those used for soft solder.

Soldering must have sufficient strength to hold pieces together satisfactorily but the solder must not show on the finished work. When an article is to be built up of a number of pieces and has to be heated many times during the construction, the first pieces are put together with hard solder which melts at a high temperature. As other parts are added, easy or medium flowing hard solder which melts at a lower temperature is used.

Types of   Hard Solders
Solders   Silver Solder
                      Silver solder sheet 28-gauge
                      Hard flowing
                      Medium flowing
                      Easy flowing
                  Gold Solder
                  Gold solder 28-gauge—the same color, three or more karats lower than the gold used in the article to be soldered

Soft Solder
 Lead and Tin
  Wire solder—50% lead and 50% tin or
  40% lead and 60% tin

Tools
and
Working
Materials

Pickle (sulphuric acid solution)
Copper pickle pan
Copper tongs
Gas plate
File or scraper
Borax slate for borax—or china saucer for other prepared flux
Prepared borax or prepared flux for hard solder
Solder
Dividers
Jeweler's shears
Charcoal block
Binding wire
Small camel's hair brush
Gas and air blow torch
Steel tweezers
Scotch stone
Flux—one part zinc chloride, one part water
Electric soldering iron or soldering iron
Soldering furnace or gas plate
Sal ammoniac
Wire solder—lead and tin
Gum tragacanth
Boric acid powder 1/3 and alcohol 2/3
Rouge paste
Borax and water solution
Soldering nest

PREPARATION FOR SOLDERING WITH HARD SOLDER

PROCESSES

Pickling
p. 22

Pickle the metal to be soldered; the surface must be clean because dirt interferes with the flow of the solder.
Wash thoroughly in water.

Filing
p. 25

File or scrape all joints to clean.

Preparing the Flux

Pour a small quantity of water into the borax slate.
Rub the prepared borax on the slate until the water becomes creamy; it should be thicker in consistency for silver and copper than for gold. This mixture called flux is painted on the metal to exclude the air and to prevent heat from forming oxides on the metal. Other flux prepared for hard solder may be used.

Cleaning the Solder

Remove the dirt and tarnish from the solder with a scraper or file.

Marking Holding Cutting the Solder

Scratch lines on the solder sheet ¹⁄₁₆ of an inch apart.

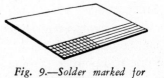

Cut across the lines as shown in Fig. 9.
Hold the solder between the thumb and first finger. Let the ball of the second finger rest under the cut edge. Now cut along the scratched lines, at right angles to the first cuts made.

Fig. 9.—Solder marked for cutting

PROCESSES

Place the small pieces of cut solder on the edge of the borax slate or saucer.

Placing
the
Article

Place the pieces to be joined by soldering on the charcoal or asbestos block. Be sure the surfaces which are to be united touch each other at all points.

Fig. 10. — *Charcoal block used when soldering and annealing*

Binding

Bind pieces together, if necessary, with annealed iron binding wire as shown in Figs. 12 and 13.

Applying
the
Flux
and
Solder

Apply the flux with a small camel's hair brush to the parts to be soldered. See Question 8.

Dampen the brush and pick up the small pieces of solder with the point of the brush.

Place the bits of solder so that they touch the pieces to be united.

Regulating
the
Flame

Light the blow torch.

Regulate the air so as to make the gas flame blue. The size of the flame to be used depends upon the weight of the metal to be united or the area to be heated or both.

SOLDERING

Applying
the
Heat
and
Soldering

Apply the heat gradually to the parts to be united, if possible on the opposite side from where the solder is placed so that the solder will be drawn toward the joint rather than away from it.

Allow the moisture in the flux to evaporate so the flux will crystallize and hold the solder in place; flux covers and protects the surface from oxidation.

Heat the article so that all parts will become hot at the same time; solder in liquid form runs to the hottest part.

Move the torch away from the metal now and then to see if any part is getting overheated; solder overheated eats into the metal.

Apply a direct flame on the solder and heat it quickly after the moisture in the flux has evaporated.

Melt the solder so that it runs and joins all parts firmly together; solder becomes solid almost immediately when the heat is removed.

Apply more solder dipped in flux to the joint with tweezers during the soldering process if necessary.

Examining the Joint — Examine the joint.

Remelting the Solder — Apply more flux and heat if the solder has not melted.

Filling the Cracks — Apply more flux, solder and heat if cracks appear which are not wider than the thickness of a sheet of paper.

Insert a piece of metal in a crack or opening too large to be filled with solder. Apply flux, solder and heat.

File off any excess metal.

Pickling — Clean in pickle.

Cleaning — Rinse in cold water.

p. 70 — Remove any excess solder with a scraper, file, or scotch stone dipped in water. The tool to be used depends upon the amount and thickness of the softer solder to be removed.

PREPARATION FOR SOLDERING WITH SOFT SOLDER

The Metal

Cleaning

Clean all surfaces to be joined with solder with a file or scraper.

The Flux

Dissolve zinc in hydrochloric acid to form a zinc chloride.

Strain and add an equal amount of water.

Electricians' paste may also be used for the flux.

The Soldering Iron

Heating

Place the soldering iron in a gas soldering furnace or gas plate or use an electric soldering iron.

Heat the soldering iron red hot.

Cleaning

File all faces of the soldering iron until they are bright copper.

Dip in zinc chloride solution.

Tinning the Soldering Iron

Place a small piece of solder on a bar of sal ammoniac.

Rub the soldering iron on the sal ammoniac and the solder until the end of the soldering iron has a thin coating of solder on each face.

Soldering

Soldering

Place flux (zinc chloride solution or soldering paste) on the metal to be joined.

Dip the hot iron in the zinc chloride.

Pick up a small amount of solder on the point of the soldering iron.

Apply the soldering iron to the metal and move along the surface to be soldered; a blow torch may be used in place of the soldering iron.

SPECIAL SOLDERING

Many problems arise in soldering. This section deals with some of the most common of these problems.

PROCESSES

Keeping Balls and Small Wires In Place While Soldering

Mix gum tragacanth with water to form a paste-like mixture.

Apply this mixture to the balls and wires before the flux and the solder have been applied; this mixture does not affect the flow of the solder.

Place the balls or other small pieces in the position in which they are to be soldered.

Place the flame on the side opposite the solder. Draw the heat through the ball and the piece to which it is soldered.

Soldering Balls Together

Place the solder so that it touches a ball and the one next to it without holding them apart.

Holding Parts Together While Soldering

Hold pieces together while soldering with iron binding wire, cotter pins, or pins made of heavy iron binding wire rolled flat and formed into pins as shown in Figs. 12 and 13.

Protecting Soldered Parts

Soldered parts frequently have to be protected from intense heat to keep them from falling apart. Surfaces also have to be protected to prevent burning. The two methods commonly used are given below:

Boric Acid Alcohol Solution

Apply boric acid and alcohol solution to the article.

Burn off the alcohol, apply solder and flux; this solution will not affect the flow of the solder and gives a slight protection to the metal.

PROCESSES *Rouge* *Paste*	Apply rouge paste to all parts to be protected. Dry out all moisture before the flux and solder are applied. Keep the rouge away from all parts to be united with solder; rouge interferes with the flow of the solder. Wash in clear water to remove the rouge before pickling.
Soldering *Gold and* *Silver* *Together*	Use silver solder when soldering gold and silver together.
Soldering *a Small* *Piece* *to a* *Large* *Piece*	In soldering a small piece of metal on a larger or heavier piece, place the larger piece on the charcoal block when possible. Direct the flame on the larger piece. The heat from the larger piece often heats the smaller piece sufficiently so that both pieces become hot at the same time which is important. Direct a blast of heat on the smaller part when the larger part has reached a dull red to bring both pieces to the same temperature at the same time.
Soldering *Hollow* *Pieces*	A small hole should be left for an air escape if hollow pieces are soldered together or on a flat surface.
Unsoldering *Joints*	Apply rouge paste to the parts which are to remain soldered. Paint the joints to be unsoldered with flux. Direct the flame on the piece to be unsoldered and the piece to which it is soldered. Melt the solder.

PROCESSES

Lift off the piece which is unsoldered. The article may have to be bound to the charcoal block and the unsoldered piece pushed off.

Soldering Copper

Bind copper pieces which are to be soldered together.
Boil in a solution of borax and water.
Let the solution dry on the surface of the metal to form a coating.
Apply flux, solder, and heat as described above.

Using the Soldering Nest

Place the metal on the soldering nest as shown in Fig. 11 to admit the flame around and under the metal evenly.

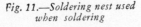

Fig. 11.—*Soldering nest used when soldering*

QUESTIONS

1. *What gauge wire is used for binding?*

Binding wire comes in many gauges; number 28 or 32 for fine work, 24 or 26 for medium weight metal, 20 or 22 for heavier work. 12-, 14-, or 18-gauge wire may be rolled flat to make pins or clamps. (Figs. 12 and 13) Fine wire can be twisted evenly to make it heavier and still flexible.

2. *Do the metal and the binding wire expand when heated?*

Both the metal and the wire expand when heat is applied.

3. *Will the wires cut into the thin metal?*

Sometimes the metal expands first and is cut by the wires. Make Z-shaped kinks in the wire to avoid cutting. (Fig. 13)

4. *Should the whole piece be heated or only the parts to be united?*

The flame should be kept moving over the whole piece until it becomes a dull red. As heat is applied remove the flame at times to see if any part is red hot and likely to burn. This part will show at once by its glow. When the whole piece is sufficiently hot, direct the flame on the joint.

5. *Why does the solder roll into a ball and not melt?*

When this happens a hotter flame is required and sometimes more flux should be applied or oil and grease may not have been removed from the metal.

6. *Is it usual to pickle the work after each soldering?*

It is best to pickle the work after each soldering to clean the metal.

7. *Is prepared borax and water always used for flux when soldering?*

There are many prepared fluxes which can be purchased at a Jeweler's Supply. See page 336.

8. *Is the solder always placed before the flame is applied?*

Often it is better to apply the flux and warm the surface enough to absorb the moisture in the flux.

BINDING WIRE—ITS USE IN SOLDERING

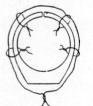

Slip four small loose loops of binding wire on the ring shank.

Insert binding wire under the loops around the ring shank.

Twist the wire tightly to join the ends of the shank.

Tighten the small loops to hold the wire in place.

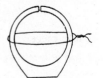

Make a loop of binding wire across the ring shank; tighten the loop until the ends of the shank meet.

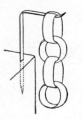

Bend flat iron binding wire at a right angle. Point and insert one end into the charcoal block.

Place the joint of the ring on the wire.

Bend 14- or 18-gauge binding wire to form a standard to hold the ring shank.

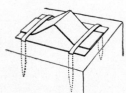

Make staples of heavy flat binding wire. Point the ends to insert in the charcoal block to hold pieces together.

Fig. 12.—Pieces bound and clamped for soldering

BINDING WIRE—ITS USE IN SOLDERING

Bind a sphere or curved surface in place with a double loop of binding wire.

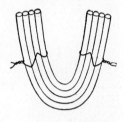

Hold wires together with a Z-formed loop of binding wire. This keeps the binding wire from cutting into the metal.

Make cotter pins of heavy flat binding wire to clamp on curved or flat surfaces.

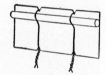

File V-shaped nicks in the edge of the metal to hold the binding wire in place.

Bind heavy flat binding wire under joints to make a firm foundation.

Loop binding wire around a cylinder. Tighten the loop in several places to bring the joint together.

Fig. 13.—*Pieces bound and clamped for soldering*

Courtesy of Cleveland Dental Mfg. Co.

Fig. 14.—Centrifugal force casting machine

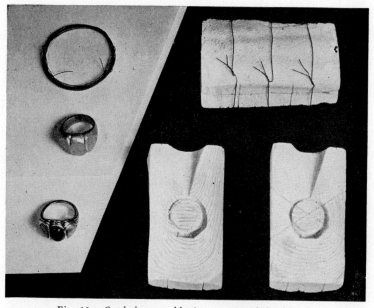

Fig. 15.—Cuttle-bone mold, tin pattern and finished ring

CASTING

Castings are made by pouring molten metal into a mold formed in cuttle-bone, sand, or plaster or by forcing molten metal into an investment. All methods require a pattern which may be made of tin, lead, or wax. Metal patterns must be filed to form and size. The wax patterns are modeled with a tool.

All methods require a mold. The cuttle-bone mold and the more recent method of casting in dental investment by means of a casting machine operated by centrifugal force are the two methods described in this book.

When cuttle-bone is used for the mold two or more pieces are required. When the soft porous side of the cuttle-bone is cut, sawed, and rubbed flat or surfaced it is ready for use. The pattern

of lead or tin is pressed into the flat surface of one piece far enough
to make the depression required. This depression, which is called
the mold, must be half the depth of the pattern. The other half
is made in the other portion of the cuttle-bone by pressing the pattern into it until the two surfaces meet. When cuttle-bone is used
the pattern must be free from undercuts which destroy the mold
when the pattern is removed. This type of casting requires a
funnel to admit the metal to the mold, also air vents in the cuttle-
bone to allow air to escape when the metal is poured into the mold
as shown in Fig. 15.

When dental investment is used for the mold, dental casting
wax is used to form the pattern. Undercuts do not interfere with
the making of the mold for investment because the wax pattern is
taken out by means of heat, hence there is no possibility of breaking. The metal is forced into the mold by centrifugal force as
shown in Fig. 14.

METAL CASTING IN CUTTLE-BONE MOLD

Tools	Bar tin
and	Rolling mill
Working	Shellac, alcohol, and dye solution
Materials	Bench pin
	Jeweler's saw frame
	Jeweler's saw blades #1
	Flat file six-inch half round
	File brush
	Chalk
	Cuttle-bone
	Graphite powdered
	Knife
	Binding wire 26-gauge
	Jeweler's shears

Tools	Jeweler's scales
and	Pickle
Working	Copper pickle pan
Materials	Copper tongs
	Gas plate
	Crucible
	Tongs
	Blow torch gas and air
	Powdered borax or other reducing flux
	Carving or chasing tools
	Emery cloth #1
	Polishing motor
	Tripoli cake
	Felt buffing wheel
	Bristle buffing wheel

PREPARATION FOR CASTING
THE METAL PATTERN

PROCESSES

Rolling Roll the bar tin the correct thickness.

Transferring the Design p. 36 Transfer the design (shellac, alcohol, and dye solution).

Sawing p. 31 Saw the outline out of bar tin.

Filing p. 25 File all surfaces, contours, and planes.

Note: The model or pattern may be modeled in surfaces or planes and the design gone over with carving or chasing tools on the casting. Undercuts must be avoided.

THE MOLD OF CUTTLE-BONE

Selecting the Cuttle-bone	Select two pieces of cuttle-bone as thick and as perfect as possible.
Sawing	Saw with a jeweler's saw blade through the soft part of the cuttle-bone at one end; remove the saw when it reaches the hard part of the bone and break off the piece.

Sawing

Saw with a jeweler's saw blade through the soft part of the cuttle-bone at one end; remove the saw when it reaches the hard part of the bone and break off the piece.

Repeat the same method with the other end and the two sides, leaving a piece rectangular in shape as shown in Fig. 15.

Repeat the above with the other piece of cuttle-bone, sawing it as nearly as possible to the size of the piece already sawed.

Facing

Saw off part of the bow on the soft side of each piece.

Rub the side thus faced on a flat smooth board to get a larger flat surface.

Powdering with Graphite

Rub a small amount of graphite on both smooth surfaces to get a cleaner impression.

Placing the Pattern

Hold the cuttle-bone in the palm of the hand. Place the pattern of tin not too near the end on the flat surface of the cuttle-bone prepared for it. The lightest end, which will be the smallest depression, should be at the top adjoining the funnel.

Forming the Mold

Press the pattern half way into the cuttle-bone. Place the other piece of cuttle-bone on top of the pattern which is embedded in the cuttle-bone.

Press slowly until the two flat surfaces of the

PROCESSES	cuttle-bone meet; the cuttle-bone should fit well into the palms to relieve the strain.
Marking to Register	Mark with the saw blade several lines on the ends and the sides so the two pieces will register exactly when put together again.
Removing the Pattern from the Mold	Separate the two pieces of cuttle-bone. Remove the tin pattern. Examine the mold to be sure that all parts have registered and the mold is clean.
Cutting the Funnel and Vents	Cut a funnel-shaped opening in both pieces with a knife to extend from the top or small end of the cuttle-bone to the mold as shown in Fig. 15. Cut vents with a saw blade in both pieces to allow air to escape from the mold as the metal is being poured.
Binding	Bind the two pieces of cuttle-bone together with 26-gauge binding wire. Be sure they register. Place the cuttle-bone mold on the bench, funnel side up.

THE METAL TO BE MELTED

Weighing	Weigh the tin pattern—the amount of silver or gold required for melting will be two and a half times this weight.
Pickling p. 22	Clean the metal to be melted for the casting in pickle. Wash in cold water.

PROCESSES	CASTING
Melting *the* *Metal*	Place the metal in a crucible. Hold the crucible firmly with tongs in the left hand. Hold the blow torch in the right hand. Direct a large hot flame directly on the metal until it is hot, then add borax or prepared reducing flux. Continue to heat the metal until it spins; add more borax or prepared reducing flux, just before pouring; this helps to fuse the metal and keeps it from oxidizing.
Pouring *the* *Metal* *into* *the* *Mold*	Play the flame on the metal during the pouring; the metal must be kept in a fluid state or the casting will be imperfect. Pour with the left hand, let the metal run into the funnel prepared for it in the cuttle-bone. Let the metal cool before removing the casting from the mold.

REMOVING THE CASTING

Removing *the Casting* *from the* *Mold*	Cut the binding wire holding the mold together. Open the mold. Remove the casting.

FINISHING

Sawing *the Button* *and* *Excess* *Metal*	Saw off any extra metal attached to the casting; the button and excess metal which has formed in the vents.

PROCESSES

Pickling	Clean in pickle.
p. 22	Rinse in cold water.
Filing	File and emery the rough surface.
Carving	Sharpen the design on the casting with a carv-
p. 87	ing or tracing tool.
Polishing	Buff with tripoli and a felt or bristle buffing
p. 71	wheel.

QUESTIONS

1. *What is undercutting?*

   To cut away or shape so as to leave an overhanging portion or relief.

2. *Why should undercuts be avoided in the pattern for a casting?*

   Undercuts in the pattern extend into the cuttle-bone beyond the outline and tear or break the form of the mold when the pattern is removed.

3. *Can metal be overheated during the melting process?*

   Yes. Overheating the metal causes more gas to be absorbed; when this gas escapes pitted marks are left in the casting.

4. *Why is a hot flame necessary for melting?*

   If the metal is heated too slowly it absorbs too much gas, which leaves pit marks in the casting.

5. *Can borax be used in place of the prepared reducing flux?*

   Borax can be used but it does not have the reducing quality of the prepared reducing flux.

METAL CASTING WITH CENTRIFUGAL
FORCE IN LOST WAX PROCESS

*Tools
and
Working
Materials*

Lubricant
Glass slab
Dental wax (hard carving, soft blending) wire
assorted shapes and gauges
Tracing paper
Steel cutting tool, knife or dental tool
Hot plate
Spatula
Ring mandrel, steel forms
Gravers
Graduated glass cylinder
Fine wire
Sprue pin
Sprue former
Small hair brush
Wax painting solution
Dental casting investment
Rubber mixing bowl
Casting flask
Asbestos strip 2 inch width
Pickle
Copper pickle pan
Copper tongs
Crucible
Centrifugal force casting machine
Furnace
Metal tray
Iron tongs
File
Gas and air blow torch
Dental reducing flux
Jeweler's saw frame
Jeweler's saw blades #1

Tools
and
Working
Materials

Files—needle and 6-inch half round
Emery cloth
Scotch stone
Polishing motor
Felt and bristle buffing wheels
Tripoli cake
Granite pan
Soda, ammonia, and water solution
Chamois or cloth buffing wheel
Rouge stick

PREPARATION FOR CASTING
THE WAX PATTERN

PROCESSES

Preparing
the
Wax sheet

Spread a thin film of lubricant on a glass slab.
Melt a portion of soft blending wax with hard
carving wax. See Question 3.
Pour the wax on the lubricated surface; more
may be added as it cools. See Question 6.
Transfer the pattern onto the wax sheet.

Cutting
the
Pattern

Cut the pattern with a sharp knife using glass or
heavy cardboard as a cutting surface.
Model or carve the surface with a graver.
Modeling may also be done by heating the cup
end of the spatula, picking up wax and applying it to the wax surface, form and smooth with
a warm spatula. Wax wires and wax units may
be sealed to a wax surface in this way. See Question 4.

Shaping
and
Doming
Polishing

Warm the cut pattern.
Press gently on the surface of a lubricated form,
to the contour desired. See Question 6.
Brush the wax pattern under cold water with a
fine brush or absorbent cotton.

*Determining
the
Amount
of Metal
Required*

Fill a graduate cylinder partly full of water as shown in Fig. 16.

Fasten a fine wire on the wax pattern.

*Fig. 16.—Graduate cylinder
containing water for
measuring*

*Fig. 17.—Measuring the
volume of the wax
pattern*

Lower the pattern into the cylinder; note the amount of water displaced by the wax pattern as shown in Fig. 17.

Remove the pattern from the cylinder; note that the water recedes to the original mark on the graduate cylinder.

Drop into the graduate cylinder enough metal to bring the water up to the line registered when the pattern was in the cylinder. Add a little more silver to raise the water about one cc. or ml. to allow for the wax used for the sprue pin and wax ball.

PROCESSES

Preparing the Sprue Former

Rub the sprue former with a wire brush to clean thoroughly.

Rub a small amount of oil on the rim of the sprue former so the invested flask can be removed easily.

Placing the Wax Ball

Place a 1/4-inch wax bead on the sprue pin to prevent porosity in the casting.

Fig. 18.—*Wax pattern held on a sprue pin and sprue former*

Placing the Pattern

Place the pattern firmly on the sprue pin.

Note: Place the ring pattern with the center of the back of the shank firmly in the point of the sprue pin and seal with wax as shown in Fig. 18.

The wax pattern plus the sprue former and the sprue pin must be about 1/2 inch below the rim of the flask.

Sealing the Ball Thickening the Sprue Pin

Seal the wax bead to the sprue pin about 1/16 inch from the wax pattern.

Thicken the section of the sprue pin between the wax ball and the pattern.

PROCESSES

Placing the Sprue Pin

Place the sprue pin in the sprue former; hold in place with a bit of wax.

Washing the Pattern

Use a soft brush and wax painting solution to paint the pattern.
Brush with water.
Repeat the above, but do not wash. See Question 7.

FORMING THE MOLD

Preparing the Flask

Line the flask with a strip of damp asbestos.
Leave 1/4 inch at each end uncovered.

Mixing the Investment

Use a rubber dish or half a rubber ball in which to mix the dental casting investment.
Add water to the investment and stir to a smooth, thick, creamy consistency.

Coating the Pattern

Paint the pattern with the mixed investment which should completely cover the pattern about 1/8 inch thick.

Placing the Flask

Place the casting flask on the rim of the sprue former which holds the sprue pin and the pattern. See Question 9.

PROCESSES

Investing
the
Pattern

Make a thin mixture of investment. Pour the investment into the flask a little at a time and vibrate until the investment is even with the top of the flask.

Run the spatula across the top of the flask to remove any excess investment.

Let the investment stand until it sets.

Removing
the
Flask
from the
Sprue
Former

Heat the base of the sprue former slightly with a loose flame.

Tap the base of the sprue former lightly.

Twist the sprue former from the flask. If the sprue pin is held in the investment, heat the pin and remove from the investment with the pliers.

Removing
Excess
Investment

Clean the investment from the inside rim of the flask where it has rested on the sprue former.

Drying
the Invested
Flask

Let the invested flask stand about one hour or more before casting. See Question 10.

THE METAL TO BE CAST

Pickling
p. 22

Pickle the metal.

Preparing
the
Crucible

Place a dampened asbestos pad in the bottom of the crucible.

Place the metal to be cast in the crucible.

Placing
the
Crucible
in the
Machine

Place the crucible on the crucible carrier, the lip end through the hole in the arm.

BALANCING THE MACHINE

Placing   Place the flask in the machine with the sprue
the   hole facing the crucible and fasten by sliding
Invested   the crucible carrier until it holds the flask firmly,
Flask   as shown in Fig. 19.
in the
Machine

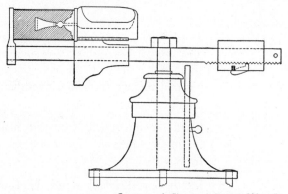

Courtesy of Cleveland Dental Mfg. Co.

Fig. 19.—*Casting machine in balance. The carrier holding the invested flask and crucible containing metal for the casting*

Balancing   Loosen the nut which holds the arm rigid.
the   Balance the arm by sliding the counterpoise to
Machine   the proper notch.
                     Tighten the nut after balancing. The machine
                     must be balanced before the hot investment
                     flask is put in place; investment cools very
                     quickly.
                     Remove the invested flask from the carrier.

FURNACE TREATMENT
OF THE MOLD

*Preheating
the
Furnace*

Preheat the furnace to 800 F.

*Burning out
the
Wax Pattern*

Place the metal tray on the furnace floor, to catch the melted wax of the pattern.

Place the prepared flask in the furnace with the feed holes on the tray.

Melt the pattern.   This forms the mold.   The temperature rises during this period.   Reverse the flask after the burnout, so the feed holes point toward the top of the furnace.

*Heating
the
Mold
for the
Casting*

Heat the mold about one hour and thirty minutes, after the temperature reaches 1200 F. or 1300 F.   Turn the flask frequently to spread an even heat.

*Placing
the
Flask
in the
Machine*

Remove the flask from the furnace with the iron tongs.
Place the flask in the machine as described above, as shown in Fig. 19.

CASTING

Winding
the
Spring
Locking
the
Carrier

Turn the arm of the carrier four times to wind the spring; this is the rule for general casting— if turned too many times the metal will spill or be thrown out of the crucible.

Push up the stop pin to lock the carrier as shown in Fig. 14.

Heating
the
Metal

Heat the metal with the blow torch.

Hold the blow torch so the flame is perpendicular to the metal; in this position the torch will not have to be changed when the metal melts into the bottom of the crucible.

Direct on the metal the part of the flame which lies just above the point of the cone; this part of the flame is hottest.

A steady heat is required until the metal has become fluid.

Lift the flame a little.

Sprinkle prepared reducing flux or borax powder on the metal to keep it from oxidizing.

Take hold of the cross bar at the counterpoise and shake to determine if the metal is in a fluid state.

Hold firmly as the stop pin has been automatically released.

Casting
the
Pattern

Release the cross bar when the metal reaches the fluid state; the arm spins and throws the molten metal from the crucible into the mold.

COOLING THE CASTING IN THE MOLD

*Removing
the
Flask
from the
Machine*

Remove the flask from the machine with the tongs.

*Cooling
the
Casting*

Pour a small amount of water into a deep pan. Hold the flask so that the investment touches the water a moment.
Remove from the water.
Repeat several times.
Stand the flask in the pan of water. Cover the flask slowly with water.

REMOVING THE CASTING

*Removing
the
Investment
from the
Flask*

Remove the investment from the flask with pressure, while wet.

*Washing
the
Casting*

Wash the investment from the casting with water and a stiff brush.

PROCESSES	FINISHING
Pickling p. 22	Place the casting on a charcoal block. Heat to a dull red glow. Immerse in pickle.
Sawing	Saw excess metal attached to the casting.
Filing	File the casting to remove any roughness.
Carving p. 87	Sharpen or carve any lines necessary with the gravers.
Polishing p. 71	Polish the surface.

QUESTIONS

1. *In what form can the wax be purchased?*
   The wax can be purchased in several forms—in sheets of various gauges, in wire, half round, and round of various gauges, in stick form and cakes of soft blending and hard carving.

2. *Is it possible to make undercuts on the wax pattern?*
   Undercuts do not affect this type of casting because the pat-tern is melted out of the mold.

3. *Can wax be carved and formed or bent?*
   Hard carving and soft blending wax may be melted together. The proportions used will control the flexibility and carving texture.

4. *Can wax wires be carved?*
   It is necessary to spread a thin coating of hard carving wax over the surface of the wires. This can be done with a warm spatula.

5. *Is the modeling and carving always executed before shaping the wax pattern?*

This depends upon the design. A ring is usually modeled and carved after it has been formed, supported on a ring mandrel during this operation.

6. *What are the various uses of lubricant?*

Lubricant is applied to—

A glass slab before pouring hot wax to form a sheet.

A stone when shaping the wax to form a setting (all stones must be removed from the wax pattern before the investment is applied).

7. *Why is the painting solution used on the wax pattern?*

The painting solution helps the flow of the investment and makes a smoother mold.

8. *What is casting investment?*

Casting investment comes in powder form. It is mixed with water to a creamy consistency and is used to encase the wax pattern. When hard it produces a smooth mold and can be heated without cracking.

9. *Are there other methods of encasing the pattern with the investment to form the mold?*

Another method of forming the mold may be used by filling the flask with investment a little above the rim and inserting the wax pattern into the filled flask until the sprue former holding the wax pattern rests on the rim of the flask.

10. *How long after the pattern has been encased in the investment can the burnout take place?*

About one hour after the pattern has been in flask it is ready for the burnout. If a long period elapses between pouring the mold material and the burnout period place the flask in water for a few minutes, this keeps the mold from cracking when heated.

CLEANING, POLISHING, AND COLORING

Cleaning, polishing, and coloring play a distinct part in the creation of a piece of jewelry. Cleaning is the basis of a good finish since no amount of coloring or polishing will cover up or remove scratches or excess solder. Coloring darkens the metal and takes away the harsh metallic look of the polished metal. Polishing creates highlights and gradations of tone and gives depth to the recessed parts.

CLEANING

Cleaning removes the fire coat, excess solder, scratches, and oil, and prepares the article for final polishing and coloring. Since the success of these two processes is dependent upon the thoroughness of the cleaning, care should be taken to have every part free of dirt and blemish.

Tools and Working Materials	Pickle of sulphuric acid for silver, gold, or copper
	Pickle of nitric acid for gold
	Copper pickle pan for sulphuric acid
	Porcelain pan for nitric acid
	Copper tongs
	File or scraper
	Scotch stone
	Fine pumice powder and oil
PROCESSES	
Pickling p. 22	Clean the metal in pickle.
	Remove the metal from the pickle with copper tongs.
Washing	Wash thoroughly in cold water.

PROCESSES
Removing
Scratches
and
Excess
Solder

Remove the deep scratches or excess solder from the surface of the metal with a file or scraper. File in the direction of the length of the scratch until the depth of the scratch has been reached. Rub the scotch stone over the metal in a circular movement; the scotch stone must be kept wet during this operation.

Repeat until all the file and scraper scratches have been removed.

Wipe the surface of the metal several times during the stoning to see that the surface is kept even.

Cleaning
Small
Recessed
Parts

Clean the surface of all small recessed parts with a piece of hard wood dipped in oil and pumice powder.

POLISHING

Polishing the metal with buffs charged with tripoli removes fine scratches and uneven surfaces. Rouge applied to a cloth or chamois buffing wheel gives a high polish to metal but does not remove blemishes. Buffs charged with rouge give the metal lustre and a foundation for coloring and for the final buffing after the color has been applied. Care must be taken to keep the metal moving on the buffing wheel as tripoli applied to a buff with a hard surface wears away the metal.

Tools
and
Working
Materials

Polishing motor
Felt or bristle buffing wheel
Tripoli cake
Soda, ammonia, and water solution
Granite pan
Soft cloth or chamois buffing wheel
Rouge stick
Gas plate

PROCESSES *Buffing*	Place the buffing wheel on the spindle of the polishing motor. Charge the felt buffing wheel with tripoli for flat surfaces. The bristle buffing wheel and tripoli are used for the recessed parts. Buff the metal until it is free from surface marks.
Washing	Wash in strong hot solution of soda, ammonia, and water. Remove and scrub with soap and a stiff brush if there are recessed parts.
Polishing	Place the chamois or cloth buffing wheel on the spindle of the polishing motor. Apply rouge stick to the buffing wheel. Buff the surface of the metal to a high polish.
Washing	Wash in a strong hot solution of soda, ammonia and water. Rinse.

COLORING

Coloring softens the tone of the metal and takes away the harsh metallic look of the polished metal. Silver is generally colored even if most of the coloring is buffed off. Gold is often just buffed but if there are recessed parts it is best to use color to give depth.

Tools *and* *Working* *Materials*	Potassium sulphide solution for silver Ammonium sulphide solution Gas plate Double boiler Small hair brush Soft cloth Whiting Cloth or chamois buffing wheel

PREPARATION FOR COLORING

Preparing
Potassium
Sulphide
Solution
and
Ammonium
Sulphide
Solution

Crush about one ounce of potassium sulphide in one quart of hot water.

Make a straw colored solution of ammonium sulphide and water. Heat the solution.

COLORING SILVER

Coloring
Silver

Method 1. Dip the silver in the warm solution of potassium sulphide or paint the solution on the silver until it becomes a blue black.

Method 2. Paint the silver with a warm solution of ammonium sulphide until it becomes a brown grey.

Washing

Wash in water.
Warm the silver dry or rub with a soft cloth.

Removing
Surplus
Color

Dip the thumb or finger in whiting.
Rub the surface of the metal to remove the oxidation; the amount to be removed depends upon the size of the piece, the design, and the stone to be set.

Polish with a cloth or chamois buffing wheel.

COLORING GOLD

Heating
the
Gold

Heat the gold until it is hot.

PROCESSES
Coloring
the
Gold

Apply the warm ammonium sulphide solution to the hot gold with a soft hair brush.
Go over the surface several times if necessary to obtain the desired color.
Wash in water.
Polish with a cloth or chamois buffing wheel.

QUESTIONS

1. *Why is silver a dull grey after heating?*
   Sterling silver has a copper alloy which oxidizes when heated.

2. *What makes the silver white after it has been pickled?*
   Pickle dissolves the copper oxides, leaving a film of pure silver over the surface.

3. *How can black spots be removed from silver?*
   Dip the piece in a solution of half nitric acid and half water; care must be taken not to leave the metal too long in the solution as it will eat into the metal.

4. *Can buffing be done without use of a polishing motor?*
   Buffing may be done by hand—using a hand buffer.

5. *Why does potassium sulphide solution sometimes turn an iridescent color on the silver instead of turning black?*
   It may be the silver has not remained in the solution long enough or the solution may be too weak.

6. *Why does potassium sulphide sometimes scale from the metal when it is dry?*
   The solution is too strong.

III. DECORATIVE PROCESSES

Chasing, Repoussé, and Modeling
Carving
Wire Working
  Wire Drawing
  Tube Drawing
  Wire Twisting
    Round Twist
    Vine or Chevron Twist
    Incised Twist
    Flat and Open Twist
    Waved Wire Smooth and Flat
    Waved Wire Broken and Flat
  Wire Coiling
    Coil of Round Rings
    Coil of Oval Rings
    Coiled Wire Cone
    Coiled Band of Overlapping Rings
    Coiled Wire Knob
    Round Rings of Wire
    Oval Rings of Wire
    Flat Coil of Wire
    Coiled Wire Unit
Domes, Balls, and Stamped Forms
Enameling
  Champlevé Enamel
  Cloisonné Enamel
  Bassetaille Enamel
  Limoges or Painted Enamel
  Plique à Jour Enamel
  Foils
Stone Setting
  Round Bezel and Bearing
  Square Mitered Bezel and Bearing
  Claw or Crown Bezel and Bearing
  Paved or Gypsy Setting

75

Fig. 20.—Chasing and Repoussé. The metal in a pitch bowl, chasing tool, and hammer in position

CHASING, REPOUSSÉ, AND MODELING

Chasing is beating a line in metal *from the front* with chasing tools and a chasing hammer. Chasing tools are much like dull chisels with rounded ends. The chasing hammer is a light, flat-faced hammer with a slender handle pear-shaped at the end that fits the hand. These tools, like many others used for jewelry and metal work, come in a number of sizes and weights.

Chasing is done on thin sheet metal or heavy metal or as a finish on castings. The metal in which the design is to be chased can be held in pitch which, when warmed and then cooled, holds the metal firmly. When comparatively little chasing is to be done, the piece may be placed on a lead or wood surface and held in position by the pressure of the tool.

Repoussé is beating the metal *from the back* with steel repoussé tools known as bossing and cushion tools. These tools are made with rounded edges and with working ends more rounded in shape than the ends of the chasing tools. A flat-faced hammer from four to six ounces in weight is used with repoussé tools depending upon the gauge of metal that is being raised.

The modeling or surface tooling for high and low relief is done *from the front* after the design has been raised. Low relief may also be obtained by beating down the background *from the front* with a modeler or grounders. Modeling tools are flat and smooth at the working end. Modeled parts are often combined with stones, enamels, and piercing to create interesting surfaces.

Chasing, repoussé, and modeling are a means of decoration rather than construction. Because the beauty of the metal surface should be evident, the work should be simple and direct. Over-worked surfaces appear mechanical and confuse or spoil the design. Undercuts made with chasing tools are sometimes used to emphasize a portion of the design.

Tools *and* *Working* *Materials*	Metal gauge Gas and air blow torch Charcoal block Copper tongs Pickle Copper pickle pan Gas plate Tracing paper . White beeswax Scratch awl Vaseline or oil Pitch bowl or block Prepared pitch Pliers Chasing and repoussé tools Chasing hammer Medium emery cloth or pumice powder

PREPARATION FOR CHASING AND REPOUSSÉ

PROCESSES

Gauging
the
Metal

Gauge the sheet metal, 24- or 26-gauge.

Annealing
p. 18

Anneal the metal to be worked.

Pickling
p. 22

Clean in pickle.

Transferring
the
Design
pp. 33, 36, 37

Transfer the design to the metal.

Note: This may be done before or after the metal is in the pitch, depending upon the method of transfer selected.

PROCESSES	Warm the metal.
Oiling the Metal	Rub a little vaseline on the surface of the metal which is to come in direct contact with the pitch.
Warming the Pitch and Metal	Warm the surface of the pitch with a soft loose flame until it becomes plastic; if heated too quickly or if the flame is too hot, it burns and becomes brittle and loses its adhesiveness. Warm the metal.
Placing the Metal on the Pitch	Place the metal with the oiled side on the pitch. Press the metal to be worked into the warm pitch. Rub vaseline on the finger tips. Bring a small amount of pitch over the edge of the metal to hold it more firmly. Let both metal and pitch cool before working.
The Position of the Worker	The position of the worker for chasing and repoussé: Sit directly in front and sufficiently above the work to look down upon it; hold the elbow up. Hold the chasing or other tools in the left hand as shown in Fig. 20. Place the tool on the line to be traced.
Holding the Chasing Tool	Tip the tool back slightly from the direction it is to move; for small curves tip the tool back at a greater angle. Place the first three fingers on the side of the tool farthest from the worker. Rest the cushion of the third finger on the metal. Hold the fourth finger out from the third finger; sometimes this finger rests on the metal beside the third finger.

PROCESSES

Place the thumb on the side of the tool nearest the worker. This position assures tool control.

Holding the Hammer

Hold the rounded pear-shaped end of the hammer in the palm of the hand; place the first finger on the top of the handle, the thumb on the side, and curve the other three fingers around the thick end with the tips pointing toward the worker.

CHASING

Chasing

Use a thin tracing tool for outlining.
Strike the tracing tool with the hammer with even, steady, and rapid strokes directly on the end with a wrist movement. As the tool moves toward the worker with each blow of the hammer, a thin, smooth grooved line should be left on the surface of the metal.
Repeat the blows, keeping the eye on the line of the design and not on the end of the tool.
Go over the line again to make smoother or deeper if necessary.
Use a wider tracing tool if a broader line is desired.

Removing the Metal from the Pitch

Warm the metal and the pitch with the loose flame of the blow torch.
Remove the metal from the pitch with pliers.

Cleaning the Pitch from the Metal

Remove, while still warm, any pitch which remains on the metal by wiping with a kerosene cloth or brush it off with melted paraffin.
Remove burned pitch by annealing the metal while still hot and plunging it into water. This

PROCESSES   may have to be repeated several times before all the pitch has been removed.

Pickling   Clean the metal in pickle.

REPOUSSÉ

Polishing the Reverse Side   Rub the raised lines on the reverse side with emery cloth or pumice powder to make the outline of the design stand out.

Oiling the Metal   Warm the metal and oil the side that has been worked.

Warming the Pitch and Metal   Warm the pitch and metal as described above.

Placing the Metal in the Pitch   Place the metal on the pitch with the raised lines of the design up.
Press the metal into the pitch as described above.

Holding the Repoussé Tool   These tools are held like the chasing tools but not at an angle.

Repoussé   Beat back between the chased lines of the design with a repoussé tool.

Removing the Metal from the Pitch   Remove the metal from the pitch as described above.

PROCESSES *Cleaning the Pitch from the Metal*	Clean any pitch from the surface of the metal as described above.
Annealing	Anneal the metal.
Pickling	Clean the metal in pickle.

MODELING

Oiling	Warm and oil the side of the metal that has just been worked.
Placing the Metal on the Pitch	Place the metal on the pitch with the side up that was first worked. Press the metal into the warm pitch as described above. Tap the surface of the metal; any hollow sound will indicate the pitch does not come in contact with the metal. Heat the metal over these spots. Press the metal further into the pitch.
Holding the Modeling Tool	Hold the tool like a repoussé tool.
Modeling	Model the design by hammering the modeling tools on the raised parts of the metal to get the contours and the planes desired.

QUESTIONS

1. *Can fine silver be used?*

   Fine silver can be used; it is softer but easier to model; if the piece is large it can be backed with sterling silver to give it strength.

2. *What is pitch prepared with to make it less brittle and more adhesive?*

Plaster of Paris and tallow are mixed with melted pitch.

3. *What is used to hold the prepared pitch?*

There are several methods of holding the pitch. A chaser's bowl or, for smaller work, a chaser's block.

4. *How is the chaser's bowl held steady while working?*

The chaser's bowl is held on a padded leather holder filled with sand, or a collar made of heavy leather belting riveted together, or a coil of rope bound together with leather. The bowl set in this may be moved at any angle.

5. *How is the pitch block held?*

The pitch block is held in the jaws of a table vise or in an engraver's ball.

6. *Why is prepared pitch the best material to beat against?*

Prepared pitch is adhesive, also it supports the metal satisfactorily while being worked, and though firm it is sufficiently plastic to produce a design in relief and of good texture.

7. *What other materials can be used to beat against?*

For low relief, hardwood closely grained, a lead block, or thick cork linoleum.

8. *If the metal has been raised in high relief, how should the metal be placed on the pitch to be modeled?*

Rub vaseline in the hollow places which have been raised in the metal and pour in melted pitch; when cool rub the same side of the metal with vaseline and place on the pitch. Warm both metal and pitch and press the metal into the pitch.

9. *Why is the handle of the repoussé hammer slender near the head of the hammer and thick and pear-shaped on the holding end?*

The thinness of the handle near the head gives a spring to each blow of the hammer and more rapid hammering is possible.

10. *If a tracing tool is held perpendicular will it move when the end is struck with the hammer?*

    The tool held in this position when struck with the hammer will not move.

11. *If a tracing tool is held at too great an angle will it run when struck?*

    If the angle at which the tool is held is too great, when struck with the hammer the tool will slip over the surface of the metal, leaving only a scratch or irregular indentations.

12. *If the blows of the hammer are uneven does this affect the work?*

    The tool will leave an uneven groove in the metal when blows are uneven.

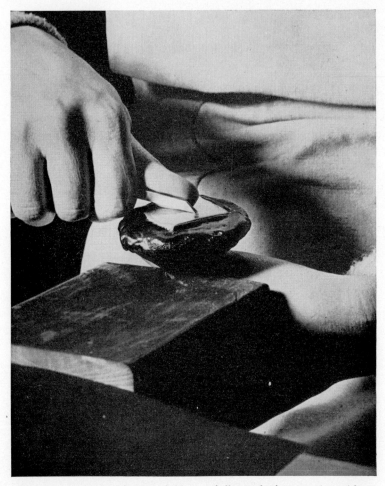

Fig. 21.—Carving. The metal held on a shellac stick, the graver in position

CARVING

Carving is cutting away metal from the surface. The forms of carving are line and low or bas relief. Fine lines are used to delineate a design as veins in a leaf and to create a design on the surface. Low relief is cutting away metal which forms the background of the design. When the design is in mass the outline of the whole is cut first and detail second. If intricate carving is to be done, the design should be made in wax or clay before cutting.

Carving tools called gravers are steel tools mounted in wooden handles. The shapes most commonly used are flat, round, and point or onglette. These tools have to be conditioned frequently as work progresses. The working end of the graver must be kept sharp and a forty-five degree angle must be maintained in order to use the tool correctly in the carving process. Because tool conditioning and carving have to be alternated frequently, the care of the tool is, in a sense, as much a part of the carving as the actual cutting of the metal.

The piece to be carved is held on a shellac stick by means of yellow flake shellac melted to form a smooth surface on the end of the stick. The metal is warmed and pressed into the shellac and allowed to cool. This holds the piece firmly.

Carving in most instances is decoration, though it is sometimes used to cut away metal on the inside of bezels and similar bits of construction.

Tools	Oil stone
and	Light oil
Working	Gravers
Materials	Kerosene cloth
	Yellow flake shellac
	Mounting stick

Tools   Gas and air blow torch
and   Steel surface plate
Working   Charcoal block
Materials   Pickle

- Copper pickle pan
- Copper tongs
- Gas plate
- Polishing motor
- Felt or bristle buffing wheel
- Tripoli cake
- Soda, ammonia, water solution
- Granite pan
- Thin tracing paper
- White beeswax
- Scratch awl
- Bench pin
- Ink eraser
- Alcohol
- Scotch stone
- Riffle file

PREPARATION FOR CARVING
THE TOOL

PROCESSES

Placing   Place a hard Arkansas oil stone on the bench,
and   the side parallel to the edge of the bench.
Oiling   Apply a few drops of light oil to the surface
the   of the stone.
Stone

Holding Hold the graver in the right hand.
the   Steady the graver with the thumb and fingers.
Tool   Place the blade so that it rests at a forty-five
While   degree angle on the oil stone.
Sharpening

PROCESSES
Sharpening
the
Tool
Blade

Keep the wrist rigid.

Bend the elbow.

Move the arm from the shoulder.

Run the blade the full length of the stone.

Press the tool on the stone during the forward stroke.

Remove the pressure on the return stroke.

Continue until all the scratches left from the grinding have been removed and the tool is true with a polished tip.

The tools will have to be sharpened at intervals during the carving process as the cutting edge wears away.

Removing
the
Burr

Jab the tool in wood to remove the burr.

Wipe the tool with a kerosene cloth; it makes the tool run more easily.

THE SHELLAC STICK

Melting
and
Moulding
the
Shellac

Melt a small amount of yellow flake shellac on a mounting stick using the direct flame of the blow torch. If heated too much the shellac burns and becomes like rubber and loses its adhesive quality.

Knead on a flat steel surface while soft.

Warm again and add more shellac to the stick.

Heat and knead as above.

Continue this process until the surface of the stick is covered well enough with well-blended shellac to hold the article to be carved.

Leave a flat surface if the base of the article to be carved is flat.

Build up the shellac while still warm if the piece to be carved is convex.

Allow to cool.

The same shellac can be used about six times, then chipped off and fresh shellac applied as described above.

THE METAL TO BE CARVED

Annealing
p. 18
Pickling
p. 22
Polishing
p. 71

Anneal the metal.

Pickle the metal.

Buff the surface with felt or bristle buffing wheel charged with tripoli.
Wash in a hot soluton of soda, ammonia, and water.

*Transferring
the
Design
to the
Metal*
p. 33

Transfer the design to the metal.　Use the wax method.
Scratch the design in the metal.
Remove the wax.
Note: Other methods of transferring may be used (See pp. 36, 37).　If the article is to be executed in repoussé and carved or pierced and carved, the work should proceed in the order given.

*Holding
the
Article
in the
Shellac*

Warm the article.　Care must be taken not to get the article too hot or the shellac will melt and run over the surface of the metal to be carved.
Place the article, while still warm, level on the shellac stick.
Press into the shellac.
Push the soft shellac around the article.　When cool the shellac hardens and holds the article firmly.

THE POSITION OF TOOLS AND MATERIAL TO BE CARVED

PROCESSES

Holding the Shellac Stick

The position of the shellac stick and the graver should be as follows: (Fig. 21)

Grasp the handle of the shellac stick in the left hand.

Hold firmly in the V of the bench pin; the hand holding the handle should be under the bench pin.

Holding the Graver

Hold the graver in the right hand; an onglette or small slightly rounded graver should be used for the initial line.

Place the handle of the graver on the joints of the second and third fingers.

Hold the part of the blade nearest the handle in the second joint of the first finger.

Close the hand.

Place the thumb with the side of the ball on the work to be carved.

Place the graver at about a fifteen degree angle on the piece to be carved; irregularities will appear in the carved line if the tool is held at too great an angle.

Support the side of the blade on the ball of the thumb; this position serves to steady and guide the tool during the carving.

CARVING

Carving

Push the graver with a forward movement of the hand without changing the position of the thumb.

PROCESSES
Carving

Move the graver firmly and evenly. Remove only a small layer of metal at a time; the lines and surfaces may be gone over several times to get the desired depth or width.

Rub the carved line during the carving with an ink eraser to make the carved line or surface stand out more clearly.

Remove any deep scratches with a scotch stone.

Outline the design with an onglette graver. Cut against this line to remove the background with a flat graver; when the tool reaches this line the metal should chip off, leaving a crisp line.

Deepen the outline.

Cut away more of the background as before.

Repeat the above until the desired depth has been reached and the design stands out in relief.

Removing the Article from the Shellac Stick

Warm the metal and shellac slightly and remove the article; sometimes the piece can be pried off without heating.

Soak the article in alcohol if any shellac remains on the surface of the metal.

FINISHING

Removing the Tool Marks
p. 71

Remove the marks of the graver from the background with a riffle file; when tool marks add to the design they should be left.

Rub the surface of the metal with a scotch stone to remove the marks of the file. Dip the scotch stone in water during this operation.

Buffing

Buff lightly with tripoli and bristle buffing wheel.

QUESTIONS

1. *What gauge metal is used for the article to be carved?*

   The gauge depends upon the design of the article and the type of carving to be executed; 18-gauge and heavier should be used for bas relief.

2. *Is the design always put on the article before the article is placed on the shellac stick?*

   This depends upon the article to be carved and the method of transferring selected.

3. *When placing the article on the shellac stick why is the metal warmed instead of the shellac?*

   The article holds to the shellac better if the metal is warmed.

4. *Is the article to be carved always held in the shellac stick?*

   Other tools can be used to hold the article during the carving; the form and the size of the article suggests the tool to be used to hold the article firmly, such as a ring clamp to hold a ring.

5. *Is the shellac stick or the tool holding the article turned during the carving?*

   In carving scrolls or curved lines, sometimes both tools are turned and the metal is moved against the carving tool.

6. *What is the initial step in carving masses?*

   The masses should be blocked out first.

7. *Should a design in relief be modeled first in wax or clay?*

   The design should first be modeled in wax, if there is much detail.

8. *Are the tool marks filed and stoned from the surface to give a smooth texture?*

   Sometimes the tool marks are removed entirely from the surface, often some are left to give varying texture and color.

9. *How is a sharp perpendicular cut made?*

   Make the outline and remove a thin layer of metal by cutting against this line. Repeat until the desired depth has been reached.

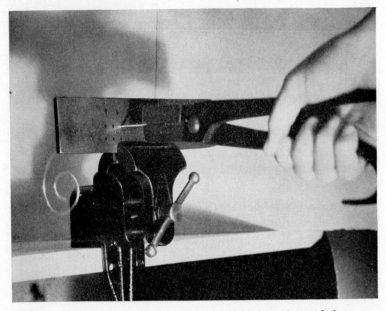

Fig. 22.—Drawing the wire through the holes in the draw plate with draw tongs

WIRE WORKING

The construction of a piece of jewelry often requires wires of various sizes and shapes. The design may also call for twisted or coiled wire to produce a broken line or to give delicacy to an edge. Ornaments for decoration such as coiled motifs, which vary the design and texture, may also be made of smooth or twisted wire. The use of the draw plates as described below makes it possible to reshape these wires into forms that add to the interest of the design.

Wires may form the foundation of a piece of jewelry such as a chain, a ring, or a bracelet, but the greatest use of wire forms and shapes is made in applied decoration. There is practically no limit to the ways wire can be used for this purpose.

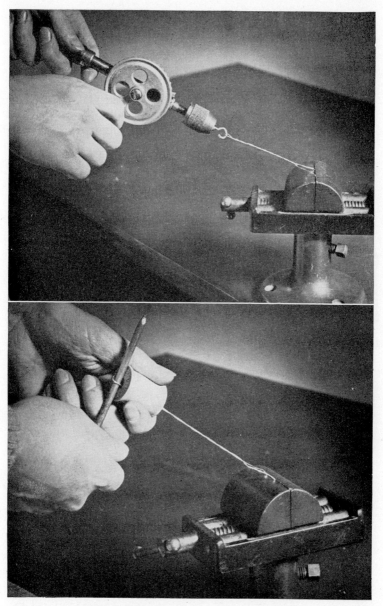

Fig. 23.—*Twisting the wire with a hand drill*
Fig. 24.—*Twisting the wire with a spool and rod*

WIRE DRAWING

Wire drawing is drawing wire through tapered and graduated holes in a steel draw plate to reduce it in size. The shape of the wire may also be changed, if desired. Some of the draw plates are made with round holes graduated and tapered; others have oval, half round, triangular, square or oblong holes.

Tools
and
Working
Materials

Charcoal block or asbestos pad
Gas and air blow torch
Pickle
Copper pickle pan
Copper tongs
Gas plate
File or emery wheel
File brush
Polishing motor
Steel hammer
Steel surface plate
Table fastened to wall or floor
Bench vise or draw bench
Round hole draw plate
Yellow beeswax
Draw tongs

PROCESSES

PREPARATION FOR WIRE DRAWING

Annealing
p. 18

Anneal the wire to be drawn; when the wire is soft it is easier to draw.

Filing
p. 25

File the end of the annealed wire to a blunt taper with a file or emery wheel placed on the polishing motor.

Hammering

Wire of heavy gauge may be hammered to a blunt taper and filed if necessary.

Placing the
Draw
Plate
in the
Vise

Hold the draw plate horizontally in the jaws of
the bench vise, the tapered end of the hole toward the worker as shown in Fig. 22; a draw
bench may also be used as shown in Fig. 25.

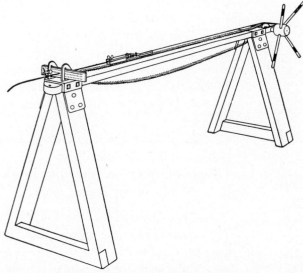

Fig. 25.—Draw bench to draw wire of heavy gauge

Waxing

Rub the length of the wire lightly with yellow
beeswax.

Coil and bind wire of light gauge as shown in
Fig. 4.

Dip in melted yellow beeswax.

Inserting
the
Wire
in the
Draw
Plate

Insert the tapered end of the wire through a
hole in the draw plate as near the diameter of
the wire as possible.

Let the wire extend through the hole about $\frac{1}{4}$
inch or more.

PROCESSES
*Holding the
Draw
Tongs*

Hold the draw tongs with the loop of the handle down as shown in Fig. 22.

DRAWING THE WIRE

Drawing

Grasp the point of wire which extends through the hole firmly with the draw tongs.

Draw the wire through the hole; the wire must come through the hole to the worker in a straight line; if drawn at an angle the edge of the hole in the draw plate will make nicks in the wire.

Continue to draw the wire through successive holes until it is the desired size.

Change the shape of the wire by drawing through holes of the desired shape.

Annealing

Anneal the wire after it has been drawn through five or six holes as the drawing has made the wire hard and brittle.

Anneal the length of the wire to straighten.

*Stretching
to
Straighten
Lengths
of
Wire*

Place one end of the wire in the jaws of the vise.

Hold the other end with the pliers.

Pull the length gently.

Rub the wire over the edge of a bench pin.

TUBE DRAWING

Tubes can be made from strips of sheet metal which are drawn through holes in a steel draw plate to form the desired size and shape.

Tools
and
Working
Materials

File
Ruler
Dividers

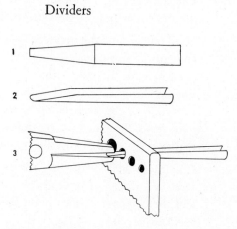

Fig. 26.—Drawing a strip of metal to form a tube

Jeweler's shears
Charcoal or asbestos block
Gas and air blow torch
Pickle
Copper pickle pan
Copper tongs
Gas plate
Block of hardwood with semicircular groove
Raising hammer with thin neck or chasing tool
Yellow beeswax
Bench vise
Draw plate
Burnisher or knife
Draw tongs
Flux
Borax slate
Solder
Small camel's hair brush

PROCESSES	PREPARATION FOR TUBE DRAWING
Filing	File the edge of the metal a little longer than the desired length of the finished tube.
Laying out the Strip	Hold one arm of the dividers against the trued edge of the metal. Scratch, with the other arm of the dividers, a line on the metal parallel with the filed edge; the width of the strip should be three and one-half (plus the gauge of the metal) times the diameter of the desired tube.
Cutting	Cut the metal with the shears along the scratched line. Cut the end to a ¾-inch blunt taper as shown in (1) Fig. 26.
Truing	File the edges true; the edges must be parallel.
Annealing	Anneal the strip.
Pickling	Clean in pickle.
Dapping	Place the block of wood in the jaws of the table vise. Place the strip of metal evenly in the groove. Tap the metal in the groove. Round the edges slightly as shown in (2) Fig. 26.
Annealing	Anneal the strip.
Waxing	Rub both sides of the strip with beeswax.
Placing the Draw Plate in the Vise	Place the draw plate horizontally in the jaws of the table vise with the tapered holes toward the worker.

PROCESSES
Inserting
the
Tapered
End
in the
Draw
Plate

Place the tapered tip through the hole in the draw plate that it most nearly fits as shown in (3) Fig. 26.

DRAWING THE TUBE

Drawing
p. 98

Draw the strip through the hole in the draw plate as if it were wire.

Continue drawing through successive holes until the edges meet.

Note: Insert a knife blade or burnisher firmly in the opening of the strip before it passes through the hole in the plate; this keeps the strip from twisting as it is being drawn.

Cleaning
the
Joint

Rub the length of the joint with a file or emery cloth.

Soldering
p. 38

Solder the joint. Be sure the solder has melted the entire length.

Note: If the tube is to be made into a hinge, the joint is not soldered until it is mounted on the article to be hinged.

WIRE TWISTING

Smooth wire is often twisted to change the texture and is used for decorative rather than for structural value. Its broken line gives a decided light and dark pattern and sometimes a feeling of delicacy as well.

ROUND TWIST

Fig. 27.—Two round wires twisted together

Tools	Charcoal block or asbestos pad
and	Gas and air blow torch
Working	Pickle
Materials	Copper pickle pan
	Copper tongs
	Gas plate
	Bench vise
	Hook of iron or steel
	Hand drill
	Spool or hand vise for heavy wire
	Flat-face steel hammer
	Steel surface plate
	File
	Draw plate
	Wax
	Draw tongs
	Snub nose pliers
	Rolling mill

PROCESSES

Annealing p. 18	Anneal the wire thoroughly.
Looping	Make a loop in the center of the wires to be twisted by bringing two ends together.
Placing	Hold the two loose ends in the jaws of the bench vise with the wires in a horizontal position.

PROCESSES

Inserting   Insert a hook in the chuck of the drill.

Holding   Catch the looped end of the wire in the hook
which has been placed in the chuck of the hand
drill as shown in Fig. 23.

Hold the wire taut and parallel to the floor.

Note: A spool and nail may be substituted for
the hand drill and hook. (Fig. 24.)
For heavy wire a hand vise is used in
place of the hook to hold and twist the
wire; twist the wire by turning the hand
vise.

TWISTING THE WIRE

Twisting   Turn the handle of the drill forward. This
should give an even right-hand twist to the wire
as shown in Fig. 27. (See Question 4.)

VINE OR CHEVRON TWIST

Fig. 28.—*Two pairs of round wires, right- and left-hand twists*

Measuring   Measure and cut two pieces of annealed wire
equal in length.

Twisting   Two steps are required to make this design.

p. 101   1. Loop one piece of wire and make a *right-
hand twist* as described above. Count the
number of full turns.

2. Loop the second piece of wire and make a
left-hand twist, this time by turning the
handle of the drill backward toward the

worker. Give the same number of full turns to the wheel as executed in step 1. place the two wires together as shown in Fig. 28.

INCISED TWIST

Fig. 29.—Twisted wire drawn through holes in the draw plate

Twisting
p. 101

Twist two annealed wires together. A tight twist is more effective than a loose twist.

Hammering
p. 96

Hammer the looped ends of the wire together on the steel plate with the steel hammer.

Filing
p. 25

File this end to a point.

Annealing
p. 18

Anneal the wire thus twisted.

Drawing
p. 96

Draw the wire through holes in the draw plate. The twist flattens out after it has been drawn through a few graduated holes. The drawing should be continued until the desired flattened spiral effect is obtained.

FLAT AND OPEN TWIST

Fig. 30.—Twisted wire rolled

Twisting
p. 101

Twist two annealed wires together; a loose twist is necessary to assure holes at intervals between flattened wires.

PROCESSES
Flattening

Roll the wires thus twisted through a rolling mill (the holes will disappear if the wire is rolled too flat) or place the wire on a steel surface plate and flatten with a planishing hammer.

WAVED WIRE SMOOTH AND FLAT

Fig. 31.—Twisted wire separated and rolled

Twisting
p. 101

Twist two annealed wires together. A tight twist is necessary to get a good waved line.

Annealing
p. 18

Anneal the wire.

Separating

Separate the wires by placing one wire in the table vise.
Hold the other wire with pliers.
Unwind the two wires without destroying the twist.

Flattening

Roll the separated wires in the rolling mill. The result should be a flat ribbon wave.

WAVED WIRE BROKEN AND FLAT

Fig. 32.—Twisted wire rolled and separated

Twisting
p. 101

Twist two annealed wires together. A tight twist is necessary.

Flattening

Roll the wires thus twisted in a rolling mill.

Annealing
p. 18

Anneal the wire.

Separating the
Wires

Separate the two wires as described above. The result should be a flat waved ribbon with slight depressions at regular intervals.

WIRE COILING

Wire coiling is winding wire around a steel mandrel which may be any size or shape. Smooth or twisted wire may be coiled and used for decorative bands or motifs. Coils as shown in Fig. 35 sawed into rings are used in the construction of a chain and often form the foundation as well as the decoration of an article as shown in Figs. 69, 94.

Tools
and
Working
Materials

Charcoal block or asbestos pad
Gas and air blow torch
Pickle
Copper pickle pan
Copper tongs
Gas plate
Steel hammer
Steel surface plate
Boards (Fig. 33)
Bench vise
C-clamp
Round split mandrel (Fig. 34)
Hand drill or jeweler's hand vise
Flat mandrel
File
File brush
Emery cloth #1
Soft wrapping paper
Shears
Binding wire 28-gauge
Pointed mandrel
Bench pin

Tools	Jeweler's saw frame
and	Jeweler's saw blade #1/0
Working	Flux
Materials	Borax slate or saucer

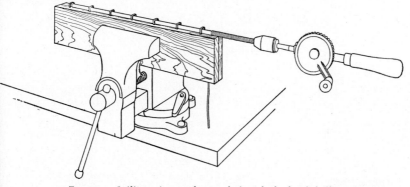

Fig. 33.—Coiling wire on the mandrel with the hand drill

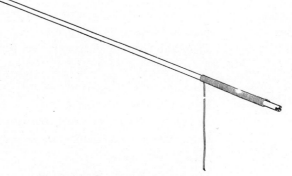

Fig. 34.—Split mandrel for wire coiling

Camel's hair brush
Solder
Mallet
Ring clamp
Jeweler's saw blades #2/0

Tools
and
Working
Materials

Wooden core
Snub nose pliers
Round nose pliers
Coiling machine (Figs. 44, 45)
Wooden block
3 Nails
Wire cutters
Sheet lead

COIL OF ROUND RINGS

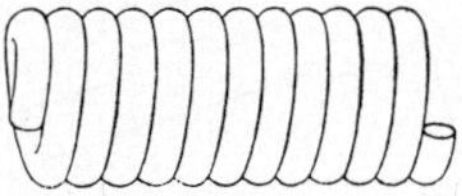

Fig. 35.—Wire coiled on a round mandrel

PROCESSES

Annealing
p. 18

Anneal the wire.

Flattening
the End
of the
Wire

Place the end of the wire on a steel surface plate.
Flatten the end ¼ inch with steel hammer.

Placing
the
Wire

Place the wire between two boards held in the bench vise as shown in Fig. 33; the boards must be held loose enough to let the wire move between them. A C-clamp may be used if necessary.

Placing
the
Mandrel

Determine the size of the mandrel by the inside diameter of the coil desired.
Insert the flattened end of the wire in the split mandrel as shown in Fig. 34.
Slip the mandrel under the staples. Boards can be prepared with staples of various sizes to hold mandrels of different sizes.

PROCESSES
*Holding
the End
of the
Wire
and the
Mandrel*

Hold the mandrel with the wire end in the chuck of the hand drill as shown in Fig. 33.

COILING

Coiling

Turn the drill handle.

Coil the wire straight around the mandrel.

Let each ring as it is wrapped touch the ring just completed.

Slip the coil from the mandrel (Fig. 35).

Note: When only a few coils are required, bend the flattened end of the wire at a right angle; clamp it on the mandrel in the vise; wind the loose end on the mandrel by hand.

COIL OF OVAL RINGS

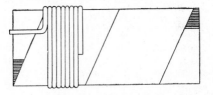

Fig. 36.—Oval mandrel and coil of oval rings

*Making
the
Mandrel*

Take a piece of metal the size of the ring desired.

Example: Copper, brass, nickel, silver, iron or steel ¼ by ⅜ inch—several inches long.

PROCESSES
Filing
p. 25

File all edges smooth.

Smooth all surfaces of the mandrel with emery cloth.

File the ¼-inch thickness slightly on one side of the ⅜-inch width.

Wrapping the Mandrel

Cut a strip of soft wrapping paper the width of the mandrel.

Dampen the paper.

Wrap the paper around the mandrel at an angle; be sure it meets without overlapping as shown in Fig. 36.

Hold both ends of the paper to the mandrel with iron binding wire or glue.

Annealing
p. 18

Anneal the wire.

Flattening the Wire

Hammer the end of the wire on the surface plate to flatten.

Holding the Wire

Place the wire between two boards held in the vise.

Hold the flattened end of the wire and the mandrel in the jeweler's hand vise on the edge of the boards.

COILING

Coiling

Coil the wire on the metal strip by turning the hand vise.

Removing

Remove the mandrel from the vise.

Annealing

Anneal the coil of wire on the mandrel.

Removing the Coil

Slip the coil from the mandrel.

COILED WIRE CONE

Fig. 37.—Tapered mandrel and coiled wire cone

PROCESSES
Coiling

Place the flattened end of the annealed wire on the shaped mandrel held in the vise; the pointed end of the mandrel should extend beyond the jaws of the vise the desired length of the cone. Coil the wire around the mandrel until the point has been reached.
Remove the coil from the mandrel.

Spacing

Pull both ends of the wire if an open spiral is desired. If the wire is of heavy gauge, anneal before spacing. A flat tool may be inserted between the rings to get the desired spacing. The wire should be of heavy enough gauge so that the cone form will be kept after it has been removed from the mandrel.

Sawing
p. 31

Saw off both ends which extend beyond the spiral with a #1/0 saw blade.

COILED BAND OF OVERLAPPING RINGS

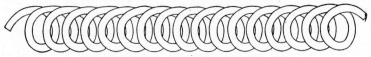

Fig. 38.—Wire coiled, spaced and flattened

Coiling
p. 106

Coil the annealed wire around the mandrel at an angle.

Spacing

Space the rings as described above.

Flattening

Place the coil on a flat surface. Tap gently with a wooden mallet.

COILED WIRE KNOB

Fig. 39.—Wire coiled and spaced to form a knob

PROCESSES

Coiling
p. 106

Coil the annealed wire straight around the mandrel as described above.

Remove the coil from the mandrel.

Forming the Knob

Form the knob by pulling the ends of the wire together until the two ends meet.

Filing
p. 25

File the ends of the wires if necessary to make an even joint and a perfect circle.

Binding
p. 46

Bind the knob with binding wire to hold in place if necessary.

Soldering
p. 38

Place the flux and solder on the joint.
Solder the joint.

Truing

The spaces between the rings may be trued after the soldering process has been completed by inserting a flat blunt tool between each ring.

ROUND RINGS OF WIRE

Coiling
p. 106

Coil the annealed wire around the mandrel shown in Fig. 33.

Note: Different methods are used in sawing coils into rings depending upon whether heavy or medium gauge wire is used.

PROCESSES
Holding

Place the coil horizontally in the ring clamp or jeweler's hand vise.

Hold the ring clamp in the jaws of the table vise.

Sawing into Rings

Saw the coil into rings with #2/0 saw blades. Care must be taken to saw the coil straight to insure an even joint.

Heavy Gauge Coil

Hold as above if the coil keeps its shape in the vise squeeze.

Light Gauge Coil

Put on a wooden core the diameter of the coil. Hold as above.
Saw the coil into rings.

Hold both ends of the wire with pliers.
Push both ends beyond each other before bringing them together as shown in Fig. 40.

RIGHT   WRONG

Fig. 40.—*Opening a wire ring*

Give the ring a gentle pressure with the pliers across the diameter if the ends do not meet.
Repeat the above in several directions to form a perfect ring if necessary.
Tap lightly with a wooden mallet on a surface plate.

Soldering
p. 38

Solder the joint.

OVAL RINGS OF WIRE

Coiling
p. 106

Coil the annealed wire around the mandrel as shown in Fig. 36.

Annealing
p. 18

Anneal the coil.

PROCESSES
Sawing
into
Rings
p. 113

SAW
CUT HERE

Saw the coil on the end of the oval as shown in Fig. 41.

Either method of holding the coil during the sawing may be used depending upon the gauge of the wire as described above. Heavy cardboard may be inserted in the coil.

*Joining
the
Ends*

*Fig. 41.—
Sawing an
oval link*

Join the ends of the ring as shown in Fig. 41.

Soldering
p. 38

Solder the joint.

FLAT COIL OF WIRE

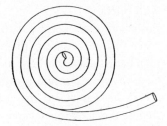

Fig. 42.—Flat coil with round center

Two methods for holding the wire can be used.

Method 1.

Flattening

Cut a length of annealed wire several inches long.
Flatten the end of the wire with a steel hammer on a steel surface plate.

Bending

Bend the wire at right angles.

PROCESSES
Holding

Place a small mandrel and the hammered wire end in the jaws of the vise or hold with snub nose pliers. The size of the mandrel depends upon the size of the hole desired for the center of the coil.

Coiling
p. 109

Coil the wire once around the mandrel.

Note: The first coil for wire of medium or light gauge may also be made with a pair of round nose pliers with or without flattening the end of the wire. (Fig. 42.)

Different methods are used from this point for wire of light or heavy gauge; if wire of light or medium gauge is used, remove the wire from the mandrel.

Sawing
p. 31

Saw or cut off the wire which extends beyond the center of the circle of wire which has been formed on the mandrel. A perfect circle should now be left with a loose end of wire. This circle forms the center of the coil.

Holding

Hold this ring flat between snub nose pliers in the right hand; the loose end of the wire in the left hand between the thumb and the first finger; the second finger is held under the pliers.

Coiling

Coil the wire around the center in successive rings that touch at all points.

Holding

Coiling wire of heavy gauge: hold the wire on the mandrel in a bench vise.

Coiling

Continue to wrap the wire around in a flat coil. The weight of the wire should be heavy enough to withstand pressure without losing form as the successive rows are coiled.

Remove from the vise.

Saw off the end of the wire which was held in the vise and extends beyond the end of the circle.

FLAT COIL OF WIRE

Fig. 43.—Flat coil with broken center

Method 2.

*Flattening
the
Wire
End*

Hammer the end of the annealed wire to flatten.

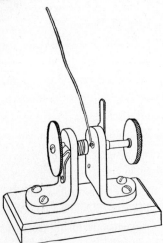

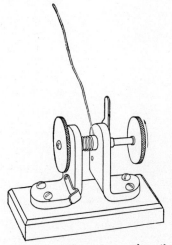

Fig. 44.—Inserting the wire end in the split mandrel of the coiling machine

Fig. 45.—Coiling wire on the coiling machine

PROCESSES
Holding

Insert the flattened end of the wire through a slit in the steel mandrel; the wire must go through the slit but not beyond it.

Coiling
p. 109

Coil the wire once around the mandrel.
Continue to make the coil as described above.
Note: The split mandrel can be held in a machine for coiling as shown in Figs. 44 and 45.

COILED WIRE UNIT

*Spacing
the
Loops*

Draw an equilateral triangle on a block of wood.
Hammer one nail at each point; the size of the nail is determined by the size of the wire and the size of the loops desired.

*Cutting
the
Nail
Heads*

Cut off the nail heads with the wire cutters.

Fig. 46.—*Wire coiled loops*

*Placing
the
Block*

Place the block of wood in the jaws of the table vise.

*Looping
the
Wire*

Coil the annealed wire around one of the nails.
Carry the left-hand wire of this coil around the nail *to the right* so the wire goes toward the center of the triangle.
Carry the right-hand wire coiled around the nail *to the left* with the end of the wire again turning toward the center of the triangle.

PROCESSES   Place the two wires together to form parallel
Joining   stems for the three loops.
the
Wires

QUESTIONS

1. *Why do the holes in the draw plate rust?*
   Rusting is sometimes caused by drawing wire which has not
   been thoroughly dried.

2. *Can half-round wire be made by using a draw plate with round
   holes?*
   Half-round wire may be made by flattening one or both sides
   of round wire slightly with a file or by rolling or drawing,
   doubling the length of wire, placing the flattened sides together and drawing as a single wire. A knife blade can be
   inserted between the two wires as they go through the plate
   to keep them from twisting.

3. *Is it possible to twist a single wire?*
   Wire which has a definite edge can be twisted.

4. *What should be done to a length of wire which has twisted un-
   evenly, some parts of the length a looser twist than other parts?*
   Anneal the wire where it has twisted loosely, return to the
   vise and continue twisting. These loose parts will tighten
   and give the full length of wire a uniform twist.

5. *Can mandrels be purchased any shape or size for coiling wire?*
   Mandrels are usually made out of wire or rod, any size or
   section, depending upon the diameter of the coil desired.

6. *Is it necessary to place the paper on all mandrels before coiling
   the wire?*
   All mandrels other than circular in form should be wrapped
   with paper before coiling the wire; when the coil is annealed
   the paper will burn and the coil can be removed easily.

7. *Will the coil be marred if it is placed in the rough jaws of the vise or pliers?*

    Sheet lead should be placed in the jaws of the vise or pliers to protect the coil for sawing.

8. *Why is the coil sometimes cut and sometimes sawed into rings?*

    The joint is neater if the coil is sawed. If the ring is to be melted into a ball the coil may be cut with the shears.

DOMES, BALLS, AND STAMPED FORMS

Domes, balls, and stamped forms used as ornaments of decora‐ tion give more weight and lustre to the design than units and motifs made of wire; they may be used as single units or may be formed into motifs for decoration. Domes are often used in place of stones and treated as the center of interest; they are made by cutting disks from sheet metal and forming them into domes, which may be decorated by piercing, carving, chasing, or by apply‐ ing wires or units of metal. The dome often forms the founda‐ tion of a piece of jewelry such as a brooch, ring, or clasp as shown in Figs. 69, 70, 86, 87, 102, 103.

Balls of the same size or graded sizes must be made of a meas‐ ured amount of material. This is accomplished by cutting coils of wire into rings. The size of the ball is determined by the gauge of the wire from which the coil is made and the size of the mandrel on which it is coiled; each ring is melted to form a ball. If balls do not have to be graded to size scraps of any gauge metal may be melted into balls.

Stamped forms are cut from light-weight metal with a flat steel tool with straight sharp edges. These forms may be domed with a tool or in a forming die and decorated by applied wire or with carved lines.

DOMES

The following silver sheet is required:
Sterling silver sheet 24-, 26-, or 28-gauge for rings or bracelets.
Fine silver sheet 24-, 26-, or 28-gauge for brooches, necklaces.

Heavier gauge silver is often used for the foundation dome.

Tools and Working Materials	Metal gauge Charcoal block Gas and air blow torch Pickle Gas plate Copper pickle pan Copper tongs Lead dapping block Hammer Dapping die cutters and punches Dapping die File Emery cloth

PROCESSES

Gauging the Metal	Gauge the metal sheet.
Annealing p. 18	Anneal the metal.
Pickling p. 22	Clean in pickle.
Cutting the Disks	Place the metal on the lead dapping die block. Strike the die cutter a sharp blow with the hammer. Repeat if the disk is not free from the metal sheet. *Note:* If the disk is larger than the dapping die cutter inscribe a circle on the metal. Saw the disk.
Doming the Disk	Select a hollow in the dapping die block which is slightly larger than the diameter of the disk. Place the disk in the center of the hollow.

PROCESSES

Place the dapping punch in the center of the disk.

Strike the dapping punch with the hammer to force the metal into the hollow. Deeper domes may be made by doming in successive smaller hollows. The metal may have to be annealed several times if the domes are to be hammered to any great depth.

Filing
p. 25

File the base of the disk even.

Smooth with emery cloth.

BALLS

*Tools
and
Working
Materials*

Fine silver wire
Table vise or jeweler's hand vise
Round mandrel
Jeweler's shears
Powdered borax
Gas and air blow torch
Charcoal block
Steel tweezers

Coiling
p. 108

Coil the wire around the mandrel.

*Cutting
the
Rings*

Cut the coil into rings.

*Melting
the
Rings
into
Balls*

Make a thick flux of borax.
Dip the ring in the flux.
Place the ring on the charcoal block.
Direct onto the ring the part of the flame just above the blue cone.
Melt the ring into a ball.
Repeat. Use the same method in melting the other rings.

STAMPED FORMS

Tools *and* *Working* *Materials*	Fine silver 26- or 28-gauge Battleship linoleum or sheet lead 10- or 12- gauge Stamping tool Hammer

PROCESSES

Stamping *the* *Forms*	Place the metal on the linoleum or sheet lead. Place the stamping tool on the metal. Strike the stamping tool a sharp blow with the hammer. Bend the linoleum or lead sheet. Remove the form which is embedded.

QUESTIONS

1. *Why is sterling used in place of fine silver for domes on rings and bracelets?*

    Fine silver dents easily and these two articles receive harder wear than brooches and pendants.

2. *Can sterling silver be melted into balls?*

    Sterling silver can be used but fine silver makes a smoother ball and has more lustre.

3. *Why are balls flat on one side when melted on the charcoal block?*

    If the metal is melted and cooled on the flat surface of the charcoal block, one side of the ball will be flat. This is often an advantage as the ball is easier to place.

4. *How can metal be melted into balls without the flat side?*

    Make small depressions in the charcoal block with a rounded tool. Melt the metal in this depression.

5. *Can balls be flattened into disks?*
   Hammer the ball directly on top to flatten it into a disk; anneal it if it starts to break around the edges.

6. *How is a large ball given a smooth surface?*
   Place the ball while slightly warm on the shellac stick. Buff the surface with tripoli and felt buffing wheel to smooth the surface.

7. *Should balls be removed from the charcoal block while still red hot?*
   Wait until the red glow disappears before removing the ball.

8. *Why is linoleum or sheet lead used to stamp the forms on?*
   This material is used so the embedded form may be removed with ease by breaking or bending the material.

9. *Is the stamping tool used for large forms?*
   This method of stamping is used only for small forms.

10. *Can sterling silver be used for stamped forms?*
    Annealed sterling silver may be used but it is more difficult to cut than fine silver, which is softer and has more lustre.

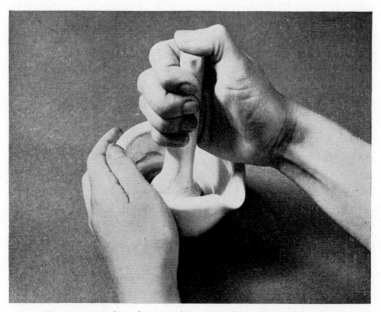

Fig. 47.—Grinding the enamel in a porcelain mortar with pestle

ENAMELING

Enameling is one of the oldest forms of metal decoration. It is used in jewelry to add richness of color, to enhance the beauty of stones, and to vary motifs. Enamels are composed of several ingredients which melt under heat to form a glazed surface either on a metal background or inserted in a network of wires without a background.

Soft enamels require less heat and fuse readily on the background, but produce a comparatively soft surface. Hard enamels require more intense heat to fuse satisfactorily, but produce a hard durable surface. Both forms of enamel are made to produce transparent, translucent, and opaque surfaces and come in varying degrees of hardness.

There are five distinct styles of enamel. Champlevé, Cloisonné, Bassetaille, and Limoges all require a foundation of metal. Plique à jour is held between cloisons of wire without a background.

It is apparent that when enamel is used design must take into account thickness, dullness, lustre, uneven surfaces, metal construction lines, color, and texture that are peculiar to enamel. When stones and enamel are combined the principles of design that apply to each medium must be adhered to but the two must be merged in such a way that each enhances the beauty of the other. In jewelry, enamel should be used in small areas to retain the jewel-like quality it should have. A few colors, and those brilliant, give the best results.

Tools	Metal—Gold 18-K or over, free from zinc in
and	the alloy
Working	Sterling or fine silver
Materials	Copper—gilding metal

Metal gauge	Tracing paper
Jeweler's saw frame	White beeswax or carbon paper
Jeweler's saw blade #1/0	Pencil
Bench pin	Scratch awl
Flat file	Pumice powder
Blow torch	Burnisher, scraper, or graver
Pickle	
Pickle pan	Enamel
Gas plate	Metal mortar and pestle or steel crusher (See Figs. 48, 49)
Copper tongs	
Wooden spatula	
Soda, ammonia, and water solution	Wedgwood or agate mortar (See Fig. 47)
Granite pan	
Scotch stone	Porcelain or agate pestle
Emery cloth	

*Tools
and
Working
Materials*

Set of shallow china dishes
Steel spatula or palette knife
Small camel's hair brush
White blotting paper
Enameling muffle furnace
Rouge paste
Palette knives, large and small
Steel cradle (See Fig. 50)
Iron tongs
Small scrub brush
Rubber, felt, or leather pad
Corundum stone
Dish lined with paraffin
Hydrofluoric acid
Pumice stone
Leather strip
Polishing motor
Felt buffing wheel
Crocus powder
Chamois cloth
Hard felt wheel or wooden wheel 6 inches diameter
Liquid shellac
Alcohol
Yellow flake shellac

Scraper or pointed steel tool
Shellac stick
Oil stone
Light oil
Gravers
Kerosene cloth
Binding wire 28-gauge
Two pieces of sheet iron 24-gauge, 4 or 6 inches
Bench vise
Draw tongs
Round hole draw plate
Round nose pliers
Blunt nose pliers
Brass block
Chisel
Hammer
Steel tweezers
Flux
Borax slate
Gold solder
Jeweler's shears
Gum tragacanth solution
Curved burnisher
Chaser's wax or modeling clay
Plate glass slab
Four wooden strips (See Fig. 52)
Plaster of Paris

*Tools
and
Working
Materials*

Binding wire 30-
   gauge
Mica sheet
Steel cotter pins
Needles mounted in cork
Glass bottles, large openings
Pickle for Silver—one part sulphuric acid, nine
   parts water
Pickle for Gold—one part nitric acid, eight
   parts water
Pickle for Copper—one part nitric acid, two
   parts water. If the metal is incised with the
   graver or tool polished do not dull the lustre
   by pickling.

Foil
Gummed tissue
Paper shears

PREPARATION FOR APPLYING THE ENAMEL
(*Choose one of the five methods*)

PROCESSES

THE METAL

Gauging
p. 346

Gauge the metal.
The gauge of the metal used will depend upon
the method of enameling chosen.

Sawing
p. 31

Saw the metal to pattern.

Filing
p. 25

File the edges.

Annealing
p. 18

Anneal the metal.

Pickling
p. 22

Clean in pickle.
Rinse in soda, ammonia, and water solution.
Remove any scratches with a file, scotch stone,
or emery cloth.

PROCESSES
*Transferring
the
Design*

Transfer the design and scratch into the surface of the metal.

*Preparing
the
Surface*

Prepare the surface of the metal to hold the enamel. This will depend upon which of the five methods is chosen.

Cleaning
p. 70

Clean the metal. (See Question 4.)

Immersing

Immerse in a bowl of clear water until ready to apply the enamels to keep the metal from oxidizing.

THE ENAMEL

Crushing

Crush the lumps of enamel in the metal crusher as shown in Figs. 48, 49.

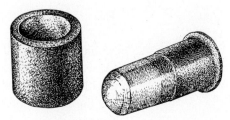

*Fig. 49.—Crushing
the enamel*

Fig. 48.—Enamel crusher

PROCESSES
*Grinding
the
Enamel
Medium
and
Fine*

Place the crushed enamel in a porcelain or agate mortar.

Wash in clear water.

Pour enough water in the mortar to cover the enamel.

Rotate the pestle firmly on the enamel in the mortar as shown in Fig. 47. Hold the elbow close to the body. Allow the ground enamel to settle.

Pour off the milky water.

Continue the grinding and washing process until the transparent or translucent enamel has been reduced to the consistency of coarse pumice powder. Opaque enamels should be ground finer. The final rinse water should be clear. Place the enamel after the final grinding and washing in a shallow porcelain dish in water ready for use.

*Very
Fine*

Use an agate mortar and pestle to grind enamels very fine; a mullar and plate glass sheet may also be used.

APPLYING THE ENAMEL TO THE METAL

(*Called Flooding In or Charging*)

*Flooding
In or
Charging*

Take a small daub of enamel on a wood or metal spatula, or a small camel's hair brush.

Saturate the ground enamel with water. If too wet, it will run off the spatula; if too dry, it will cling to the spatula.

Lay the enamel thinly and evenly on the metal. Tap the edge of the charged piece lightly to spread the enamel more evenly, in the small

PROCESSES

*Absorbing
the
Moisture*

*Removing
Surplus
Enamel
From the
Surrounding
Metal*

spaces; press the enamel into large areas with a small palette knife.

Apply the edge of a small strip of white blotting paper to the edges of the enamel to absorb any moisture.

Remove any surplus enamel from the metal with a fine camel's hair brush slightly dampened.

Note: Enamel too thickly applied chips when fired; if too thinly applied, bare spaces appear on the enameled surface.

PREPARATION FOR FIRING

*Heating
the
Kiln*

*Protecting
the
Soldered
Joints*

*Placing
the
Charged
Piece
for
Firing*

Heat the kiln—1400° F. or more. Hot enough to fuse the enamel.

Protect any soldered joints with rouge paste; care must be taken to keep the rouge away from the enamel.

Place the piece charged with enamel in the center of the cradle as shown in Fig. 50.

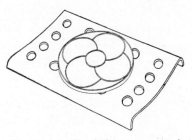

Fig. 50.—Cradle of sheet iron or steel

PROCESSES	FIRING THE ENAMEL
Drying the Enamel	Place the cradle in front of the open furnace and dry the enamel thoroughly.
	Grasp the cradle with the long tongs and insert it in the furnace. Withdraw quickly.
	If enamel is steaming repeat the above process; the enamel must be thoroughly dry before firing.
Firing the Enamel	Place the piece thoroughly dried in the center of the furnace.
	Watch carefully and remove when the enamel has fused and the surface has become glossy.
Cooling	Allow to cool in a warm place.

FINISHING

Pickling p. 22	Pickle the enameled piece—gold or copper in nitric acid pickle, silver in sulphuric acid pickle.
Cleaning	Scrub well with a stiff brush charged with fine pumice powder; wash well under running water.
Recharging	Apply the enamel and dry out as above.
Refiring	Place the enamel on a hot cradle and fire before the cradle cools.
	Examine the enamel. If the surface is uneven or the color is lost or if the enamel is too thick the surface will have to be stoned and cleaned in acid and refired; if the enamel has shrunk, the surface will have to be recharged.
Stoning	Place the enameled piece on rubber, felt, or leather. This will relieve the strain on the enamel.

PROCESSES

Rub a corundum stone over the surface if uneven or if the color is lost. Keep both the stone and the enamel wet—running water is best. The surface of the enamel should be even with the metal surface.

Dipping
in
Acid

Wash in clear water.
Paint a coat of paraffin on the inside of a saucer or bowl.
Pour hydrofluoric acid in the saucer.
Dip the article in the hydrofluoric acid to remove any residue left after stoning. Care must be taken not to inhale the fumes of this acid. It must be kept in a covered container of guttapercha or paraffin.
Rinse in clear running water.
Dry the piece.

Recharging
Refiring

Recharge the surface if the enamel has shrunk.
Refire to bring back the lustre after stoning or recharging.

Pickling
Washing

Pickle the metal.
Wash the metal in water. The piece may have to be charged and fired several times.

Polishing
by
Machine
for
High Polish

Hold the article to be polished on a piece of leather.
Cover the enameled surface with fine wet pumice powder.
Buff with a felt buffing wheel.
Add more pumice as it is buffed off by the action of the wheel. Continue until the desired lustre has been obtained.
Wash thoroughly in clear water.
Care must be taken not to wear down the metal which is softer than the enamel.

PROCESSES
Finishing
Mat with
Abrasives

Rub the surface with pumice powder and water. Clean with scotch stone; rub in a circular movement; keep the scotch stone wet during this operation.

Finishing
Mat with
Acids

Dip the stoned and washed piece in a solution of hydrofluoric acid to make the enameled surface dull.

Combining
Mat and
Polished
Surfaces

If only parts of the surface are to be dull, cover the parts to remain polished with shellac.
Dip in hydrofluoric acid for a few minutes until the surface of the exposed enamel is dull.
Wash thoroughly in water.
Soak in alcohol to remove the shellac.

REPAIRING FLAWS IN THE ENAMELED SURFACE AFTER FIRING

Repairing
Holes
and
Uncovered
Spots

Clean out any holes in the enamel with a scraper or graver or pointed steel tool.
Scrape any uncovered spots in the metal and remove any discoloration on the enameled edge.
Rub with a corundum stone.
Dip in hydrofluoric acid.
Wash in clear water with a stiff brush.
Recharge holes or the entire surface with enamel if necessary.
Refire as described above.

CHAMPLEVÉ ENAMEL

The enamel is fused into a sunken surface of metal in which the design has been carved, stamped, pierced, or soldered to a background, or etched with acid. Casting is also used although the cast surface is rather porous for this type of work.

The following metal sheet and enamel are required:

Silver or gold 18-gauge
Copper 16- to 18-gauge
Transparent, translucent, or opaque enamel

PROCESSES

Preparing the Metal p. 128	Prepare the metal for enameling.
Carving to Prepare the Surface p. 87	Carve the scratched outline of the design with an onglette graver. Carve the design in the metal with a blunt graver about $\frac{1}{30}$ to $\frac{1}{20}$ inch below the surface. A small edge of metal the original thickness should be left around the design. Roughened surfaces act as keys to hold the enamel. Care must be exercised in cutting the metal as flaws will be magnified if transparent or translucent enamel is used.
Preparing the Enamel p. 129	Prepare the enamel.
Charging p. 130	Charge the sunken surfaces with enamel.
Preparing for Firing p. 131	Prepare for firing.
Firing p. 132	Heat the enamel until it fuses.

PROCESSES

Repairing   Remove any flaws on the enameled surface.
p. 134

Recharging and   Recharge and refire the enamel; repeat several
Refiring   times if necessary until the enamel is flush with
p. 132   the metal surface.

Finishing   Finish the enameled surface.
p. 132

CLOISONNÉ ENAMEL

Cloisonné is made in sections formed of flattened wire set edgewise to form boxes or cloisons into which the enamel is fused. The cloisons are arranged to form the design.

The following metal sheet, wire, solder, and enamel are required:

> Sterling or fine silver or gold sheet, 24- to 26-gauge
> $\frac{1}{32}$ inch wide 32-gauge wire
> Transparent, translucent, or opaque enamel
> Solder 9-K, 18-K gold wire for pure gold

PROCESSES

Preparing   Sterling silver sheet, 24-gauge.
the   Prepare the metal background.   The metal may
Metal   be raised slightly toward the center if desired.
p. 128

Annealing   Sterling silver wire $\frac{1}{32}$ inch wide, 32-gauge.
the   Make a coil of wire and bind as shown in
Wire   Fig. 4.
p. 20   Place the coil of wire between two pieces of
          sheet iron to anneal.

Winding   Wind the wire tightly on a spool to keep it
the   from kinking.
Wire

PROCESSES

Forming the Cloisons

Form the wire cloisons with small pliers to follow the outline of the design.

Cutting the Wire

Place the wire on a block of brass.
Use a small sharp chisel to cut wire units.

Applying the Cloisons

Dip the cloison in gum tragacanth solution and flux.
Place the cloisons on the metal background; follow the scratched line of the design. Continue this with the other cloisons.

Soldering
p. 38

Place small pieces of solder on the joints of wire and the background; use as little solder as possible.
Solder in place.
Note: Often just the outer cloisons or the main part of the cloisons are held on with solder.

Pickling
p. 22

Clean in pickle.

Cleaning

Clean the metal background between cloisons with a scraper or burnisher.

Immersing

Immerse in a bowl of cold water.

Preparing the Enamel
p. 129

Prepare the enamel.

Charging
p. 130

Charge the metal background until the enamel is level with the rim of the cloison.

Preparing for Firing
p. 131

Prepare for firing.

PROCESSES

Firing   Fire the enamel until it fuses.
p. 132

Removing   Remove any flaws from the enameled surface.
Flaws
p. 134

Recharging   Recharge and refire the enamel.   This may
and   have to be done several times until the enamel
Refiring   is flush with the top of the cloisons.

Finishing   Finish the enameled surface.
p. 132

BASSETAILLE ENAMEL

Bassetaille enamel is much like champlevé enamel. The design is carved or executed in repoussé in low relief about $\frac{1}{30}$ inch below the surface. Transparent enamel is fused over the design, possibly several times, until a uniform surface is obtained. For this method gold or silver should be used as the reflecting quality is better than copper. The design may be concave or convex and must be executed with great care; interesting shadow effects are obtained as the depth of the enamel varies. One or more colors may be used.

The following metal sheet and enamel are required:

Silver or gold sheet, 18-gauge or heavier ⎱ for a carved
Copper sheet, 18-gauge or heavier   ⎰ design

Silver or gold 26- or 27-gauge ⎱ for a repoussé design
Copper 24- or 25-gauge   ⎰

Transparent enamel

PROCESSES

Preparing   Prepare the metal.
the
Metal
p. 128

PROCESSES

*Preparing
the
Surface
Carving*
p. 87
*or
Repoussé*
p. 77

Model the design either by carving or repoussé. The higher part should be about $\frac{1}{30}$ inch below the rim which remains the original thickness of the metal.

Burnishing

Burnish the surface to clean.
If the surface has been incised with the graver this will be sufficient.

Immersing

Immerse in a bowl of cold water until ready to apply the enamel.

*Preparing
the
Enamel*
p. 129

Prepare the enamel.

Charging
p. 130

Charge the piece with enamel. If several colors are used let each one dry before adding another as there is no retaining wall between colors. A small amount of gum tragacanth can be mixed with the enamel to keep it from spreading.
If the design has been executed in repoussé the metal must be keyed on the back with a graver and enamel mixed with a little gum tragacanth painted on. Absorb the moisture with blotting paper before charging the other side.

*Preparing
for
Firing*
p. 131

Prepare for firing.

PROCESSES

Firing p. 132	Fire the enamel until it fuses.
Removing *Flaws* p. 134	Remove any flaws on the enameled surface.
Recharging *and* *Refiring* p. 132	Recharge and refire the enamel until it is even with the outside rim. The last layer of enamel should be crystal clear.
Finishing p. 132	Finish the surface.

LIMOGES OR PAINTED ENAMEL

Limoges or painted enamel is used mainly for pictorial work. The enamel, ground very fine, is painted and fused on the metal without a retaining wall to separate colors or parts of the design.

The following metal sheet and enamel are required:

Silver and gold sheet, 26-, 27-, or 28-gauge

Copper sheet, 24-, 25-, or 26-gauge

Transparent, translucent, or opaque enamel

PROCESSES

Preparing *the* *Metal* p. 128	Prepare the metal for enameling.
Preparing *the* *Surface*	Raise slightly toward the center using a curved burnisher, or place it on a stake, and planish the surface. Turn the edge down at an angle. Key the under side of the dome with a graver.

	File the edges until they rest evenly on a flat surface. Leave the rough edge or burr on the edge; it helps to hold the enamel in place.
	Transfer the design and scratch the outline into the metal; use the carbon method.
	Anneal the metal.
	Clean in pickle.
	Scrub with a brush and fine pumice powder.
	Prepare the enamel. (See Question 6.)
	Place the raised metal on a piece of white blotting paper, convex side down. Mix a little solution of gum tragacanth with the enamel. Charge the keyed surface evenly with the enamel. Absorb the moisture with a strip of white blotting paper.
	Turn the enameled piece over; let it rest on a clean piece of blotting paper. Charge each section with enamel and absorb the moisture with strips of white blotting paper. Each section should be nearly dry before placing a new color next to it. This precaution will keep the colors from running into each other.

PROCESSES

Preparing for Firing p. 131	Prepare the piece for firing.
Firing p. 132	Fire the enamel until it fuses.
Repairing p. 134	Remove any flaws which occur in the enameled surface.
Recharging and Refiring p. 132	Recharge and refire. The piece may have to be recharged and refired several times to get a smooth surface or the desired depth of color.
Finishing p. 132	Finish the enameled surface.

PLIQUE À JOUR ENAMEL

Plique à jour enamel is the name given to enamel set in wire filigree or pierced metal sheet which forms a fretwork for the enamel and remains a part of the design in the finished piece. When held to the light it has the appearance of stained glass surrounded by metal frames.

The following metal sheet or oblong wire and enamel are required:

     Silver or gold sheet, 18- to 20-gauge
     Copper sheet, 16- to 18-gauge
     Oblong wire
     Transparent enamel

PROCESSES

Annealing p. 18	Anneal the wire.
Wire Drawing p. 96	Draw the flat wire through the round draw plate to curve the edges slightly to form a slight hollow. This acts as a key to hold the enamel.

PROCESSES
Shaping

Shape the wire according to the design with the pliers and tweezers, the hollow side of the wire on the inside.

Cutting
p. 137

Cut the wires, where necessary, to form units with the chisel.

Placing
the
Units
in
Wax

Place chaser's wax or modeling clay on a glass surface, the area a little larger than the design. Level the top of the wax or clay.

Place the units to form the design on the wax or clay. Under each unit place pieces of binding wire 28- or 30-gauge. Let the ends extend upward and beyond the wire edge of the unit about ¼ inch.

Press the units into the wax or clay, only a small edge extending above as shown in Fig. 51.

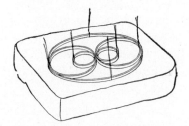

Fig. 51.—Wire units pressed into clay or wax

Boxing

Wet four strips of wood in water and place around the wax to form a box; let them extend an inch or more above the wax or clay surface as shown in Fig. 52.

Making
the
Mold

Mix some plaster of Paris with water; stir slowly until the mixture is of creamy consistency.

Pour in a small amount of plaster and blow

PROCESSES

over the surface of the embedded motif; continue with the pouring until the plaster is level with the top of the box.

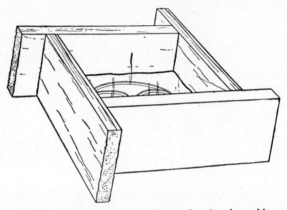

Fig. 52.—Wooden strips to form a box for the mold

Let the plaster set, remove the boards, and draw out the wax or clay. The binding wires should be firm in the plaster to hold the units in place as shown in Fig. 53.

Bake to remove all moisture from the plaster.

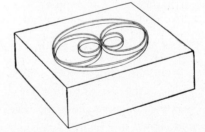

Fig. 53.—Wire units embedded in a plaster of Paris mold

Cleaning
the
Motif

Remove all plaster and oxidation from the wires with a scraper.

	Cover all joints and points of contact with flux. Apply small pieces of solder or solder filings. Solder.
	Soak the mold in water to release the wire design.
	Clean in pickle.
	Clean the wires with a scraper or burnisher.
	Immerse in a bowl of cold water until ready to charge with enamel.

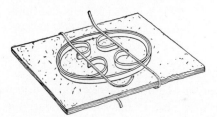

Fig. 54.—Motif held to a mica sheet with nickel cotter pins

	Prepare the enamel.
	Place the motif on a piece of mica—the mica may first be laid on a piece of sheet iron. If the motif is large it should be held to the mica with U-shaped wires made of nickel, as shown in Fig. 54.

PROCESSES *Charging* p. 130	Charge the cells made by the wires; more enamel can be placed in the center than at the edges.
Firing p. 132	Fire the enamel until it fuses.
Repairing	Remove any flaws on the enameled surface.
Recharging and Refiring	Recharge and refire until the enameled cells are full.
Finishing p. 132	Finish the enamel on both sides of the piece.
Piercing p. 35	*Note*: The design may be pierced from metal sheet to form a fretwork.
Keying	Incise the sides of the metal in several places on each side of all openings with the graver. This is called keying and holds the enamel in place.

FOILS

Gold, silver, or platinum foils can be used in many decorative ways. Transparent enamel may be fused over the foil to give it greater brilliancy or the foil may be cut into decorative motifs and applied to the enamel and a clear transparent enamel fused over the surface for protection. Care must be taken not to change the brilliancy or color of the enamel when it is used over the foil. Yellow, green, red, or green blue may be used over gold foil and blue and violet over silver or platinum foil to produce the best color values.

PROCESSES *Charging and Firing*	Charge the metal with enamel. Fire the piece.

PROCESSES

Holding the Foils	Place the foil between gummed tissue paper.
Pricking the Surface	Prick the entire surface with needle points.
Transferring the Design	Transfer the design to be cut on the tissue paper.
Cutting	Cut the pattern with the shears.
Removing the Tissue	Soak the foil in water to remove the tissue.
Holding the Foil	Hold the foil unit to the enameled surface with a solution of gum tragacanth.
Shading	Soften the outline of the foil by shading with finely ground enamel painted on with a brush. This will not be necessary if the foil is used in cloisonné or champlevé enamel where there is a definite edge of metal.
Firing	Fire the piece until the foil holds firmly and smoothly to the enameled surface.
Recharging and Refiring p. 132	Recharge and refire the enameled piece.
Finishing p. 132	Finish the enameled surface.

Questions

1. *Is it always necessary to have a furnace to melt the enamels?*
   A blow torch can be used for some types of enameling though care must be taken to keep the direct flame from the enamel surface.
2. *What kind of heat is usually used for the furnace?*
   Electricity or gas are preferred; oil and coke are also used.
3. *What metals should be used for enamel work?*
   Gold, 18-K or finer; silver, sterling or fine silver; copper; gilding metal or fine bronze.
4. *If the metal has been incised with a graver or tool polished should it be pickled?*
   Pickling dulls the lustre of the tool finish. Care must be taken not to touch the surface. Immerse immediately in water until the piece is ready to charge the enamel.
5. *How are enamels purchased?*
   Enamels are purchased from the factory in lump form by the pound, ounce, or quarter ounce in almost any color.
6. *How is enamel ground into a powder?*
   An agate mortar and pestle are used with a small amount of water to grind the enamel to the consistency required.
7. *Should fused samples of the enamels be made before using?*
   Samples should be made of the enamels before using to test the fusing point of each enamel and its color.
8. *Can enamels be combined to change the color?*
   Enamels of the same fusing can be mixed together, charged and fired, but a better effect will be obtained by fusing a transparent color over an opaque color.
9. *How can fired enamel be removed from the surface of the metal?*
   Hold the enameled piece in cold water and tap the obverse side with a steel hammer. Place in hydrofluoric acid.

10. *Can ground enamel be kept?*

Ground enamel can be kept in water for short period of time, if kept in a wide-mouthed bottle well corked.

11. *Does gum tragacanth change the color of the enamel?*

Gum tragacanth used in liquid form and only a small quantity in the enamel or on the foils does not discolor the enamel.

12. *What is enamel flux?*

Enamel flux is the clear substance into which oxides are mixed to form the colored enamels.

13. *Why are fluxes used?*

Transparent enamels are more brilliant if fired over a coating of flux.

14. *What solder should be used?*

To prevent discoloration in the enamel gold solder should be used. For general soldering 9-K is used; for fine gold 18-K gold wire is used.

15. *What metal is used for the cradles?*

Nickel is preferred for the cradles as it does not scale. Iron may be used but should have a coating of rouge on the surface.

16. *Why are the cradles equally perforated?*

To obtain a uniform heat for the enameled piece under fire.

17. *How is the tarnish removed from the foil?*

Anneal the foil in the furnace.

18. *Why do the foils crinkle when they are fired?*

Foils should be annealed before being applied to the enamel. Many of the foils are annealed when purchased.

19. *Why is the foil perforated with holes?*

To make it easier to handle and less likely to crinkle, also to allow air to escape.

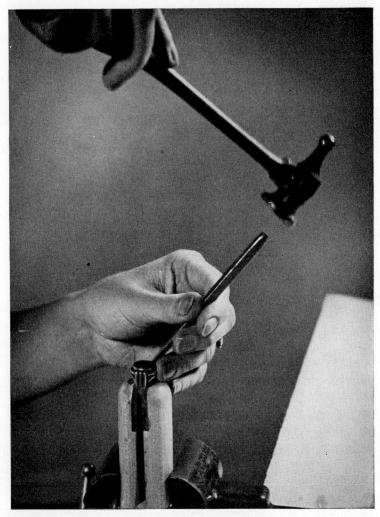

Fig. 55.—Setting the stone

STONE SETTING

Stones are set in jewelry to give color and lustre. They are selected to suit the design or the design is made to fit around the stone, thus making the setting and the design a single unit. The method to be used for settings is determined by the shape and cut of the stone and the construction and design of the article. Four methods used for setting stones in hand-made jewelry are the round bezel as shown in Fig. 56, the mitered bezel as shown in Fig. 58, the claw or crown setting as shown in Fig. 59, and the paved or gypsy setting as shown in Fig. 62.

The round and mitered bezels require a set-in bearing of flat metal or wire, which not only strengthens the bezel but insures an even base for the stone when the bezel is soldered on a curved surface. It also raises the stone high enough to allow for a decoration at the base of the bezel if desired. The bearing for a gypsy setting is carved into the metal. The bearing for a claw or crown setting can either be carved or set in.

The following silver sheet is required:

Sterling silver sheet 26-gauge for the round bezel
Sterling silver sheet 26- or 28-gauge for the bearing
Sterling silver sheet 16- or 18-gauge for the claw or crown setting
Sterling silver sheet 10-gauge or heavier for the paved or gypsy setting

Tools	Dentimetre	Charcoal block
and	Binding wire	Gas and air blow torch
Working	26-gauge	Pickle
Materials	Jeweler's shears	Copper pickle pan
	Dividers	Copper tongs
	Metal gauge	Gas plate

*Tools
and
Working
Materials*

Flat nose pliers
Binding wire
   28-gauge
Flux
Borax slate or saucer
Solder
Camel's hair brush
Bench vise
Round mandrel
Wood or rawhide
   mallet
Wax stone lifter
Half round file
Steel hammer
Cotter pins
Scotch stone
Emery cloth
Polishing motor
Felt buffing wheel
Tripoli cake
Soda, ammonia, and
   water solution
Granite pan
Cloth or chamois buf-
   fing wheel
Rouge stick
Potassium sulphide so-
   lution

Whiting
Bench pin
Jeweler's saw frame
Jeweler's saw blade
   #1/0
Small square file
Ruler
Scratch awl
Pencil compass
Tracing paper
Soft pencil
White beeswax
Soft cloth
Yellow flake shellac
Shellac stick, ring
   clamp, or hand vise
Gravers
Oilstone
Light oil
Kerosene cloth
Center punch
Hand drill
Twist drill
Small repoussé tool
Chasing hammer
Pusher
Burnisher
Soft cloth buffing
   wheel

ROUND BEZEL AND BEARING

A round bezel is made of a band of metal formed into a collar to fit closely around the stone. A strip of metal or wire the same gauge or lighter than the bezel, cut narrower, is set inside and fitted closely to the bezel for the girdle of the stone to rest upon. Enough of the bezel is allowed to extend above the bearing to be tapped and burnished over the stone to hold the setting firmly in place.

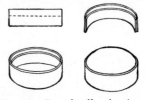

Fig. 56.—*Round collar, bearing, and cabochon stone*

Type of Stone

Round cabochon stone.

PROCESSES

Measuring the Circumference of the Stone

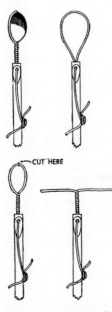

CUT HERE

Fig. 57.—*Measuring the girdle of a stone with the dentimetre and binding wire*

Make a loop of 26-gauge binding wire. Run the two ends of the wire into the holes of the dentimetre. Place the stone in the loop. Twist the wire until it fits the girdle of the stone. Cut the loop in the center. Spread the ends to determine the length to cut the strip for the bezel.

PROCESSES
*Measuring
the
Depth
of the
Stone*

Determine the width of the strip for the bezel. If the bezel is set on a curved surface, measure from the girdle of the stone well over the curve.

BEZEL

Gauging
p. 346

Gauge the metal, sterling silver sheet 26-gauge.

Annealing
p. 18

Anneal the metal.

Pickling
p. 22

Clean in pickle.

Filing
p. 25

File one edge straight.

*Laying
out
the
Pattern*

Place one arm of the dividers over the straight edge of the silver sheet.

Cutting

Cut the strip thus marked.

Fitting

Bend the strip so the two ends meet; file if necessary to make an even joint.

Binding
p. 44

Bind together as shown in Fig. 13.

Soldering
p. 38

Solder the joint to form a collar or bezel.

Pickling

Clean in pickle.

Forming

Place the bezel on a round mandrel.
Tap lightly with wooden or rawhide mallet to form into a circle.

PROCESSES *Fitting* *the* *Stone* *in the* *Bezel*	Warm the wax stone lifter sufficiently for it to adhere to the top center of the stone. See Question 13. If the bezel is too large for the stone see Question 3. If the bezel is too small to fit the stone see Question 4.
Truing	True the edges with a file or emery cloth.

BEARING

Measuring *the* *Bezel*	Measure the inside circumference of the bezel to determine the length of the bearing; the width should be narrower than that of the bezel.
Gauging	Gauge the metal, sterling silver sheet 28-gauge.
Annealing	Anneal the metal.
Pickling	Clean in pickle.
Making *the* *Bearing*	Follow the directions given in making a round bezel.
Inserting *the* *Bearing* *in the* *Bezel*	Insert the bearing in the bezel; leave enough of the bezel above the bearing to turn over the curve of the stone. The rim of the bearing must be parallel with the top rim of the bezel as shown in Fig. 56.
Binding	Hold together with cotter pins as shown in Fig. 13.
Soldering	Place flux and small pieces of solder on the lower rim of the bezel and bearing. Solder together.

PROCESSES
Filing

File the base of the bezel and bearing to true if necessary.

File the thickness of the upper edge which is to be hammered or burnished over the stone to 28-gauge.

Cleaning

Remove any scratches or excess solder with a file and scotch stone.

Polishing
p. 71

Buff with a felt buffing wheel and tripoli.

Polish with a cloth buffing wheel and rouge.

Coloring
p. 72

Color in potassium sulphide solution.

Remove excess color with whiting.

Polish with a cloth buffing wheel.

SQUARE MITERED BEZEL AND BEARING

A mitered bezel is used for square, oblong, or other angular stones. The mitered bezel, as its name indicates, is made of a strip of metal cut in sections which are fitted together to form the size and the shape of the stone to be set. The bearing required for

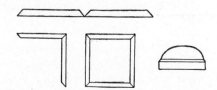

Fig. 58.—Square bezel, bearing, and cabochon stone

this setting may be made from a strip of metal scored and bent to fit inside the bezel or it may be formed of pieces mitered together the same way the bezel was made.

Type
of
Stone

Square cabochon stone.

PROCESSES   BEZEL

Measuring the Circumference of the Stone p. 153	Measure one side of the stone at the girdle to determine the length to cut the strip for the bezel.
Measuring the Depth of the Stone p. 154	Measure with the dividers over the curve of the stone to determine the width of the strip for the bezel. If the bezel is to be set on a curved surface see Question 10.
Gauging p. 346	Gauge the metal, sterling silver sheet 24-gauge.
Annealing p. 18	Anneal the metal.
Pickling p. 22	Clean in pickle.
Laying out the Pattern	Place the dividers over the straight edge of the 24-gauge metal. Scratch a line on the metal, a little more than twice the length of one side.
Sawing p. 31	Saw two strips this measured length.
Marking	Scratch a line across the center of each strip.
Scoring	File about 7/8 inch through the silver with the corner of the square file; keep the angle of the file straight.
Bending	Bend each piece of silver at a right angle at the filed angle.

PROCESSES	Solder the seams.
Soldering	
p. 38	
Measuring	Place one section just soldered around two sides of the stone.
	Measure diagonally across the stone from corner to corner.
	Mark the silver at this angle.
	Repeat with the second section.
Sawing	Saw the silver on the marked line.
Fitting	Place the two sections together to form a frame to fit around the stone.
	Remove the stone.
	File the ends of each bent piece to make an even joint.
Holding	Place the two sections on the charcoal block.
	Hold to the charcoal block with staples made of binding wire as shown in Fig. 12.
Soldering	Solder the mitered joints.
Pickling	Clean in pickle.
p. 22	
Fitting	Fit the stone in the bezel.
	Warm the wax stone-lifter sufficiently for it to adhere to the top center of the stone and hold it in position for repeated fittings. See Question 13.
	If the bezel is too large for the stone see Question 3.
	If the bezel is too small for the stone see Question 5.
Truing	True the edges with a file and emery cloth.

PROCESSES	BEARING
Measuring the Bezel	Measure the inside circumference of the bezel to determine the length of the bearing. The width should be narrower than that of the bezel.
Gauging	Gauge the metal, sterling silver sheet 28-gauge.
Annealing	Anneal the metal.
Pickling	Clean in pickle.
Making the Bearing	Follow the directions given in making a square mitered bezel.
Inserting the Bearing in the Bezel	Insert the bearing in the bezel and leave enough of the bezel above the bearing to turn over the curve of the stone. The rim of the bearing must be parallel with the rim of the bezel.
Binding	Hold together with cotter pins as shown in Fig. 13.
Soldering	Place flux and solder on the lower rim of the bezel and bearing. Solder together.
Filing p. 25	File the base of the bezel and the bearing to true, if necessary. File the thickness of the upper edge of the bezel which is to be hammered or burnished over the stone to 28-gauge.
Cleaning p. 70	Remove scratches and excess solder with a file and scotch stone.
Polishing p. 71	Buff with a felt buffing wheel and tripoli. Polish with a cloth or chamois buffing wheel and rouge.

PROCESSES
Coloring
p. 72
Color in potassium sulphide solution.
Remove excess color with whiting.
Polish with a soft cloth buffing wheel.

CLAW OR CROWN BEZEL AND BEARING

A claw or crown setting is made in the form of a frustum of a hollow cone as shown in Fig. 60, to fit the stone. After the number of prongs has been determined they are made by sawing or filing the sections to form, usually of uniform size or shape and long enough to be burnished over the stone to hold it in place.

The bearing for this type of setting may be carved in the bezel or set in. The bezel may be carved, pierced, or sawed if the design requires this decoration.

Fig. 59.—Crown setting pierced, carved bearing, faceted stone

*Type
of
Stone*

Round brilliant cut.

PROCESSES   **BEZEL**

*Measuring
the
Circumference
of the
Stone*
Measure the circumference of the stone at the girdle as shown in Fig. 57.

*Measuring
the
Depth
of the
Stone*
Measure the stone from the base or point over the girdle of the stone.

Gauging
p. 346
Gauge the metal, sterling silver sheet 16- or 18-gauge.

PROCESSES

Annealing p. 18	Anneal the metal.
Pickling p. 22	Clean in pickle.

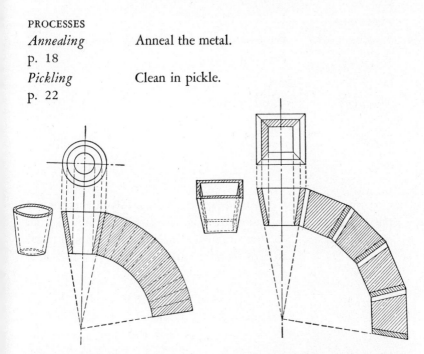

Fig. 60.—*Pattern for a frustum of a hollow cone*   Fig. 60.—*Pattern for a frustum of a hollow pyramid*

Laying out the Pattern	Lay out the frustum of a hollow cone as shown in Fig. 60. When the pattern has been sawed, soldered, and shaped it should fit the girdle of the stone.
Transferring the Design p. 33	Transfer the pattern to the metal. Use the wax method.
Sawing	Saw to pattern.
Bending	Bend so the two ends meet.
Filing	File to make an even joint.

PROCESSES

Binding   Bind firmly together as shown in Fig. 13.

Soldering   Solder the joint.
p. 38

Pickling   Clean in pickle.

Polishing   Buff with a felt buffing wheel and tripoli.
p. 71

BEARING

Carving   Carve the bearing for the girdle of the stone to
the   rest upon. It should be carved far enough from
Bearing   the top rim of the bezel to leave enough metal
p. 87   to turn over the stone.

PRONGS

Transferring   Paint the metal with shellac alcohol dye so-
the   lution.
Design   Block the prongs and the design with the
p. 36   scratch awl.

Filing   File the metal between the blocked prongs.
                             File the end of the prongs a lighter gauge.

Carving   Carve the prongs to hold the stone.   The bezel
                             may be ornamented by sawing, piercing, carv-
                             ing, and by appliqué.

Cleaning   Remove any scratches with a file and scotch
p. 70   stone.

Polishing   Buff with a felt buffing wheel and tripoli.
p. 71   Polish with a cloth buffing wheel and rouge.

Coloring   Color with potassium sulphide solution.
p. 72   Remove excess color with whiting.
                             Polish with a chamois buffing wheel.

PAVED OR GYPSY SETTING

The paved setting, or gypsy setting, as this type of setting is sometimes called, is carved into the metal to form a recess the exact size of the girdle of the stone and to form the base on which it is to rest. This type of setting necessitates enough metal above the bearing to be tapped and burnished over the stone to hold it in place. The thickness of the upper edge of a gypsy setting is usually somewhat great and should be filed at an angle so that the burnished edge will mold over it and blend with the surfaces of the stone.

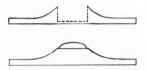

Fig. 62.—*Paved setting, carved bearing, and cabochon stone*

Type	Round cabochon stone.
of	
Stone	

PROCESSES	SETTING
Gauging p. 346	Gauge the metal, sterling silver sheet 10-gauge or heavier. The gauge must be thick enough to leave enough metal above the bearing to tap over the curve of the stone.
Transferring the Pattern p. 33	Transfer the pattern to the metal. Use the wax method.
Sawing p. 31	Saw to pattern.
Annealing p. 18	Anneal the metal.
Pickling p. 22	Clean in pickle.
Shaping	Shape the article before carving the setting.

PROCESSES	
Holding	Place the metal to be carved in the shellac stick, ring clamp, or hand vise, or any other tool which will hold the article firmly during the carving process.
Transferring the Size of the Girdle of the Stone on the Metal	Place the stone on the metal. Scratch the exact size of the girdle of the stone on the metal to be carved.
Carving the Box for the Setting p. 87	Carve just below the surface of the metal on the line just scratched with an onglette graver. Remove the metal from the inside of the box with the flat graver; let the graver meet the first carved line so as to chip off the metal. Make the first line of the outline deeper. Remove the metal with the flat graver as before. Continue the above until the required depth of the box has been reached.
Filing p. 25	File away the metal around the box at an angle; keep the original depth of the metal around the top of the box as shown in Fig. 62. *Note:* The box may be open under the stone by piercing the metal, leaving a ledge for the stone to rest upon.
Cleaning p. 70	Remove any scratches with a file and scotch stone.
Polishing p. 71	Buff with a felt buffing wheel and tripoli. Polish with a cloth buffing wheel and rouge.

PROCESSES
Coloring
p. 72

Color with potassium sulphide solution.
Remove excess color with whiting.
Polish with a chamois buffing wheel.

SETTING THE STONES

Stones are set after the article has been colored and buffed.

The edge of the bezel is then tapped or burnished over the stone to hold it in place.

*Holding
the
Article*

Hold the article on a shellac stick or in ring clamp, depending upon the size and the shape of the article.

Place the tool selected to hold the article in the jaws of the table vise.

*Setting
the
Stone*

Place the stone in the set with the stone lifter; be sure the girdle of the stone rests on the bearing.

Tap the metal around and over the stone with a small repoussé tool and chasing hammer as shown in Fig. 55.

Smooth with a file or graver.

Burnish the metal thus hammered with a burnisher.

Remove the article from the tool which holds it; if held in a shellac stick see Question 14.

*Setting
Small
Stones*

Small stones may be set by pushing the bezel over with the pusher and finishing with a burnisher.

Finishing

Remove any marks left by the setting tool.

Retouch with a small brush and color.

Rub with a chamois cloth or buffing wheel for the final polish. A burnisher may also be used.

FORMS FOR HOLDING THE BEZELS

FRUSTUM OF A CONE, PYRAMID, AND WIRE GALLERY

Frustum of a hollow cone

 Sterling silver sheet 20-gauge.

 Lay out and saw a form as shown in Fig. 60.

 Solder the joint and shape.

 Sterling silver sheet 22-gauge.

 Solder the large opening to silver sheet.

 Saw and file the edges even.

 Bind and solder the bezel on the covered end of the cone.

 File the base as shown at A.

 Fit and solder to the shank as shown at B.

 Two cones may be made and soldered together.

Fig. 63.—*Frustum of a hollow cone holding a bezel*

Frustum of a hollow pyramid

 Sterling silver sheet 18-gauge.

 Lay out and saw a form as shown in Fig. 61.

 File and bend on the angles as shown in Fig. 58.

 Solder the joint.

 Sterling silver sheet 20-gauge.

 Solder the large opening to the silver sheet.

 Saw and file the edges even.

 Bind and solder the bezel to the flat surface.

 File the base as shown at A.

 Fit and solder as shown at B.

 Two pyramids may be soldered together.

Fig. 64.—*Frustum of a hollow pyramid holding a bezel*

Gallery

Make two rings.

Solder the joints and shape into a circle.

Make the desired number of small rings to fit the circumference of the large ring.

Solder the small rings into a band as shown in Fig. 77.

Bend the band so the two end rings meet.

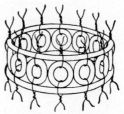

Bind and solder.

Shape the band into a circle.

Bind and solder to the two rings.

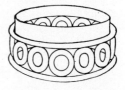

Solder the bezel to the gallery.

Fig. 65.—*Wire gallery holding a bezel*

Questions

1. *Can the girdle of a stone with a curved contour be measured with any other tool than the dentimetre?*
   A piece of binding wire doubled, held and twisted with snub nose pliers, or a strip of paper may also be used to measure around the stone.

2. *When the bezel is made of 18-gauge or heavier, is the strip of metal cut longer than the circumference of the girdle of the stone?*
   Bezels made of 18-gauge or heavier are cut the length of the circumference of the stone plus the thickness of the metal.

3. *Is it possible to make the bezel smaller if it is found to be too large for the stone after it has been soldered and shaped?*
   Measure the bezel and cut out the excess metal at the joint, solder, and shape.

4. *If the bezel is too small to fit the stone is it possible to enlarge it?*
   The bezel can be made larger by slipping it on the steel mandrel and tapping it lightly with a steel hammer. If it is hammered on a tapered mandrel it should be reversed at intervals so that it will stretch evenly on both edges. If it has to be stretched much it should be annealed.

5. *Is it possible to enlarge a mitered bezel?*
   Slip the bezel on a flat mandrel. Tap the bezel with a steel hammer, taking care to tap all sides evenly.

6. *What gauge metal is used for small bezels?*
   28-gauge metal is used for a round or mitered bezel.

7. *Is sterling or fine silver used for very small bezels?*
   Fine silver is used.

8. *Can several bezels be made the same size at the same time?*
   Metal can be formed into a tube, soldered, and cut the

desired width for a round bezel. A mitered bezel may be made wider than desired and sawed into sections the desired width.

9. *Should the piece be cleaned, buffed, and colored before the stone is set?*

Scratches and solder should be removed and the piece polished and colored before the stone is set to avoid scratching or discoloring the stone.

10. *How is a bezel made to fit a curved surface?*

The pattern for the bezel must be wide enough to allow for filing the base the contour of the curve. The bezel must touch at all points.

11. *If the bezel has a backing of metal should it be pierced under the stone?*

If the stone is transparent or translucent the metal should be pierced under the stone. Sometimes it is pierced to reduce the weight of the article.

12. *When should the piercing be done?*

It should be pierced after the article has been shaped and the bezel soldered in place.

13. *What tool is used to pick up the stone when fitting it in the bezel?*

A stone lifter is used which is made by heating and modeling a small piece of dental sticky wax on a stick. Warm the wax slightly and press firmly on the top center of the stone.

14. *How can the article be removed from the shellac after the stone has been set?*

The shellac can be warmed slightly and the article lifted from the shellac stick.

Necklace of coiled wire and looped wire units

IV. JEWELRY MAKING

Finger Rings
  Ring with Double Knot
  Ring with Square Knot, Wire, and Balls
  Ring with Decorated Flat Ornament
  Ring with Decorated Domed Ornament, Wire, and Balls
  Ring with Round Stone, Wire, and Sawed Units
  Ring with Round Stones, Rings, and Domes
  Ring with Round Stone, Built-up Dome
  Ring with Oblong Stone, Metal Plate, and Wire Units
  Ring with Three Stones and Carved Design
  Ring with Round Stone and Carved Design

Brooches and Clips
  Brooch Pierced and Decorated with Wire and Balls
  Brooch Built Up with Metal Units
  Clip with Stone, Wire, and Balls

Bracelets
  Bracelet of Twisted Wire
  Bracelet Band with Applied Wire Units

Chains
  Chain of Round and Oval Links
  Chain of Interwoven Links
  Chain of Flat Coiled Units
  Round Coiled Units and Oval Links

Clasps
  Clasp—Ring Socket and Swivel Catch
  Clasp—Tube Socket and Spring Catch
  Clasp—Square and Oblong Sockets and Spring Catch

Beads
  Open Work Bead of Wire Units and Balls
  Round Bead Decorated with Wire and Domes
  Oval Bead Decorated with Wire and Balls

JEWELRY MAKING

Jewelry consists mainly of four principal articles: rings, brooches, bracelets, and chains. No matter what the prevailing mode of dress may be these articles of jewelry are worn. From the standpoint of jewelry construction and, to some extent, design, these four articles are important because they involve basic processes of construction which are used in all forms of jewelry work.

Modern tools and equipment have brought about simplification of certain processes and improvement in others but the basic processes used in making jewelry have been essentially the same since early historic days. Since the essential tools and materials can be secured at low cost the fabrication of articles from such metals as gold and silver easily comes within the reach of creative craft work for beginners.

Design in jewelry is always important, since much of the beauty of an article is determined by the form, proportion, balance, unity, harmony, and repetition of line and mass. Craftsmanship, however, is often the key to a beautiful design because workmanship not only creates texture which is essential to the beauty of the article, but quite frequently it is the only way to bring out the details of a well-developed design. A good craftsman knows that good workmanship, in itself, is a thing of beauty.

In order to carry through a piece of work from the design to the completed article the worker must follow through a series of processes in order. A beginner may find it necessary to write out the directions at first but later, as he advances, he should learn how to keep his working plan and order of processes in mind. In this event only a few notes and sketches need be used as reminders.

The following problems are presented in the form of work sheets to show the order in which the various parts of the work are done and to indicate the relation of one part to another and one process to another. Directions must be read through and sequence and procedure carefully noted. Procedure is memorized after several articles have been made. Learning to follow oral and written directions cannot be emphasized too strongly because it is only in this way that the worker can learn to anticipate what comes next. As the beginner comes to understand the various procedures he can outline the work to be done on any piece of jewelry he is capable of undertaking.

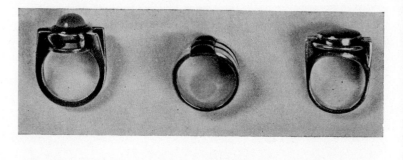

Silver rings with black onyx settings

FINGER RINGS

Finger rings are made up of two parts, the shank which is the band that fits around the finger, and the ornament which is applied to the shank for decoration.

The shank may be made of wire as shown in Figs. 66, 67, 68, 69, and 70, or it may be sawed or cut to pattern from flat metal as shown in Figs. 72, 73, 77, 78, 79, 80, 81, and 82. Metal cast in a mold as shown in Figs. 83, 84, and 85 is another method used to form a ring shank. The type of shank is determined by the size and design of the ornament to be used.

Ornaments vary considerably in type. A solid decoration as shown in Figs. 69 and 70 may be made entirely of metal or of metal and stones combined. A stone set in a collar or bezel which forms a box setting is shown in Figs. 72, 73, 77, 78, 79, and 80. Still another form of setting is a stone set between wires with metal bands on two sides as shown in Figs. 81 and 82. Another setting which makes a very attractive frame for a stone is the paved or gypsy setting which is shown in Figs. 83, 84, and 85.

Several important principles govern the design of any ring: (1) the size of the band in relation to the size of the ornament must be proportional; (2) the finished ring must be a single unit of design; (3) the ornament must be short enough from top to bottom to allow the finger knuckle to bend with ease, and (4) the raised part of the ornament, if it extends around the curve of the shank, must be short enough to insure comfort when worn.

Other methods of forming shanks and setting stones in rings may be used but these are the types most commonly used. A beginner who can execute pieces of jewelry successfully by these methods can work out other ways of forming shanks and setting stones as they suggest themselves.

RING DESIGN

CONSTRUCTION

RING WITH DOUBLE KNOT

Shank—Wire rings.
Ornament—Knotted wires.
  Sterling silver wire annealed 14-gauge.
  Cut two 4-inch lengths.
  Make a loose knot in the center of one length.

Insert the other 4-inch length of wire through the knot.

Knot the inserted piece.
Pull the loose ends to tighten the knots.

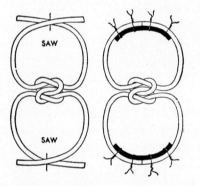

Shape the wires around the ring mandrel the desired size.
Saw the wire at the point where they overlap.

Bind each ring.
Solder the joints.

True on the mandrel.
Clean, polish, and color.

Fig. 66.—Wire shank with double knot

RING WITH DOUBLE KNOT
Fig. 66

Type	Shank—Wire bands.
of	Ornament — knotted wires.
Ring	The following wire is required:
	Sterling silver wire 14-gauge.

Tools	Metal gauge	File
and	Charcoal block	Flux
Working	Gas and air blow torch	Borax slate or saucer
Materials	Pickle	Solder
	Copper pickle pan	Camel's hair brush
	Copper tongs	Scotch stone
	Gas plate	Polishing motor
	Jeweler's shears	Felt buffing wheel
	Table vise	Tripoli cake
	Snub nose pliers	Soda, ammonia, and
	Jeweler's hand vise	water solution
	Ring sizes	Granite pan
	Ring gauge	Chamois buffing wheel
	Ring mandrel	Rouge stick
	Mallet	Potassium sulphide so-
	Bench pin	lution
	Jeweler's saw frame	Whiting
	Jeweler's saw blade	Cloth buffing wheel

PROCESSES	RING SHANK
Gauging	Gauge the wire, sterling silver 14-gauge.
Annealing	Anneal the wire.
p. 18	
Cutting	Cut the wire in two 4-inch lengths.
Knotting	Make a loose knot in the center of one wire.
	Place the end in the jaws of the table vise.
	Hold the other end with the jeweler's hand vise.
	Give the wire an even pull.

PROCESSES *Knotting*	Keep the knot in the center of the wire by reversing the ends held in the table vise; continue until a loose knot has been formed in the center of the wire. Insert the other length of wire through the knot. Knot the inserted wire as described above; the knot must be left open to let the wires swivel.
Measuring the Finger	Measure the finger for size.
Shaping	Shape the wires around the ring mandrel the desired size. Tap lightly with a mallet.
Sawing p. 31	Saw the wires where they overlap.
Binding	Bind the wires to make even joints as shown in Fig. 66.
Soldering p. 38	Solder the joints.
Truing the Rings	Place the rings on the mandrel. Tap with a mallet to true.
Cleaning p. 70	Remove any excess solder with a file and scotch stone.
Polishing	Buff the joints with a felt buffing wheel and tripoli. Polish with a chamois buffing wheel and rouge.
Coloring	Color with potassium sulphide solution. Remove any excess color with whiting. Polish with a soft cloth buffing wheel.

Silver rings with black onyx and coral combined with turquoise

RING DESIGN

RING SHANK

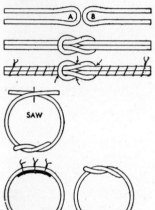

ORNAMENT

JOINING THE ORNAMENT AND THE FOUNDATION

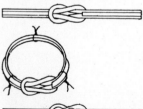

Fig. 67.—Wire shank with square knot, wire, and balls

RING WITH SQUARE KNOT, WIRE, AND BALLS

Shank—Wire rings.

Ornament—Knot, wire band, and balls.

Shank—Sterling silver wire annealed 14-gauge.

    Cut two 4-inch lengths.

    Loop each length in the center A and B.

    Insert the ends of loop A through loop B and the ends of loop B through loop A.

    Pull the ends to tighten the loops.

    Bind and solder together.

    Shape the wires around the ring mandrel the desired size.

    Saw the wires at the center back.

    Bind and solder together.

Ornament

    Fine silver wire.

    Make three graduated balls.

    Sterling silver wire 14-gauge, drawn half round.

    Cut 1½-inch length.

Joining the Ornament and Foundation

    Bind and solder the wire to the shank to end under one loop and over the other loop.

    Solder the three balls in the loops.

    Clean, polish, and color.

RING WITH SQUARE KNOT, WIRE, AND BALLS
Fig. 67

Type
of
Ring

Shank—Two wire rings.
Ornament—Square knot, band, and balls.
The following wire is required:
  Sterling silver wire annealed 14-gauge for the shank.
  Sterling silver wire 14-gauge, drawn half round, for the band on the shank.
  Fine silver wire for the balls.

Tools
and
Working
Materials

Metal gauge	Ring mandrel
Ruler	Rawhide mallet
Charcoal block	Bench pin
Gas and air blow torch	Jeweler's saw frame
Emery cloth	Jeweler's saw blade
Jeweler's shears	#1/0
Round nose pliers	Binding wire
Bench vise	14-gauge flat
Jeweler's hand vise	Binding wire
Binding wire	26-gauge
24-gauge	Powdered borax
Flux	Round graded man-
Borax slate or saucer	drels
Solder	Steel tweezers
Small camel's hair	Half round hole draw
brush	plate
Pickle	Draw tongs
Copper pickle pan	Yellow beeswax
Copper tongs	File
Gas plate	File card
Ring sizes	Scotch stone
Ring gauge	Polishing motor

Tools	Felt buffing wheel	Chamois buffing wheel
and	Tripoli cake	Potassium sulphide so-
Working	Soda, ammonia, and	lution
Materials	water solution	Whiting
	Granite pan	Soft cloth or chamois
	Rouge stick	buffing wheel

PROCESSES

RING SHANK

Gauging
p. 346

Gauge the wire, sterling silver wire 14-gauge.

Annealing
p. 18

Anneal the wire.

Cutting

Cut the wire in two 4-inch lengths.

Looping

Loop each of the two pieces of wire in the center.

Curve each wire slightly.

Inserting

Bring the ends of each loop together.

Insert the two ends at A through the loop B.

Insert the two ends at B through the loop A.

Holding

Place the ends of B in the jaws of the bench vise.

Hold the ends of A with draw pliers or the jeweler's hand vise.

Tightening
the
Knots

Pull the wires until the loop is tight. The wire ends may have to be reversed, the ends of A held in the bench vise and the ends of B pulled to keep the loop knotted in the center of the wires.

Binding

Bind the wires together.

Soldering
p. 38

Solder the wires.

Measuring the
Finger

Measure the finger for size.

PROCESSES *Shaping*	Place the wires on the ring mandrel. Strike the knot with a rawhide mallet. Shape around the mandrel the desired size.
Sawing p. 31	Saw the wire ends where A overlaps B at the center back.
Binding	Bind the wires together to form an even joint.
Soldering	Solder the joint.
Truing	Place on the ring mandrel. Tap with a rawhide mallet to true.

ORNAMENT

Ball *Making* p. 122	Fine silver wire. Make three graduated balls.
Wire *Drawing* p. 96	Sterling silver wire 14-gauge. Draw the wire half round.

JOINING THE RING SHANK AND THE ORNAMENT

Binding	Bind the wire to the shank; let the ends finish over one loop and under the other loop.
Soldering	Solder the wire and balls in place.
Cleaning p. 70	Remove any excess solder with a file and scotch stone.
Polishing p. 71	Buff with a felt buffing wheel and tripoli. Use the bristle buffing wheel for recessed parts. Polish with a soft cloth or chamois buffing wheel and rouge.
Coloring p. 72	Dip in potassium sulphide solution. Remove any excess color with whiting. Polish with a soft cloth or chamois buffing wheel.

RING DESIGN

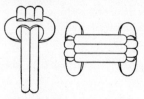

RING SHANK

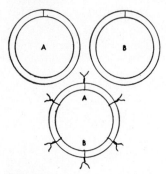

ORNAMENT

**JOINING RING SHANK
AND THE ORNAMENT**

Fig. 68.—*Wire shank with decorated
flat ornament*

RING WITH DECORATED FLAT ORNAMENT

Shank—Wire rings.

Ornament—Sawed unit with applied wire bands.

Shank—Sterling silver wire half round annealed 10-gauge.

> Make two rings A and B.
> Solder the joints.
> Shape round.
> Bind and solder A and B together.
> Clean and polish.

Ornament—Sterling silver sheet 16-gauge.

> Saw to pattern.
> Sterling silver wire 10-gauge drawn half round.
> Saw three pieces of equal length.
> File the ends of the wires.
> Bind and solder together.
> Shape the sawed unit and wire to fit the contour of the shank.
> File the wire ends true.
> Bind and solder the wire unit on the sawed unit.

Joining the Ring Shank and the Ornament

> Bind the joint of the ring underneath the ornament.
> Solder in place.
> Clean, polish, and color.

RING WITH DECORATED FLAT
ORNAMENT
Fig. 68

Type
of
Ring

Shank—Wire rings.

Ornament—Flat unit with bands of wire.

The following wire and flat metal are required:
   Sterling silver wire 10-gauge drawn half
   round for the shank and ornament.
   Sterling silver sheet 16-gauge for the base
   of the ornament.

Tools
and
Working
Materials

Ring sizes	Copper tongs
Ring gauge	Gas plate
Metal gauge	Ring mandrel
Charcoal block	Mallet
Blow torch	Scotch stone
Emery cloth	Polishing motor
Flat file	Felt buffing wheel
Bench vise	Felt ring buff
Half round hole draw	Tripoli cake
plate	Soda, ammonia, and
Yellow beeswax	water solution
Draw tongs	Granite pan
Bench pin	Tracing paper
Jeweler's saw frame	Scratch awl
Jeweler's saw blade	White beeswax
Snub nose pliers	Forming blocks
Binding wire	Bristle buffing wheel
Flux	Chamois buffing wheel
Borax slate or saucer	Rouge stick
Solder	Potassium sulphide so-
Jeweler's shears	lution
Camel's hair brush	Whiting
Pickle	Cloth buffing wheel
Copper pickle pan	

PROCESSES	RING SHANK
Measuring the Finger	Measure the finger for size.
Gauging the Metal p. 346	Gauge the metal sheet and wire.
Annealing p. 18	Anneal the wire.
Drawing the Wire p. 96	Draw the 10-gauge wire through the half round hole draw plate.
Sawing p. 31	Saw two pieces of wire the measured length.
Bending	Bend A so the two ends of the wire meet. Repeat with B.
Fitting	Saw through the joints to insure a perfect fit.
Binding	Bind each ring as shown in Fig. 67.
Soldering p. 38	Solder the joints.
Shaping	Shape A on the ring mandrel; tap lightly with a mallet to form a perfect circle. Repeat with ring B.
Binding	Bind A to B firmly.
Soldering	Solder A and B together.
Cleaning p. 70	Remove excess solder with a file and scotch stone.
Polishing p. 71	Polish with a felt and bristle buffing wheel and tripoli for the outside and a felt ring buff for the inside.

PROCESSES	ORNAMENT
Transferring the Pattern	Sterling silver sheet 16-gauge. Transfer the pattern for the sawed unit to the metal.
Sawing	Saw the metal to pattern.
Annealing	Anneal the metal.
Sawing	Sterling silver wire half round 10-gauge. Saw three pieces of wire to fit the sawed unit.
Filing	File the ends of the wires at an angle.
Binding	Bind the three wires firmly together.
Soldering	Solder the wires on the flat side.
Shaping	Shape the sawed unit in the forming block to the contour of the shank as shown in Fig. 75. Shape the wire unit in the wooden forming block as shown in Fig. 74 to fit the contour of the sawed unit.
Filing	File the ends of the wires to true.
Binding	Bind the wire unit to the sawed unit.
Soldering	Solder together.

JOINING THE RING SHANK AND ORNAMENT

Binding	Bind the joint of the ring shank under the center of the ornament.
Soldering	Solder points of contact.
Cleaning	Remove excess solder.
Polishing	Buff with a bristle buffing wheel and tripoli. Polish with a chamois buffing wheel.
Coloring p. 72	Color with potassium sulphide solution. Remove any excess color with whiting. Polish with a soft cloth buffing wheel.

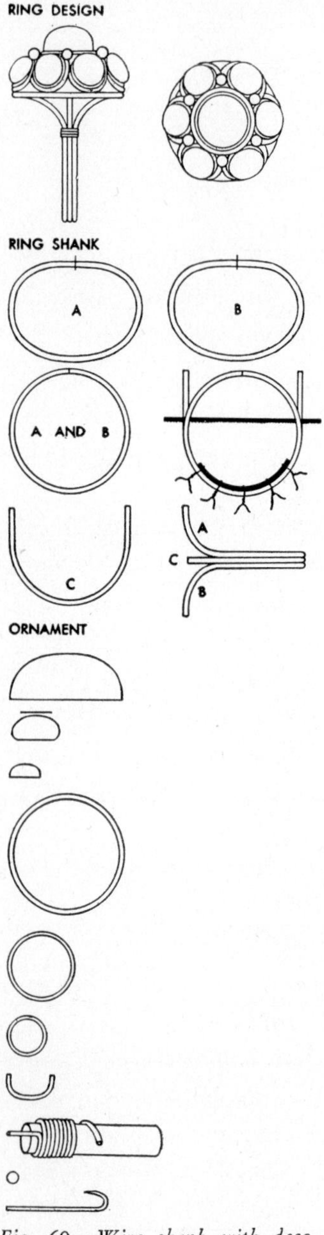

RING DESIGN

RING SHANK

A

B

A AND B

C

C
A
B

ORNAMENT

Fig. 69.—*Wire shank with decorated domed ornament*

RING WITH DECORATED DOMED ORNAMENT, WIRE, AND BALLS

Shank—Wire bands.

Ornament—Domes, rings, and balls.

Shank—Sterling silver wire annealed 18-gauge.

> Saw three lengths, A, B, and C.
> Bend and solder A and B.
> Shape A, B and C.
> Bind A, B, and C together.
> Insert binding wire between A, B and C; solder together.
> Curve A and B.

Ornament—Sterling silver sheet annealed 26-gauge.

> Cut and dome one large disk the diameter of the spread A-B.
> Cut and dome six small disks.

Sterling silver wire 18-gauge.

> Make one ring the diameter of the large dome.

Fine silver wire 20-gauge.

> Make six rings the diameter of the small dome and one ring twice the diameter.
> Solder the joints.

Fine silver wire 26-gauge.

> Make six half rings.
> Make one ball to fit the medium size ring, and six small balls.

Fine silver wire 22-gauge.

> Make two hooks with wire ends.

Assembling Parts of the Ornament

Bind and solder the large dome on the large ring.

Solder the six small rings around the medium size ring to form a motif.

Dome the motif to fit the large dome.

Bind and solder the dome of rings to the large dome.

Pierce the large dome inside the center ring.

Drill air holes in the large dome inside the six rings.

File grooves in the center ring between the small rings.

Solder the large ball in the center opening.

Solder the balls in the grooves and the domes on the rings.

Solder the half rings in place.

Joining the Ring Shank and the Ornament

Bind and solder A, B, and C under the ring of the ornament.

Place the hook of wire over the shank at the spread and coil three times.

Solder in place.

Clean, polish, and color.

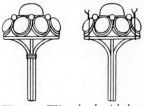

Fig. 70.—Wire shank with decorated domed ornament

RING WITH DECORATED DOMED
ORNAMENT, WIRE, AND BALLS
Figs. 69, 70

Type
of
Ring

Shank—Wire bands.

Ornament—Large dome mounted with small domes, rings, and balls.

The following metal sheet and wire are required:

Sterling silver wire 18-gauge for the shank and the ring to hold the large dome of the ornament.

Sterling silver sheet 26-gauge for the domes.

Fine silver wire 20-gauge for the rings around the large ball and small domes.

Fine silver wire 26-gauge for the half rings and balls.

Fine silver wire 22-gauge for the wires to bind the shank.

Tools
and
Working
Materials

Ring sizes	Flux
Ring gauge	Borax slate or saucer
Metal gauge	Solder
Gas and air blow torch	Jeweler's shears
Charcoal block	Camel's hair brush
Pickle	Binding wire
Copper pickle pan	26-gauge
Copper tongs	Ring mandrel
Gas plate	Mallet
Ruler	Flat file
Bench pin	Scotch stone
Jeweler's saw frame	Polishing motor
Jeweler's saw blades	Felt buffing wheel
#1/0	Felt ring buff
Snub nose pliers	Tripoli cake

Tools *and* *Working* *Materials*	Soda, ammonia, and water solution Granite pan Lead dapping block Dapping die cutters and punches Dapping die Round mandrels—2 sizes Surface plate Tweezers Shellac stick Flake shellac Round nose pliers Alcohol	Center punch Bristle buffing wheel Riffle file Graver Oil stone Oil Gum tragacanth Chamois buffing wheel Rouge stick Potassium sulphide so- lution Whiting Soft cloth buffing wheel

PROCESSES

SEPARATE PARTS OF THE RING SHANK

Measuring
the
Finger

Measure the finger for size.

Gauging
the
Metal
p. 346

Gauge the metal to be used.

Annealing
p. 18

Anneal the metal.

Sawing
p. 31

Sterling silver wire 18-gauge. Saw three lengths of wire A and B long enough to allow spread to hold the base of the large dome as shown in Fig. 69. C should be long enough to fit under the dome.

Bending

Bend A so the two ends meet.
Repeat with B.

PROCESSES
Fitting

Saw through the joints formed by the meeting of the two ends to insure a perfect fit.

Soldering
p. 38

Solder the joints.

Shaping

Shape A and B on the ring mandrel.
Form C half round on the mandrel.

ASSEMBLING PARTS OF THE RING SHANK

Binding

Bind A, B, and C together.
Curve A and B slightly outward.
Insert flat binding wire between the rings where they spread.

Soldering

Solder A, B, and C together.

Cleaning
p. 70

Remove any excess solder with a file and scotch stone.

Polishing
p. 71

Buff with a felt buffing wheel and tripoli for the outside and the inside with a felt ring buff and tripoli.

SEPARATE PARTS OF THE ORNAMENT

Disk
Cutting
and
Doming
p. 120

Sterling silver sheet 26-gauge.
Cut one large disk the diameter of the spread between A and B with the dapping cutter. Saw if a larger cutter is not available.
Cut six small disks with the dapping cutter.
Dome the disks in the dapping die.

Ring
Making
p. 112

Sterling silver wire 18-gauge.
Make one ring the diameter of the large dome.
Fine silver wire 20-gauge.
Make six rings the diameter of the small dome.
Make one ring twice the diameter of the small dome.

PROCESSES

Soldering	Solder the joints.
Truing	Tap the rings lightly on a round mandrel and surface plate to true.
Ring Making	Fine silver wire 26-gauge. Make six half rings.
Ball Making p. 120	Make one large ball to fit the center ring. Make six small balls to fit between the domes.
Polishing p. 71	Hold the large ball in a shellac stick. Polish with a felt buffing wheel and tripoli to make smooth.
Cutting	Fine silver wire 22-gauge. Cut two lengths of wire $1\frac{1}{2}$ inches. Make a small hook on the end of each with round nose pliers.

ASSEMBLING PARTS OF THE ORNAMENT

Binding	Bind the large dome on the large ring.
Soldering	Solder in place. Solder the six small rings around the medium sized ring to form a motif.
Shaping the Motif	Dome the motif by pressing it in the dapping die to fit the large dome.
Binding	Bind the motif to the large dome.
Soldering	Solder together.
Piercing p. 35	Pierce the inside of the large dome inside the center ring.

PROCESSES

Drilling
p. 35

Drill small air holes in the large dome inside the six small rings.

Cleaning

Remove any excess solder with a file and scotch stone.

Polishing

Buff with a bristle buffing wheel and tripoli.

Filing
p. 25

File or carve a groove in the center ring between the six rings to hold the small balls; a small opening must be left under the balls.

Soldering

Solder the large ball in the center opening.
Solder the small balls in the groove.
Solder the domes on the rings.

Filing

File the ends of the half circles of wire to a point, place under ball and around the ring which holds the dome as shown in Figs. 70, 71.

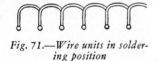

Fig. 71.—*Wire units in soldering position*

Binding

Bind in place.

Soldering

Solder the wires.

JOINING THE RING SHANK AND THE ORNAMENT

Shaping

Fit the shank to the dome so that the wires A, B, and C fit inside the wire ring at the base of the large dome.

Binding

Bind the dome to the shank.

Soldering

Solder together.

Coiling

Hook the 22-gauge wire on the shank where A and B spread on each side of the ornament; coil three times around the shank. Let the ends finish on the inside of the shank.

PROCESSES	
Soldering	Solder the coil to the shank.
Filing	File the wires smooth on the inside of the shank.
Cleaning p. 70	Remove any scratches or excess solder with a file and scotch stone.
Polishing p. 71	Buff with a bristle buffing wheel and tripoli Polish with a cloth or chamois buffing wheel and rouge.
Coloring p. 72	Color with potassium sulphide solution. Remove any excess color with whiting. Polish with a cloth or chamois buffing wheel.

RING DESIGN

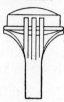

RING SHANK

ORNAMENT

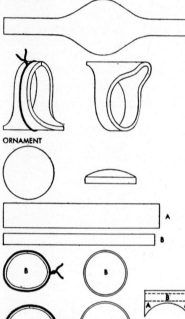

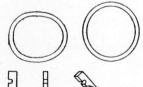

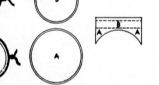

Fig. 72.—Shaped metal shank with round stone, wire, and sawed units

RING WITH ROUND STONE, WIRE, AND SAWED UNITS

Shank — Shaped band of silver.

Ornament — Round stone set, ring, and sawed units.

Shank—Sterling silver sheet 12- or 14-gauge.

Saw to pattern.

Anneal the metal.

Bend so the ends meet.

Bind and solder.

Shape round.

Ornament—Sterling silver sheet 26-gauge.

Cut A for the bezel and B for the bearing.

Bend A so the two ends meet and repeat with B.

Solder the joints.

Shape round.

Solder B inside of A.

File the lower edge the contour of the shank.

Sterling silver wire 14-gauge.

Make a ring to fit the bezel.

Solder the joint.

Sterling silver sheet 12- or 14-gauge.

Saw six units to pattern.

Joining the Ring Shank and the Ornament

Bind and solder the bezel to the shank.

File the upper edge of the bezel to 28-gauge.

Solder the wire ring to the bezel to touch the shank at two points.

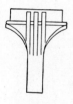

Place the three units on one side so as to touch the shank and bezel and to fit over the wire ring.

Solder in place.

Repeat on the other side with the other three units.

Clean, polish, and color.

Set the stone.

Fig. 73. — *Shaped metal shank with round stone, wire, and sawed units*

RING WITH ROUND STONE, WIRE, AND SAWED UNITS
Figs. 72, 73

Type of Ring

Shank—Shaped metal band.

Ornament—Round cabochon stone and applied silver units.

The following flat metal, wire, and stone set are required:

Sterling silver sheet 12- or 14-gauge for the shank and ornamental units.

Sterling silver sheet 26-gauge for the bezel and bearing.

Sterling silver wire 14-gauge for the ring around the bezel.

Stone—Round cabochon, black onyx.

Tools and Working Materials

Ring sizes
Ring gauge
Metal gauge
Pumice powder
Pencil
Ruler
Tracing paper
Blow torch
White beeswax
Soft cloth
Scratch awl
Bench pin
Jeweler's saw frame
Jeweler's saw blade
  #1/0
File
File card

Hand vise
Charcoal block
Pickle
Copper pickle pan
Copper tongs
Gas plate
Forming block
Ring mandrel
Mallet
Jeweler's saw blade
  #3/0
Binding wire
  24-gauge
Flux
Borax slate or saucer
Solder
Jeweler's shears

*Tools
and
Working
Materials*

Small camel's hair
   brush
Scotch stone
Polishing motor
Tripoli cake
Felt buffing wheel
Felt ring buff
Soda, ammonia, and
   water solution
Granite pan
Dentimetre
Dividers
Round mandrel
Stone lifter

Wax
Bristle buffing wheel
Potassium sulphide so-
   lution
Whiting
Cloth or chamois buf-
   fing wheel
Pusher
Ring vise
Repoussé tool
Chasing hammer
Burnisher
Soft cloth buffing
   wheel

PROCESSES

RING SHANK

*Measuring
the
Finger*

Measure the finger for size.

*Gauging
the
Metal*
p. 346

Gauge the metal to be used.

*Drawing
the
Pattern*

Draw the pattern for the shank; the size of the shank must be wide enough to carry the ornament.

*Transferring
the
Pattern
to the
Silver*
p. 33

Sterling silver 12- or 14-gauge.
Transfer the traced pattern to the silver; use the wax method.

PROCESSES
Sawing
p. 31

Saw the metal following the scratched line of the pattern.

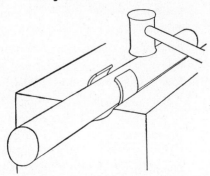

Fig. 74.—*Bending a ring blank in a wooden forming block*

Annealing
p. 18
Bending

Anneal the blank just sawed.

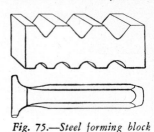

Fig. 75.—*Steel forming block*

Bend the blank in the forming block as shown in Figs. 74 and 75.

Bring the two ends together to form the shank as shown in Fig. 76.

Fitting

Saw through the joint formed by the meeting of the two ends with a 3/0 saw blade to insure a perfect fit.

Binding

Bind the shank firmly.

Soldering
p. 38

Solder the joint.

Shaping

Shape the shank on the ring mandrel.

Tap lightly with a mallet; re-

Fig. 76 — *Joining the ends of the blank*

verse several times on the tapered mandrel to form a perfect circle.

Remove any excess solder with a file and scotch stone.

Buff the outside with a felt buffing wheel and tripoli, and the inside with a felt ring buff and tripoli.

SEPARATE PARTS OF THE ORNAMENT

Measure the girdle of the stone as shown in Fig. 57.

Sterling silver sheet 26-gauge.
Make a round bezel and bearing as shown in Fig. 72.

File the lower edge of the bezel the contour of the ring shank to touch at all points as shown in Fig. 72.

Sterling silver wire 14-gauge.
Make a ring to fit the outside circumference of the bezel.

Solder the joint.

Transferring
the
Pattern,
for the
Units
to the Metal

Sterling silver sheet 12- or 14-gauge. Transfer the pattern for the six units onto the silver; use the wax method.

Sawing
p. 31

Saw out the units.

Filing

File the edges.

JOINING THE RING SHANK AND THE ORNAMENT

Binding

Bind the bezel to the shank.

Soldering

Solder together.

Filing
the
Bezel

File the upper edge of the bezel to about 28-gauge.

Soldering

Place the ring of wire around the bezel so that it touches the ring shank at two points.
Solder in place.
Place the three units on one side so as to touch the shank and bezel and to fit over the wire ring.
Solder in place.
Repeat on the other side of the shank with the other three units.

Filing

File to true.

Cleaning

Remove excess solder with a file and scotch stone.

PROCESSES

Polishing	Buff with a felt buffing wheel and tripoli and a bristle buffing wheel and tripoli for recessed parts.
	Polish with chamois buffing wheel and rouge.
Coloring	Color with potassium sulphide solution.
p. 72	Remove any excess color with whiting.
	Polish with a soft cloth buffing wheel.
Setting the Stone	Set the stone.
p. 165	

RING DESIGN

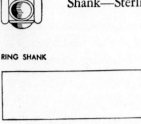

RING WITH ROUND STONES, RINGS, AND DOMES

Shank—Straight band of silver.

Ornament—Three stones, rings, and domes.

Shank—Sterling silver sheet annealed 22-gauge.
> Saw to pattern.
> Bend so ends meet.

RING SHANK

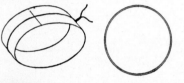

> Bind and solder the joint.
> Shape round.

Ornament—Fine silver sheet 28-gauge.
> Make three bezels.

Fine silver wire 24-gauge.
> Make three rings for bearings.

ORNAMENT

Sterling silver sheet annealed 26-gauge.
> Cut and dome six disks the diameter of the bezel.

Fine silver wire 24-gauge.
> Make nine rings the outside circumference of the bezel.

> Solder the nine rings together.

> Bend so the two end rings meet.
> Bind and solder.

Sterling silver wire 10-gauge drawn half round.
> Make two rings to fit the outside of the shank.
> Solder the joints.
> Shape the rings to fit the shank.

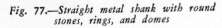

Fig. 77.—Straight metal shank with round stones, rings, and domes

Joining the Ring Shank and the Ornament.

Bind and solder the band of rings to the center of the shank.

Clean and polish.

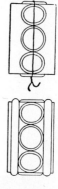

Place the two rings of half round wire on the shank to touch the band of rings.

Solder in place.

File the shank on both sides flush with the wire rings.

Place the six domes in the six consecutive rings on the shank.

Solder in place.

Place the three bezels in the three remaining rings, the bearings in the bezels.

Solder in place.

Clean, polish, and color.

Set the stones.

Fig. 78 — Straight metal shank with round stones, rings, and domes

RING WITH ROUND STONES, RINGS
AND DOMES
Figs. 77, 78

Type
of
Ring

Shank—Straight band.

Ornament—Round stones, domes, and rings.

The following metal sheet, wire, and stone sets are required:

Sterling silver sheet 22-gauge ½ inch wide for the shank.

Fine silver sheet 28-gauge for the bezels.

Fine silver wire 24-gauge for the rings and the bearing.

Sterling silver sheet 26-gauge for the domes.

Sterling silver wire 10-gauge drawn half-round for the rings to edge the shank.

Stones—Three round cabochon.

Tools
and
Working
Materials

Ring sizes	Binding wire
Ring gauge	26-gauge
Metal gauge	Flux
Charcoal block	Borax slate or saucer
Gas and air blow torch	Solder
Pickle	Jeweler's shears
Copper pickle pan	Camel's hair brush
Copper tongs	Ring mandrel
Gas plate	Mallet
Ruler	Emery cloth
Dividers	Scotch stone
File	Polishing motor
Bench pin	Felt buffing wheel
Jeweler's saw frame	Felt ring buff
Jeweler's saw blade	Tripoli cake
Snub nose pliers	Granite pan

Tools and Working Materials

Soda, ammonia, and water solution
Round mandrel—size of the stone
Binding wire 28-gauge
Dentimetre
Stone lifter
Round mandrel—size smaller than the bezel
Dapping die cutter
Lead dapping block

Dapping die punch
Dapping die
Bristle buffing wheel
Chamois buffing wheel
Rouge stick
Potassium sulphide solution
Whiting
Ring clamp
Pusher
Burnisher
Soft cloth buffing wheel

PROCESSES

RING SHANK

Measuring the Finger

Measure the finger for size. A loose fit for this type of ring is necessary.

Gauging p. 346

Gauge the metal.

Annealing p. 18

Anneal the metal.

Laying out the Pattern

Sterling silver sheet 22-gauge.
Place one arm of the dividers over the straight edge of the silver sheet.
Scribe a line with the other arm on the metal $\frac{1}{2}$ inch wide, parallel with the edge and to loose-fit ring size; $\frac{1}{16}$ inch of this width is for construction purposes.

Sawing p. 31

Saw the strip of metal the measured length and width.

PROCESSES

Bending	Bend the strip so the two ends meet to form the shank.
Fitting	Join the ends to form a perfect fit.
Binding	Bind the shank firmly.
Soldering p. 38	Solder the joint.
Shaping	Shape the shank on the ring mandrel. Tap lightly with a mallet; reverse several times on the tapered mandrel to insure a perfect circle.
Truing	True both edges with a file and emery cloth.
Cleaning p. 70	Remove excess solder and scratches with a file and scotch stone.
Polishing p. 71	Buff the outside with a felt buffing wheel and tripoli and the inside with a felt ring buff and tripoli.

ORNAMENT

Making the Bezel p. 153	Fine silver sheet 28-gauge. Make three round bezels to fit the stones as shown in Figs. 56, 57.
Making the Bearing p. 155	Fine silver wire 24-gauge. Make three wire rings to fit inside the bezels for the bearing.
Ring Making p. 112	Make nine rings the outside circumference of the bezel. Bring the ends together to make an even joint as shown in Fig. 77.

PROCESSES

Disk *Cutting* *and* *Doming* p. 120	Sterling silver sheet 26-gauge. Cut and dome six disks the diameter of the bezel.
Wire *Drawing* p. 96	Sterling silver wire 10-gauge. Draw the wire half round.
Ring *Making*	Make two rings the outside circumference of the shank. Bring the ends together to make an even joint.
Placing *the* *Small* *Rings*	Place the nine rings on the charcoal block in a straight line so the joint of each ring touches the preceding ring.
Soldering	Solder the joints of the two large rings. Solder the nine rings together.
Bending	Bend the band so the two end rings meet.
Binding	Bind the two end rings.
Soldering	Solder the joint.
Shaping	Place the soldered band of rings on a round mandrel. Tap lightly with a mallet; reverse several times on the tapered mandrel to form a perfect circle to fit the shank. Shape the two large rings in the same way. True on the surface plate.

JOINING THE RING SHANK AND THE ORNAMENT

PROCESSES	
Binding	Bind the band of rings in the center of the shank.
Soldering	Solder in place.
Polishing	Buff with a bristle buffing wheel and tripoli.
Binding the Large Rings	Place the outside rings of wire to touch the band of small rings; hold in place with binding wire. $\frac{1}{32}$ inch of the shank will be left on each edge outside the rings.
Soldering	Solder in place.
Filing	File off the $\frac{1}{32}$ edges flush with the wire rings.
Placing the Domes	Place the domes in the rings (these will have to be placed and soldered separately or in groups depending upon the curve of the ring shank). Three adjoining rings are left open to hold the bezels for the stones.
Soldering	Solder in place.
Placing the Bezels and Bearing	Place the bezels in the three remaining rings. Place the bearings in the bezels.
Soldering	Solder in place.
Cleaning	Remove any excess solder and scratches with a file and scotch stone.
Polishing	Buff with a bristle buffing wheel and tripoli. Polish with a cloth or chamois buffing wheel and rouge.

PROCESSES

Coloring
p. 72

*Setting
the
Stone*
p. 165

Color the ring with potassium sulphide solution.   Method number two.

Polish with a soft cloth or chamois buffing wheel.

Push the silver of the bezels over the edge of the stones with the pusher.

Burnish the metal around the stones to smooth with the burnisher.

RING WITH A ROUND STONE AND BUILT-UP DOME

RING DESIGN

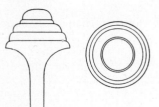

RING SHANK.

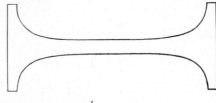

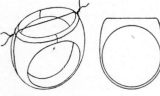

ORNAMENT

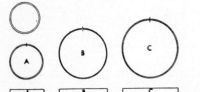

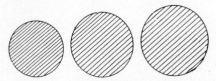

Shank—Shaped band.
Ornament — Three collars and round stone set.
Shank — Sterling silver sheet 16-gauge.

Saw to pattern.
Anneal the metal.
Bend so the ends meet.
Bind and solder.
Shape the shank.

Ornament — Sterling silver sheet 26-gauge.

Cut a strip $\frac{1}{16}$ inch wide into three lengths

A the circumference of the stone.

B $\frac{1}{4}$ inch longer than A.

C $\frac{1}{4}$ inch longer than B.

Join the ends of each length.
Bind and solder.
Shape round.

Sterling silver wire 26-gauge.

Make a bearing to fit inside of A.

Sterling silver sheet 24-gauge.

Saw three disks $\frac{1}{8}$ inch larger than A, B, and C.

Fig. 79.—Shaped metal shank with round stone and built-up dome

Assembling Parts of the Ornament

Bind and solder A, B, and C on the three disks and the bearing inside of A.

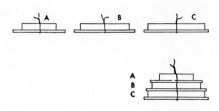

Pierce the center of each disk.

Bind and solder A, B, and C together.

Joining the Ring Shank and the Ornament

Bind the ornament to the shank.

Solder in place.

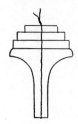

Buff the edges of the disks which extend beyond A, B, and C.

Clean, polish, and color.

Set the stone.

Fig. 80.—Shaped metal shank with round stone and built-up dome

RING WITH A ROUND STONE AND BUILT-UP DOME
Figs. 79, 80

Type
of
Ring

Shank—Shaped metal band.

Ornament—Round cabochon stone on raised steps.

The following metal and stone set are required:

Sterling silver sheet 16-gauge for the shank.

Sterling silver sheet 26-gauge for the collars of the disks and for the bezel.

Sterling silver wire, 26-gauge for the bearing. Sterling silver sheet 24-gauge for the disks.

Stone—Round cabochon.

Tools
and
Working
Materials

Ring size
Ring gauge
Metal gauge
Ruler
Thin tracing paper
Pencil
Fine pumice powder
White beeswax
Gas plate
Scratch awl
Bench pin
Jeweler's saw frame
Jeweler's saw blade
　#1
Gas and air blow torch
Charcoal block
Pickle
Copper pickle pan
Copper tongs

Mallet
Forming block
Ring mandrel
Binding wire
　26-gauge
Jeweler's saw blade
　#3/0
Flux
Borax slate or saucer
Solder
Jeweler's shears
Camel's hair brush
Round mandrel
Scotch stone
File
Felt buffing wheel
Felt ring buff
Polishing motor
Tripoli cake

*Tools
and
Working
Materials*

Soda, ammonia, and
water solution
Granite pan
Dentimetre
Dividers
Emery cloth #1
Center punch
Hand drill
Twist drill
Chamois buff
Rouge stick
Whiting

Potassium sulphide so-
lution
Ring clamp
Bench vise
Stone lifter
Pusher
Repoussé tool
Chasing hammer
Burnisher
Soft cloth buffing
wheel

PROCESSES

RING SHANK

*Measuring
the
Finger*

Measure the finger for size.

*Gauging
the
Metal
p. 346*

Gauge the metal to be used.

*Transferring
the
Design
p. 33*

Sterling silver sheet 16-gauge.
Transfer the traced pattern to the silver; use
the wax method.
Note: The distance between the two points at
the end of the curve determines the size
of the ring shank; the spread between
the ends of the curved lines should equal
half the circumference of the largest
disk of the ornament.

*Sawing
p. 31*

Saw the metal following the scratched line of
the pattern.

*Annealing
p. 18*

Anneal the blank just sawed.

PROCESSES *Bending*	Bend the blank in the forming block as shown in Figs. 74 and 75. Bring the two ends together as shown in Fig. 79 to form the shank.
Fitting	Saw through the joints formed by the meeting of the four ends with a 3/0 saw blade to insure perfect joints.
Binding	Bind the shank firmly, as shown in Figs. 12, 79.
Soldering p. 38	Solder the joints.
Shaping	Shape the shank on the ring mandrel. Tap lightly with a mallet; reverse several times on the tapered mandrel to form a perfect circle. Shape the front opening on a round mandrel. Tap lightly with a mallet to form a perfect circle.
Cleaning p. 70	Remove any excess solder with a file and scotch stone.
Polishing p. 71	Buff the outside with a felt buffing wheel and tripoli and the inside with a felt ring buff and tripoli.

SEPARATE PARTS OF THE ORNAMENT

| *Making*
a Round
Bezel
and
Bearing
and
Collars
p. 153 | Sterling silver sheet 26-gauge $\frac{1}{16}$ inch wide.
Make a bezel A as shown in Figs. 56, 57.
Make two collars B and C following directions under bezel making; one collar should be $\frac{1}{4}$ inch longer and the other $\frac{1}{2}$ inch longer than the strip cut for the bezel.
Sterling silver wire 26-gauge.
Make a ring with the inside diameter of A for the bearing. |

PROCESSES	Sterling silver sheet 24-gauge.
Inscribing	Inscribe three circles on the silver with dividers.
Circles	The diameter of the three disks should be $\frac{1}{8}$ inch greater than the diameter of the bezel A and the two collars B and C.
Sawing	Saw out the disks.

ASSEMBLING PARTS OF THE ORNAMENT

Binding	Place the bearing inside the bezel A.
	Bind A in the center of the smallest disk.
	Bind B in the center of the medium-sized disk.
	Bind C in the center of the largest disk.
Soldering	Solder A, B, and C on the disks and the bearing inside A.
Piercing	Pierce the center of the disks.
p. 35	
Binding	Bind A, B, and C together firmly.
Soldering	Solder together.

JOINING THE RING SHANK AND THE ORNAMENT

Binding	Bind the ornament ABC to the ring shank. Let disk C rest over the opening.
Soldering	Solder in place.
Cleaning	Remove any excess solder with a file and scotch stone.
Polishing	Buff the edges of the disks with a felt wheel and tripoli.
	Polish with a cloth buffing wheel and rouge.
Coloring	Color with potassium sulphide solution.
p. 72	Remove any excess color with whiting.
	Polish with a chamois buffing wheel.

RING DESIGN

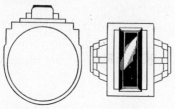

RING SHANK

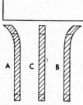

A   C   B

ASSEMBLING PARTS OF THE SHANK

A
C
B

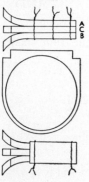

Fig. 81.—*Shaped and pierced metal shank with oblong stone, metal plate, and wire units*

RING WITH OBLONG STONE, METAL PLATE, AND WIRE UNITS

Shank—Three sawed silver forms.

Ornament—Opaque oblong stone, flat plate, and wires.

Shank—Sterling silver sheet 14-gauge.

Pierce and saw three pieces to pattern.
Anneal the metal.
Curve A and B slightly.

Sterling silver 20-gauge.

Cut a band of silver about four times the gauge of the metal.

Assembling Parts of the Shank

Bind and solder A, B, and C together.

File inside of the ring to size, the outside circumference the desired width.

Bind and solder the band to the shank.

File the applied band even with A and B.

File A, B, and C flat on top to hold the ornament.

ORNAMENT

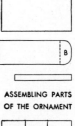

Ornament—Sterling silver sheet 14-gauge.

Saw a rectangle longer and wider than the stone.

Sterling silver sheet 24-gauge.

Saw a rectangle the width of the stone and the length plus twice the depth of the stone and add to this length ⅛ inch. File the corners round.

Mark length of the stone on the small rectangle as shown at A and B.

Anneal the smaller rectangle.

Score the marked line.

Bend the ends at a right angle.

Solder at the angles.

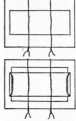

ASSEMBLING PARTS OF THE ORNAMENT

Sterling silver wire ¹⁄₁₆-inch square.

Saw two pieces the length of the bent rectangle.

Assembling Parts of the Ornament

Bind and solder the bent form to the large rectangle.

Bind and solder the two pieces of square wire in place.

JOINING RING SHANK AND THE ORNAMENT

Joining the Ring Shank and the Ornament

Bind and solder the ornament to the shank.

Clean, polish, and color.

Set the stone.

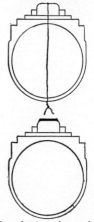

Fig. 82.—*Shaped and pierced metal shank with oblong stone, metal plate, and wire units*

RING WITH OBLONG STONE, METAL
PLATE, AND WIRE UNITS
Figs. 81, 82

Type
of
Ring

Shank—Three flat forms cut to shape.

Ornament—Oblong opaque stone set, flat plate, and wires.

The following metal, wire, and stone are required:

Sterling silver sheet 14-gauge for the shank and the flat plate for the ornament.

Sterling silver sheet 20-gauge for the outside band of the shank.

Sterling silver sheet 24-gauge for the rectangle to hold the stone.

Sterling silver wire 10-gauge drawn $\frac{1}{16}$ inch square to hold the stone at the sides.

Stone—Oblong black onyx.

Tools
and
Working
Materials

Ring sizes	Bench pin
Ring gauge	Jeweler's saw frame
Metal gauge	Jeweler's saw blade
Drawing paper	#1
Compass	File
Thin tracing paper	Charcoal block
Soft pencil	Gas and air blow torch
Pumice powder	Pickle
Gas plate	Copper pickle pan
White beeswax	Copper tongs
Pliers	Dividers
Scratch awl	Round mandrel
Center punch	Forming block
Hammer	Bench vise
Twist drill	Mallet
Hand drill	Ruler

Tools and Working Materials

Binding wire 24-gauge
Flux
Borax slate or saucer
Solder
Jeweler's shears
Camel's hair brush
Ring clamp
Half round file, 6-inch
Scotch stone
Polishing motor
Felt buffing wheel
Felt ring buff
Tripoli cake
Granite pan
Soda, ammonia, and water solution
Small square file
Snub nose pliers

Steel hammer
Steel surface plate
Square hole draw plate
Draw tongs
Boric acid and alcohol solution
Chamois buffing wheel
Rouge stick
Potassium sulphide solution
Whiting
Stone lifter
Pusher
Small repoussé tool
Chasing hammer
Soft cloth buffing wheel
Burnisher

PROCESSES

Measuring the Finger

Gauging the Metal p. 346

Drawing the Pattern

RING SHANK

Measure the finger for the size.

Gauge the metal sheet and wire to be used.

Draw a circle on paper with a compass one size smaller than the measured size of the ring.
Draw the outline for the inside of the ring around this circle.
Draw the outline of the outer contour a little wider than the desired size of the finished ring, as shown in Fig. 81.

PROCESSES

Tracing	Make three tracings of the shank.
Transferring the Design p. 33	Sterling silver sheet 14-gauge. Transfer the tracings to the silver; use the wax method.
Piercing and Sawing pp. 31, 35	Pierce and saw three pieces to pattern.
Annealing p. 18	Anneal the blanks just sawed.
Shaping	Curve A and B slightly in the forming block (Fig. 75).
Measuring	Sterling silver sheet 20-gauge. Scribe a line over the straight edge of the sheet $\frac{1}{16}$ inch wider than the thickness of A, B, and C, long enough to reach around the shank to $\frac{3}{8}$ inch on each side of the sawed step in the shank.
Sawing	Saw the measured length.

ASSEMBLING PARTS OF THE SHANK

Binding	Bind A, B, and C together as far as the curve of A and B.
Soldering p. 38	Solder A, B, and C together.
Truing	True the curve of A and B if necessary.
Filing p. 25	File the inside of the ring to size and the outside the desired width.
Binding	Bind the band of silver around the shank. Each end should measure $\frac{3}{8}$ inch from the first step in the shank. Solder in place.

PROCESSES	
Filing	File the applied band even with A and B.
	Hold the back of the shank in the ring clamp. File A, B, and C flat on top to hold the ornament.
Cleaning p. 70	Remove any excess solder with a file and scotch stone.
Polishing p. 71	Buff with a flat felt buffing wheel and tripoli outside. Use the felt ring buff and tripoli inside.

ORNAMENT

Measuring	Measure the length and the width of the stone with the dividers.
	Sterling silver sheet 14-gauge.
	Inscribe on the silver a rectangle wider and longer than the stone.
	Sterling silver sheet 24-gauge.
	Measure a rectangle the width of the stone and the length of the stone plus twice the depth— to this add $\frac{1}{8}$ inch.
Sawing	Saw out both rectangles.
Filing	Round the ends of the small rectangle with a file.
Annealing p. 18	Anneal the smaller rectangle.
Scoring p. 157	Score the annealed silver with the angle of the small square file the length of the stone; leave an equal margin on each end as shown in Fig. 82.
Bending	Bend the ends at a right angle on the scored lines.
Soldering	Solder at the bent angles.

PROCESSES

Wire	Sterling silver wire 10-gauge.
Drawing	Draw the wire $\frac{1}{16}$ inch square.
p. 96	
Sawing	Saw the two pieces of wire the length of the bent rectangle.
Filing	File the ends to true.

ASSEMBLING PARTS OF THE ORNAMENT

Binding	Bind the bent form to the center of the large rectangle.
Soldering	Solder in place.
Binding	Bind the two pieces of square wire on each side of the bent form; the wires must be flush with both ends.
Soldering	Solder in place.

JOINING THE RING SHANK AND THE ORNAMENT

Binding	Bind the ornament to the ring shank.
Soldering	Solder in place.
Cleaning	Remove any excess solder with a file and scotch stone.
Polishing	Buff with felt buffing wheel and tripoli. Polish with a chamois or cloth buffing wheel and rouge.
Coloring p. 72	Dip in a solution of potassium sulphide. Remove any excess color with whiting. Polish with a soft cloth or chamois buffing wheel.

PROCESSES

Holding Hold the shank in a ring clamp.
the Place the clamp in the jaws of the table vise.
Ring

Setting Set the stone between the wires and the ends
the of the bent rectangle.
Stone Tap the ends over the stone.
p. 165 Smooth with a file.
Burnish the metal to polish.

RING DESIGN

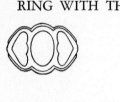

PATTERN

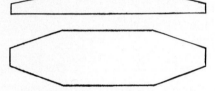

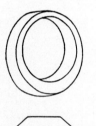

CASTING

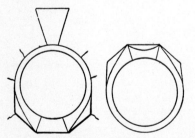

RING WITH THREE STONES AND CARVED DESIGN

Shank — Casting.

Ornament — Three stones and carved design.

Pattern of tin.

Roll the bar of tin at each end the thickness of 12-gauge.

Saw to pattern.

Bend so the two ends meet.

Solder the joint with soft solder.

Shape round.

File the inside surface of the shank a little smaller than the desired size.

File the planes for the stones and the outline and the contour of the shank.

Mold of cuttle-bone as shown in Fig. 14.

Prepare the cuttle-bone.

Press the pattern in the cuttle-bone to form the mold.

Cut the funnel and vents.

Casting.

Melt the metal in the crucible.

Pour the metal into the mold.

Saw off the button and the vents.

File the inside to ring size.

Smooth with a file.

Polish the surfaces.

Fig. 83.—Cast shank with three stones, and carved design

Ornament

Transfer the outline of the stone girdles and the lines to be carved.

Center punch and drill holes in each space.

Pierce the openings the exact size of the girdles of the stones.

Carve the wall of the center setting above the bearing straight down.

Carve the walls above the bearings next to the center setting at an angle; cut the other two walls straight down.

Polish.

Carve the lines around the shank.

Carve and file the edges around the bezels for a gypsy setting.

Carve the motif at the end of the two side stones.

Color.

Set the stones.

Retouch with color and polish.

Fig. 84.—Cast shank with three stones, and carved design

RING WITH THREE STONES AND
CARVED DESIGN
Figs. 83, 84

Type
of
Ring

Shank—Casting.
Ornament—Three stones and carved design.
The following metal and stone sets are required:
Sterling silver or 18 karat gold 2½ times the weight of the tin pattern.
Stone sets—One oval, cabochon stone, two matching stones, irregular in form, flat base.

Tools
and
Working
Materials

Ring sizes
Ring gauge
Dividers
Paper shears
Bar of tin
Rolling mill
Shellac, alcohol dye solution
Soft brush
Scratch awl
Bench pin
Jeweler's saw frame
Jeweler's saw blade #1
Forming block
Ring mandrel
Wooden mallet
Flux (electrician's paste)
Brush

Soft solder (lead and tin)
Gas and air blow torch
Flat and half round files
File card
Two pieces of cuttlebone
Powdered graphite
Knife
Binding wire 26-gauge
Jeweler's scales
Jeweler's shears
Pickle
Copper pickle pan
Copper tongs
Gas plate
Crucible #3
Iron tongs

<table>
<tr><td>

Tools
and
Working
Materials

</td><td>

Prepared reducing flux
  or powdered borax
Emery cloth #1
Polishing motor
Felt buffing wheel
Tripoli cake
Felt ring buff
Soda, ammonia, and
  water solution
Granite pan
Stone lifter
Center punch
Twist drill #60
Hand drill
Wooden core
Ring clamp
Gravers

</td><td>

Oil stone
Light oil
Kerosene cloth
Ink eraser
File card
Bristle buffing wheel
Chamois buffing wheel
Rouge stick
Potassium sulphide so-
  lution
Whiting
Small repoussé tools
Chasing hammer
Burnisher
Soft cloth or chamois
  buffing wheel

</td></tr>
</table>

PREPARATION FOR CASTING

PROCESSES

THE PATTERN

Measuring

Measure the finger two sizes larger than the size desired; this will be the required length of the pattern to be cut.

Measure with the dividers the depth and width of the stones to be set.

Making
the
Paper
Pattern

Make a paper pattern the measured length, wide enough to take care of the settings and the carved lines of the ornament.

Rolling

Roll a piece of bar tin to about 12-gauge on the ends, leaving a heavier gauge in the center, thicker than the depth of the stones.

PROCESSES

Transferring the Pattern to the Metal p. 36	Transfer the pattern. Use the painted method. Place the paper pattern on the tin, the center of the pattern on the thickest part. Scratch the pattern in the metal.
Sawing p. 31	Saw the metal, following the scratched line of the pattern.
Bending	Bend the blank in the forming block as shown in Fig. 74 to bring the two ends together.
Fitting	Saw through the joint.
Soft Soldering p. 43	Solder the joint with soft solder (lead and tin).
Shaping the Shank	Shape the shank on the ring mandrel. Tap with a mallet, reversing several times on the tapered mandrel to form a perfect circle.
Filing p. 25	File the inside of the shank a little smaller and the back a little wider than the desired size. File the outline, contours, and planes.

THE MOLD

Preparing the Cuttle-bone p. 54	Prepare the cuttle-bone.
Placing the Pattern	Hold the cuttle-bone in the palm of the hand. Place the tin pattern of the shank in the center of the smooth surface of the cuttle-bone with the back of the shank one inch from the end.

PROCESSES

Forming
the
Mold
p. 54

Press the front of the shank into the cuttle-bone until the back of the shank rests on the surface of the cuttle-bone.

Press the shank evenly until half is embedded. Place the other piece of cuttle-bone so that it registers with the first piece.

Hold between the palms and press slowly until the two flat surfaces of the cuttle-bone meet.

Marking
to
Register
p. 55

Mark lines on the cuttle-bone on both ends and sides with a saw blade.

Removing the
Pattern
from the
Mold
p. 55

Remove the tin pattern.

Cutting
the
Funnel
and the
Vents

Cut the funnel and vents in the cuttle-bone as shown in Fig. 15.

Binding

Bind the two pieces of cuttle-bone together.

CASTING THE PATTERN

Weighing
the
Pattern
and the
Silver

Weigh the tin pattern.
Weigh the metal, $2\frac{1}{2}$ times the weight of the pattern.

Pickling
p. 22

Clean in pickle.

PROCESSES

Melting   Place the metal in a crucible.
the   Melt the metal until it spins; add borax or re-
Metal   ducing flux just before pouring.
p. 56

Pouring   Direct the flame on the metal while pouring.
the   (The metal must be kept in fluid state.)
Metal   Pour the metal into the funnel of the cuttle-
into the   bone.
Mold

Removing   Remove the casting from the mold.
the
Casting
from the
Mold

Sawing   Saw off the button and the vents.
Pickling   Clean in pickle.
Filing   File to true and to remove any rough surfaces.
Polishing   Buff the outside with a felt buffing wheel and
p. 71   tripoli and the inside with a felt ring buff and
tripoli.

CARVING THE ORNAMENT AND SETTINGS

Transferring   Transfer the design. Use the painted method.
the   Scratch a line with the dividers in the center
Design   around the shank.
for   Scratch a line at right angles to the above di-
Carving   viding line at the widest part of the shank.
and   Pick up the oval stone with the stone lifter.
Settings   Center the stone on these two dividing lines.
p. 36   Scratch into the metal around the girdle of the
stone.

PROCESSES	Place the stones on the side planes. Center the point of the stone on the dividing line. Leave a space between the center and the side stones. Scratch around the girdles of the stones. Scratch the lines to be carved in the shank.
Center *Punching*	Locate and mark three points within the spaces marked by the girdles of the stones. Slip the shank on a wooden core. Center punch each of the located marks.
Drilling p. 35	Drill three holes as marked with the punch.
Piercing p. 35	Pierce the openings just drilled. They should be the exact size of the girdles of the stones.
Carving *the* *Bearings* p. 164	Place the shank in a ring clamp. Carve the walls for the center stone straight. Carve the walls for the side stones nearest the center stone at an angle to slope inward. Carve the other walls straight.
Filing	File the metal but keep the original gauge around the stone.
Polishing	Buff with a bristle buffing wheel and tripoli. Polish with chamois buffing wheel and rouge.
Carving *the* *Shank* p. 87	Carve the lines in the shank. Round off the metal with the graver between the carved lines, also the edge, to give the appearance of rounded wires. Carve the motif at the end of each of the pointed stones as shown in Fig. 84.
Coloring p. 22	Color the ring with potassium sulphide solution. Remove any excess color with whiting.
Setting the *Stones* p. 165	Set the stones as shown in Fig. 55.

RING DESIGN

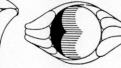

WAX PATTERN

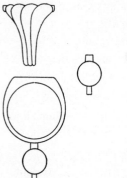

INVESTED PATTERN

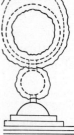

CASTING

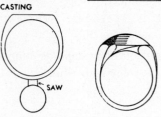

Fig. 85.—Cast shank, round stone, and carved design

RING WITH ROUND STONE AND CARVED DESIGN

Shank—Casting.

Ornament—Round stone set and carved design.

Pattern of Wax

Cut the pattern from the wax sheet.

Shape on the mandrel one size smaller than desired.

Press the stone into the wax.

Carve the wax around the stone and the design in the pattern.

Remove the stone.

Determine the amount of metal required for the casting as shown in Figs. 16, 17.

Place a $\frac{1}{4}$-inch ball of wax on the sprue pin; insert the pin through the back of the shank.

Seal the pattern to the pin.

Seal the wax ball to the pin $\frac{1}{16}$ inch from the pattern.

Double the thickness of the sprue pin with wax between the ball and the pattern.

Place the sprue pin in the sprue former and seal with wax.

Clean the wax surface with wax painting solution.

Rinse with water.

Paint the surface again do not rinse.

Investing the Pattern.

Paint the wax ball and pattern $\frac{1}{8}$ inch thick with mixed investment.

Line the flask with asbestos.

Place the flask on the sprue former.

Invest the pattern. Remove the sprue former and sprue pin when the investment has set.

Bake the invested flask.

Casting

Cast the pattern.

Wash and clean in pickle.

Saw off any excess silver.

Polish and smooth the surfaces.

Color.

Set the stone.

RING WITH ROUND STONE AND CARVED DESIGN
Fig. 85

Type of Ring

Shank—Casting.

Ornament—Round cabochon stone and carved design.

The following metal and stone set are required:

Sterling silver—The same volume of metal as wax, adding about two dwts. of metal to this measurement.

Stone—Round cabochon.

Tools and Working Materials

Ring sizes	Lubricant
Bunsen burner or gas flame	Ring mandrel
Dental casting wax	Steel tool (knife or flat dental tool or graver).
Soft blending and Hard carving	

*Tools
and
Working
Materials*

Graduate cylinder (1 inch or more diameter)
Sprue pin
Sprue Former
Wax painting solution
Soft brush
Dental casting investment
Rubber dish
Wire brush or steel wool
Spatula
Small paint brush
Casting flask
Hot plate
Asbestos sheet 2" wide
Crucible
Centrifugal casting machine
Electric furnace
Flat file
Iron tongs
Gas and air blow torch

Prepared reducing flux or borax
Pan 4-inch depth or more
Jeweler's saw frame
Jeweler's saw blades #1
Half-round 6-inch file
Scotch stone
Polishing motor
Bristle buffing wheel
Felt buffing wheel
Felt ring buff
Tripoli cake
Granite pan
Soda, ammonia, and water solution
Soft cloth or chamois buffing wheel
Rouge stick
Gravers
Oilstone
Light oil
Kerosene cloth
Potassium sulphide solution
Stone lifter
Ring clamp
Table vise
Small repoussé tool
Chasing hammer
Burnisher
Soft cloth buffing wheel

PREPARATION FOR CASTING

PROCESSES	THE PATTERN
Measuring	Measure the finger for the size.
Preparing the Wax Sheet p. 59	Spread a thin film of lubricant on a glass slab. Melt a small portion of soft blending wax and hard carving wax. Pour the melted wax on the glass surface.
Shaping the Shank p. 59	Model the wax pattern around a lubricated steel ring mandrel to form the shank a size smaller than desired and about $\frac{1}{16}$ inch thicker than the ting (Fig. 62). See Question 6, p. 69.
Forming the Bezel	Place the stone and press into the warm wax; be sure the wax is left heavy enough around the stone so the casting can be filed for a gypsy setting (Fig. 62). See Question 6, p. 69.
Carving the Design	Carve the design in the wax pattern. Remove the stone from the wax. *Note:* If the stone is transparent or translucent, cut the wax out under the set, leaving a small ridge for the stone to rest upon.
Polishing the Pattern p. 59	Remove the pattern from the mandrel. Brush the wax pattern under cold water with a fine brush or absorbent cotton.

Measuring the Amount of Metal Required p. 60	Measure the amount of metal necessary for the casting as shown in Fig. 17.
Placing the Wax Bead on the Sprue Pin p. 61	Place a $\frac{1}{4}$-inch wax bead on the sprue pin.
Placing the Pattern on the Sprue Pin	Place the back center of the wax pattern on the sprue pin.
Sealing the Bead	Seal the bead to the pin $\frac{1}{16}$ inch from the pattern.
Thickening the Sprue Pin	Thicken the sprue pin with wax, twice its diameter between the ball and the pattern.
Sealing the Sprue Pin on the Former	Place the sprue pin in the hole of the sprue former. Seal with wax. Care must be taken to have the pattern $\frac{1}{8}$ inch or more below the top of the flask.

PROCESSES

*Washing
the
Pattern*

Paint the pattern with a soft brush, wax paint-ing solution. Rinse in water. Repeat the above but do not rinse. See Question 7, p. 69.

FORMING THE MOLD

*Mixing
the
Investment*
p. 62

Mix the investment with water to a smooth, thick, creamy consistency.

*Coating
the
Pattern*
p. 62

Paint the pattern with the mixed investment.

*Preparing
the
Flask*
p. 62

Line the flask with a strip of damp asbestos. Leave $\frac{1}{4}$ inch at one end uncovered.

*Placing
the
Flask*

Place the flask on the rim of the sprue former. See Question 9, p. 69.

*Mixing
the
Investment*

Mix the investment to a thin pouring con-sistency.

*Investing
the
Pattern*
p. 63

Pour the mixture into the flask.

PROCESSES

*Removing
the
Flask
from the
Sprue
Former*
p. 63

Remove the flask from the sprue former when
the investment has set.

*Removing
Excess
Investment*
p. 63

Remove any excess investment from the inside
rim of the flask.

BALANCING THE MACHINE

*Preparing
the
Crucible*

Place damp asbestos sheet cut to pattern in the
crucible.

*Placing
the
Metal
in the
Crucible*

Place the metal to be cast in the crucible.

*Balancing
the
Machine*
p. 64

Balance the machine as shown in Fig. 19.

FURNACE TREATMENT
OF THE MOLD

*Preheating
the
Furnace*

Preheat the furnace to 800 F.

PROCESSES

Burning
out the
Wax Pattern
p. 65

Place the prepared flask in the furnace, with the feed holes on the tray. Reverse this position when the wax has been burned out.

CASTING

Placing
the
Flask
in the
Machine
p. 64

Place the flask in the machine.

Winding
the
Spring
of the
Machine
p. 66

Wind the spring.

Locking
the
Carrier
p. 66

Lock the carrier as shown in Fig. 14.

Heating
the
Metal
p. 66

Heat the metal and sprinkle with borax or prepared reducing flux when it becomes red hot and again when it reaches the fluid state just before it is cast.

PROCESSES

*Casting
the
Pattern*
p. 66

Release the carrier when the metal reaches a fluid state.

*Removing
the
Flask*

Remove the flask from the carrier.

*Cooling
the
Casting*
p. 67

Cool the casting by degrees in water.

FINISHING

*Removing
the
Casting*

Remove the casting from the investment.

*Washing
the
Casting*

Wash the casting in water to remove the investment.

Pickling

Clean in pickle.

Sawing
p. 31

Saw off any excess metal attached to the casting with the jeweler's saw blade.

Filing
p. 25

File the casting to remove any roughness if necessary. File the inside of the ring with a six-inch half round file.

*Preparing
the Box
for a
Gypsy
Setting*

File away the metal around the top of the bezel at the angle. Keep the original depth of the metal around the stone as shown in Fig. 62.

Cleaning

Remove any scratches with the file and scotch stone.

PROCESSES

Polishing
p. 71

Buff the outside surfaces with a bristle buffing wheel and tripoli and the inside surface with a felt ring buff and tripoli.

Polish with a cloth or chamois buffing wheel.

Carving
p. 87

Carve any surfaces to sharpen with the graver.

Coloring
p. 72

Color the ring with potassium sulphide solution.

Setting the Stone
p. 165

Set the stone as shown in Fig. 55.

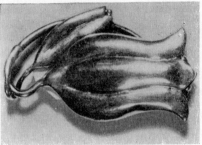

Brooch of wire, bead and sawed
forms

Brooch—chased and repoussé

Brooch of looped wire

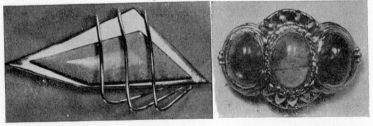

Brooch—Enameled forms and wire loops

Brooch of looped wire

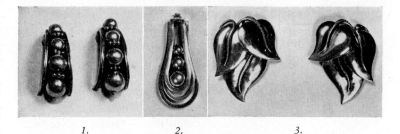

1.   2.   3.

1.—*Clips of beads, balls, and wire*
2.—*Clip of wire loops and beads*
3.—*Clips of silver leaves*

BROOCHES AND CLIPS

The brooch is a useful as well as an ornamental piece of jewelry. Brooches vary in size and form. The greatest size in this piece of jewelry was reached in the Scottish brooch used to pin the plaid in place on the shoulder. A brooch is made up of three parts: the foundation, the ornament, and the fastening.

The foundation, as its name indicates, is the base to which the fastening is attached and upon which the ornament rests. The foundation often forms part of the ornament (Figs. 86, 87 illustrate this method) although some brooches are so constructed that the foundation serves only that purpose. The fastening is composed of the joint, the catch, and the pin stem. These are always attached under the base and concealed by it.

Like other pieces of jewelry a brooch may be decorated with the material of which it is made or with stones set into the foundation or resting upon it. Flat metal or wire in different forms appliquéd on the foundation may be used to ornament the background. All silver, or silver combined with gold, or silver combined with copper can be used with good effect.

BROOCH DESIGN

FOUNDATION

ORNAMENT

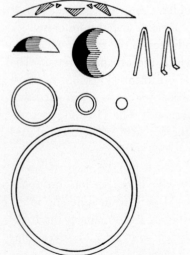

Fig. 86.—*Domed brooch pierced and decorated with wire and balls*

BROOCH PIERCED AND DECORATED WITH WIRE AND BALLS

Foundation—Dome.

Ornament — Pierced, applied wire and balls.

Foundation—Sterling silver sheet 20-gauge.

 Inscribe a 1½-inch circle on the silver.

 Saw out the disk.

 Anneal the disk.

 Transfer the design.

 Dome the disk about ⅜ inch.

 Drill a small hole in the center.

Ornament

 Pierce twelve triangles in the foundation.

Fine silver sheet 24-gauge.

 Cut and dome a disk.

Sterling silver wire annealed 16-gauge.

 Cut six 1-inch lengths of wire.

 Bend in the center.

 Make a hook on each end.

Sterling silver wire 14-gauge.

 Make two rings, one the diameter of the large dome and one the diameter of the small dome.

 Solder the joints.

 File one side flat.

Fine silver wire.

 Make six balls.

Joining the Ornament and the Foundation

Insert the hooked ends of one bent wire unit in two small pierced triangles in the foundation.

Bind to the foundation.

Repeat with the other five wires.

Solder in place.

Saw out the outline of the foundation.

File the edges smooth.

Bind the flat side of the large ring under the foundation.

Place the small dome on the flat side of the small ring.

Bind in the center of the foundation.

Solder together.

Solder the six balls over the wires around the center dome.

Solder the joint and catch to the rim of the foundation a little above center.

Clean, polish, and color.

Rivet the pin stem in the joint.

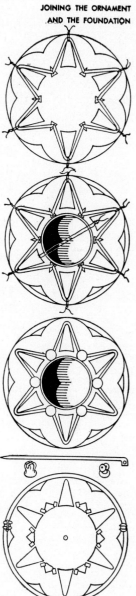

Fig. 87. — *Domed brooch pierced and decorated with wire and balls*

BROOCH PIERCED AND DECORATED
WITH WIRES AND BALLS

Type
of
Brooch

Figs. 86, 87

Foundation—Dome.

Ornament—Pierced, applied wire, and balls.

The following sheet metal, wire, and brooch fittings are required:

Sterling silver sheet 20-gauge for the foundation dome.

Fine silver sheet 24-gauge for the center dome.

Sterling silver wire 16-gauge to outline the pierced triangles.

Sterling silver wire 14-gauge for the base rings of the two domes.

Fine silver wire for the balls.

Brooch fittings—joint, catch, and pin tongue.

Tools
and
Working
Materials

Metal gauge	White beeswax
Ruler	Soft cloth
Dividers	Scratch awl
Bench pin	Dapping die or lead dapping block
Jeweler's saw frame	
Jeweler's saw blade #1/0	Large round head steel stake
Flat file	Raising hammer
Charcoal block	Mallet
Gas and air blow torch	Center punch
Pickle	Twist drill #70
Copper pickle pan	Hand drill
Copper tongs	Dapping die cutter— half-inch
Gas plate	
Pliers	Dapping die punch
Thin tracing paper.	Emery cloth

*Tools
and
Working
Materials*

Jeweler's shears
Round nose pliers
Steel surface plate
Steel hammer
Round mandrels
(three sizes for the
balls, base of large
dome and small
dome balls)
Flux
Borax slate or saucer
Solder
Camel's hair brush
Scotch stone
Polishing motor
Felt buffing wheel
Tripoli cake
Soda, ammonia, and
water solution

Granite pan
Binding wire
26-gauge
Bristle buffing wheel
Soap and water solu-
tion
Scrub brush
Chamois buffing wheel
Rouge stick
Potassium sulphide so-
lution
Whiting
Soft cloth buffing
wheel
Reamer
Nickel silver wire 18-
gauge for rivet
Cutters
Small riveting hammer

PROCESSES

FOUNDATION

*Gauging
the
Metal*
p. 346

Gauge the metal.

*Inscribing
a Circle*

Sterling silver sheet 20-gauge. Inscribe a $1\frac{1}{2}$-
inch circle on the silver sheet.

Sawing
p. 31

Saw out the disk.

Annealing
p. 18

Anneal the disk.

PROCESSES	
Pickling p. 22	Clean in pickle.
Transferring *the* *Design* *to the* *Metal* p. 33	Transfer the design on the metal; use the wax method.
Doming p. 121	Dome the disk to form the foundation.
Drilling p. 35	Drill a small hole in the center.

ORNAMENT

Piercing p. 35	Pierce the twelve triangles in the foundation.
Cutting *and* *Doming* p. 121	Fine silver sheet 24-gauge. Cut and dome a disk for the center of the foundation.
Truing	File the base to straighten. Rub on emery cloth to smooth.
Cutting *Lengths* *of Wire*	Sterling silver wire 16-gauge. Cut six lengths of wire 1 inch long.
Bending *the* *Wire*	Bend each length in the center with the round nose pliers. Hammer the ends to flatten with a steel hammer on a steel stake.
Annealing	Anneal the wire.

PROCESSES

Making a Hook

Form a small hook on each of the flattened ends with the pliers.

Ring Making
p. 112

Sterling silver wire 14-gauge.
Make a ring the diameter of the large dome.
Make a ring for the small dome to rest on; the ring should extend a little beyond the edge of the dome.

Soldering
p. 38

Solder the joints of the rings.

Truing

Tap the rings on a round mandrel with a mallet to true.

Filing
p. 25

File the base of both rings to flatten.
Smooth on emery cloth.

Cleaning
p. 70

Remove any excess solder with a file and scotch stone.

Polishing

Buff with a felt buffing wheel and tripoli.

Ball Making
p. 120

Fine silver wire.
Make six balls of equal size.

JOINING THE ORNAMENT AND THE FOUNDATION

Binding

Insert two hooked ends of a wire unit in two small pierced holes on each side of a large pierced triangle.
Bind the wire unit so as to frame the pierced triangle; it must touch the foundation at all points.
Repeat the above with the other five units.

PROCESSES	
Soldering	Solder in place.
Sawing	Saw the outline of the foundation.
Filing	File all edges smooth.
Binding	Bind the large ring under the foundation. Bind the small ring and the dome in the center of the foundation.
Soldering	Solder the rings and domes in place. Solder the six balls over the wire ends spaced evenly around the center dome.
Pickling	Clean in pickle.
Cleaning p. 70	Remove any excess solder or scratches with a file and scotch stone.
Polishing p. 71	Buff with felt buffing wheel and tripoli around the outer edge of the foundation and to flatten the wire units slightly on top. Buff the recessed parts with a bristle buffing wheel and tripoli.
Placing the Joint	Place the right side of the brooch on the charcoal block—the top away from the worker. Care must be taken to keep a geometrical or a balanced design straight. Place the joint a little above the center on the right side of the brooch close to the outer edge.
Placing the Catch	Place the catch directly opposite the joint with the opening down.
Binding	Bind the joint and the catch in place.
Soldering	Place the flux and a small piece of solder on one side of the joint and catch. Solder in place.

PROCESSES	Inspect the solder to be sure it has run completely around the base of the joint and the catch.
Pickling	Clean in pickle.
Polishing p. 71	Polish with a cloth or chamois buffing wheel and rouge stick.
Coloring p. 72	Color with potassium sulphide solution. Remove any excess color with whiting. Polish with a chamois or soft cloth buffing wheel.
Reaming	Ream out the holes in the pin stem slightly larger than the joint.
Making the Rivet	Select a piece of nickel wire slightly larger than the hole in the joint. File one end of the wire about $\frac{1}{4}$ inch to a blunt point to fit through the holes of the joint and the pin stem. Place the pin stem in the joint. Place the wire through the holes of the joint and the pin stem. Cut the thick end of the wire with the wire cutters so as to leave a small head. Cut the filed end shorter and leave enough to make a head.
Riveting the Pin Stem in Place	Rivet the wire ends with a small riveting hammer. Finish with a file and emery if any sharp edge is left on the edge of the rivet.

BROOCH DESIGN

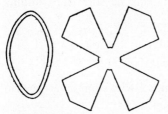

**ASSEMBLING PARTS
OF THE FOUNDATION**   ½ **SIZE**

ORNAMENT

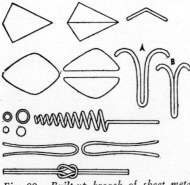

*Fig. 88.—Built-up brooch of sheet metal
and wire units*

BROOCH BUILT UP WITH METAL UNITS

Foundation—Wire and flat metal.
Ornament—Repoussé motifs, wires, and balls.
Foundation—Sterling silver sheet 20-gauge.
    Saw to pattern.
    Drill a hole in the center.
Sterling silver wire 14-gauge.
    Make four oval rings.
Assembling Parts of the Foundation
    Bind and solder the four oval rings together to form a motif.
Solder to the foundation.
Ornament—Sterling silver sheet 20-gauge.
    Saw four triangles to pattern.
Sterling silver sheet 24-gauge.
    Saw four orals to pattern.
      Bend the triangles.
        Repoussé the ovals.
        Sterling silver wire annealed 20-gauge.
            Cut eight 1½-inch and eight 1¼-inch lengths of wire.
        Bend the units A and B.
        Make four wire cones.
    Fine silver wire 18-gauge.
        Make eight small balls and four large balls.
        Make a square knot.

Assembling Parts of the Ornament

Bind and solder A and B.

Bind and solder the eight cupped units.

Drill a hole in the base of each cup.

Bind and solder the AB unit inside the cup, the wire ends of A on the point of the cup, the wire ends of B to the edge of the cup.

Repeat the above with the other AB units and cups.

Solder the small balls over the wire ends of A.

Solder the large ball on the point of each cone.

Place a cone inside each cup with the wire through the hole in the base.

Joining the Ornament and the Foundation

Bind and solder the four triangles to the four oval rings.

Bind the cupped motifs to the foundation.

Insert the wire ends of the coils and knot through the hole in the center of the foundation.

Bend the wire ends over the back of the foundation and cut off excess wire.

Solder all points of contact.

Solder the joint and catch in place.

Clean, polish, and color.

Rivet the pin stem in the joint.

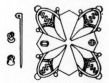

Fig. 89.—*Built-up brooch of sheet metal and wire units*

BROOCH BUILT UP WITH METAL UNITS
Figs. 88, 89

Type
of
Brooch

Foundation—Shaped form and wires.
Ornament—Repoussé units, bent, coiled, and knotted wires, and balls.
The following metal sheet, wire, and brooch fittings are required:

Sterling silver sheet 20-gauge for the foundation and the triangular pieces of the ornament.

Sterling silver wire 14-gauge for the oval rings of the foundation.

Sterling silver wire 20-gauge for the wire coils and wire units.

Sterling silver sheet 24-gauge for the repoussé cups.

Fine silver wire 18-gauge for the balls and knot.

Brooch fittings—Joint, catch, and pin tongue.

Tools
and
Working
Materials

Metal gauge	Emery cloth
Thin tracing paper	Center punch
Soft pencil	Hand drill
White beeswax	Twist drill
Gas plate	Charcoal block or asbestos pad
Scratch awl	
Soft cloth	Gas and air blow torch
Bench pin	Oval mandrel
Jeweler's saw frame	Pickle
Jeweler's saw blades #1/0	Copper pickle pan
	Copper tweezers
Medium flat file	Jeweler's shears
File brush	Round nose pliers

*Tools
and
Working
Materials*

Cotter pins of 18-
gauge binding wire
Flux
Borax slate or saucer
Solder
Camel's hair brush
Binding wire
26-gauge
Steel ruler
Scoring tool
Hand vise
Dapping block
Repoussé tool
Chasing hammer
Polishing motor
Felt buffing wheel
Tripoli cake
Soda, ammonia, and
water solution
Granite pan

Scrub brush
Round mandrels—two
sizes
Pointed mandrel
Scotch stone
Fine emery cloth
Bristle buffing wheel
Boric acid and alcohol
solution
Rouge paste
Soft cloth or chamois
buffing wheel
Rouge
Potassium sulphide so-
lution
Whiting powder
Soft cloth
Nickel wire for rivet
Riveting hammer
Steel block

PROCESSES

FOUNDATION

*Gauging
the
Metal
p. 346*

Gauge the metal.

*Transferring
the
Design
p. 33*

Sterling silver sheet 20-gauge. Transfer the
design to the metal. Use the wax method.

*Sawing
p. 31*

Saw to pattern.

PROCESSES

Drilling
p. 35

Drill a hole in the center of the sawed foundation.

Annealing
p. 18

Sterling silver wire 14-gauge.   Anneal the wire.

*Making
Oval
Rings*
p. 113

Make four oval rings.

ASSEMBLING PARTS OF THE FOUNDATION

Binding

Bind the four rings together on the charcoal block with staples as shown in Fig. 12.

Soldering
p. 38

Solder the rings together to form a motif.

Binding

Bind the wire motif to the sawed foundation as shown in Fig. 13.

Soldering

Solder together.

Pickling
p. 22

Clean in pickle.

SEPARATE PARTS OF THE ORNAMENT

*Transferring
the
Design*

Sterling silver sheet 20-gauge.
Transfer four triangles to the silver.   Use the wax method.
Sterling silver sheet 24-gauge.
Transfer eight ovals to the silver.   Use the wax method.

Sawing

Saw to pattern.

Annealing

Anneal the metal.

Pickling

Clean the metal in the pickle.

PROCESSES	
Scoring p. 157	Score the triangles lengthwise in the center with a triangular file.
Bending	Bend on the scored line.
Repoussé p. 77	Raise the ovals slightly on a lead block using a broad repoussé tool. Bend the edges of each to measure ¼ inch apart to form a cupped unit.
Polishing p. 71	Polish with a felt buffing wheel and tripoli.
Annealing	Sterling silver wire 20-gauge. Anneal the wire.
Cutting	Cut eight 1½-inch lengths of wire. Cut eight 1¼-inch lengths of wire.
Bending	Bend the wires in the center with round nose pliers. Curve the ends of the wires as shown in A and B (Fig. 88).
Coiling p. 111	Coil four cones of wire; leave about 1 inch of wire on the end of each cone.
Ball	Fine silver wire 18-gauge.
Making p. 120	Make eight small balls and four large balls.
Knotting	Make a square knot.

ASSEMBLING PARTS OF THE ORNAMENT

Binding	Bind B on A so the two looped ends are even. Insert flat binding wire between A and B a little above center to keep the solder from flowing beyond this point as shown in Fig. 89. Bind with cotter pins the eight cup-shaped units so they overlap as shown in Fig. 89.

PROCESSES

Soldering

Solder the AB motif.
Solder the seam of the cup-shaped unit.

Pickling

Clean in pickle.

Drilling
p. 35

Drill a hole in the center base of each of the cup-shaped units, large enough to admit 20-gauge wire.

Binding

Place two AB units inside the cup over the two soldered seams.   Hold in place with cotter pins as shown in Fig. 89.
Let the wire ends of the A unit meet the point of the cup.
Let the ends of the B unit rest on the edge of the cup about ¼ inch from the point of the cup. Bind in place if necessary.
Repeat with the other six AB units.

Soldering

Solder in place.
Solder the small balls to the points of the cup over the wire ends of A.
Solder the large balls on the end of the cones of wire.

Placing the Coil inside the Cup

Place the cones of wire inside the cups.
Let the wire ends extend through the small drilled holes of the cups.

JOINING THE ORNAMENT TO THE FOUNDATION

Binding

Bind the four triangles to the oval rings of the foundation.

Soldering

Solder in place.

PROCESSES

Pickling	Clean in pickle.
Binding	Bind the four cup-shaped motifs to the foundation. The ball on the end of the cone should rest on the point of the oval ring of the foundation.
	Insert the wire ends which extend from the coiled cones through the center hole in the foundation.
	Draw the four ends of the square knot through the same hole.
	Spread the wires on the back of the foundation.
Soldering *Brooch* *Fittings* p. 252	Solder the motifs and wires to the foundation. Solder the joint and the catch on the back of the foundation.
Cleaning p. 70	Clean in pickle and remove any excess solder with a file and scotch stone.
Polishing p. 71	Buff with a bristle buffing wheel and tripoli. Polish with a chamois or cloth buffing wheel.
Coloring p. 72	Color with potassium sulphide solution. Remove any excess color with whiting. Polish with a chamois or cloth buffing wheel.
Riveting *Pin* *Stem* p. 253	Rivet the pin stem in the joint.

CLIP DESIGN

CLIP WITH STONE, WIRE, AND BALLS

Foundation—Flat metal form.

Ornament—Stone set, applied wire, and balls.

Foundation

Sterling silver sheet 18-gauge.

FOUNDATION

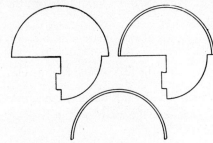

Saw to pattern.

Sterling silver wire annealed 16-gauge.

Bend and saw a length of wire to fit the half-circle of the foundation. File slightly to flatten.

Bind and solder to the foundation.

Ornament

Sterling silver sheet 24-gauge.

Make a bezel.

Sterling silver sheet 26-gauge.

ORNAMENT

Make a bearing.

Fine silver wire 18-gauge.

Bend the wire to pattern.

Make five balls.

Sterling silver wire 16-gauge.

Saw four lengths and bend to pattern.

Bind and solder.

Make a waved wire.

Fig. 90.—Flat clip decorated with a stone, wire, and balls

Joining the Ornament and the Foundation

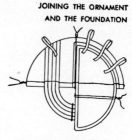

Bind the bezel, bearing, and wires to the foundation.

Solder together.

Bind and solder the waved wire and balls to the foundation.

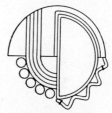

Pierce the metal inside the bezel.

Solder the joint of the clip at the center top with the hook up.

Clean, polish, and color.

Set the stone.

Fasten the clip in the joint and the spring on the hook.

CLIP

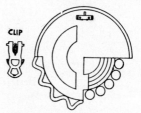

Fig. 91.—*Flat clip deco-rated with a stone, wire, and balls*

CLIP WITH STONE, WIRE, AND BALLS
Figs. 90, 91

Type
of
Clip

Foundation—Flat metal form.
Ornament—Stone set, wire, and balls.
The following flat metal, wire, stone, and clip fittings are required:

Sterling silver sheet 18-gauge for the foundation.
Sterling silver wire 16-gauge for the foundation and ornament.
Sterling silver sheet 24-gauge for the bezel.
Sterling silver sheet 26-gauge for the bearing.
Fine silver wire 18-gauge for the wire around the bezel for the balls.
Clip fittings—Joint and clip.
Stone—Translucent agate.

Tools
and
Working
Materials

Metal gauge
Thin tracing paper
Soft pencil
White beeswax
Gas and air blow
   torch
Soft cloth
Scratch awl
Bench pin
Jeweler's saw frame
Jeweler's saw blade
   #1/0
Flat file
Charcoal block
Emery cloth #0
Round nose pliers

Snub nose pliers
Cotter pins of 18-
   gauge flat iron wire
Flux
Borax slate or saucer
Solder
Jeweler's shears
Camel's hair brush
Copper tweezers
Copper pickle pan
Pickle
Gas plate
Binding wire
   26-gauge
Dentimetre
Dividers

*Tools
and
Working
Materials*

Round mandrel—⅛-
   inch
Bench vise
Drill stock
Iron or steel hook
Alcohol and boric acid
   solution
Center punch
Hand drill
Twist drill
Scotch stone
Polishing motor
Bristle buffing wheel
Tripoli cake
Granite pan
Soda, ammonia, and
   water solution

Scrub brush
Soap
Rouge paste
Rouge stick
Chamois buffing wheel
Light oil
Yellow flake shellac
Shellac stick
Alcohol
Potassium sulphide so-
   lution
Whiting
Soft cloth
Soft cloth buffing
   wheel

PROCESSES

FOUNDATION

*Gauging
the
Metal*
p. 346

Gauge the metal.

*Transferring
the
Design*
p. 33

Sterling silver sheet 18-gauge. **Transfer the**
outline. Use the wax method.

Sawing
p. 31

Saw to pattern.

Annealing
p. 18

Sterling silver wire 16-gauge.
Anneal the wire.

Bending

Bend the wire to fit the half circle of the foundation as shown in Fig. 90.

PROCESSES

Sawing   Saw the wire ends.

Filing   File the base slightly flat.
p. 25

Placing   Place the wire with the flattened side on the
                    sawed foundation, the outer edge of wire flush
                    with the edge of the metal foundation.

Binding   Bind the wire in place with cotter pins.

Soldering   Solder together.
p. 38

ORNAMENT

Making   Sterling silver sheet 24-gauge.
the   Make a bezel to fit the stone.
Bezel   Sterling silver sheet 26-gauge.
and   Make a bearing to fit the bezel.
Bearing
p. 156

Bending   Fine silver wire 18-gauge.
Wire   Bend the wire to fit the half of the bezel as
                    shown in Fig. 90.

Ball   Make five balls.
Making
p. 120

Sawing   Sterling silver wire 16-gauge.
and   Saw four lengths of wire.
Bending   Bend to pattern.

Binding   Bind together as shown in Fig. 90.

Soldering   Solder together.

PROCESSES *Making* *Smooth* *Waved* *Wire* p. 105	Make a waved wire smooth and flat as shown in Fig. 31.

JOINING THE ORNAMENT AND THE FOUNDATION

Binding	Bind the bezel, bearing, and wires to the foundation.
Soldering	Solder together.
Shaping	Curve the waved wire to touch the bezel and one end of the foundation wire.
Soldering	Solder the waved wire and balls in place.
Piercing p. 35	Pierce the silver inside the bezel if the stone is transparent or translucent.
Soldering *the* *Clip*	Solder the joint of the clip at the center top with the hook up.
Cleaning p. 70	Clean in pickle and remove excess solder and scratches with a file and scotch stone.
Polishing p. 71	Buff with bristle buffing wheel and tripoli. Polish with a cloth buffing wheel and rouge.
Coloring p. 72	Color with potassium sulphide solution. Remove any excess color with whiting.
Setting *the* *Stone* p. 165	Set the stone.
Setting *the* *Clip*	Fasten the two protruding ends on the clip in the joint; fasten the spring on the hook.

Silver band wire and balls   *Chevron twist and balls*   *Silver band wire and domes*

Sawed and twisted bracelet   *Crimped bracelet*   *Silver wire bracelet*

Twisted linked bracelet with decorated silver beads

BRACELETS

Bracelets are bands of metal or interwoven links of wire made to fit the arm or wrist. They have been worn through the ages to symbolize power, or wealth, or to provide a setting for a stone or an insignia which may or may not have symbolic significance. The bracelet has also been used as an ornament valued for its beauty of design and workmanship.

Recently the use of bracelets as costume jewelry has attached them to prevailing modes of dress which, in turn, influences both design and materials used to produce them. Like all other types of jewelry bracelets vary in design and construction depending upon the mode in vogue. The simplest form of construction is the band of metal or wire with an opening large enough to slip over the wrist. The bracelet made by the American Indian is a well-known example of this type. More elaborate bracelets may be made of chain or hinged pieces of metal.

Ornamentation may be added by piercing or carving the design in the band of the bracelet. A design in relief may be executed in repoussé. Still another method of ornamentation is a stone in a suitable setting applied to the band. This type of ornament may be set also in the clasp. Piercing, carving, or repoussé may be used to create pieces to be applied on the band for decoration or to form decorative motifs to be linked together as a bracelet. Stones in effective settings also may be used to ornament one or more of the units of the linked bracelets.

Ornaments, like the settings for rings, must be proportionate to and suitable in design to the size, width, shape, and construction of the bracelet. When decorated at intervals the repeats should be close enough together to be pleasing at all angles of the curved surface.

BRACELET DESIGN

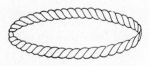

BRACELET OF TWISTED WIRE

Foundation and ornament
Band of twisted wire.

CONSTRUCTION

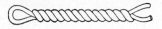

Construction

Sterling silver wire annealed 10-gauge 18 inches long.

Loop the length of wire in the center.

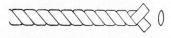

Twist the two wires together, about twenty-four full turns to make a tight twist.

Draw through the oval hole draw plate to flatten the twist.

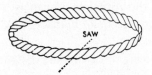

Bend the wires so the ends overlap to form a circle about 2½ inches in diameter.

Saw at an angle so there is no break in the twist.

File to make a perfect fit.

Bind together on a piece of flat binding wire to make an even joint.

Solder the joint.

Shape round.

Clean, polish, and color.

Fig. 92.—Bracelet of twisted wire drawn oval

BRACELET OF TWISTED WIRE
Fig. 92

Type
of
Bracelet

Twisted wire bracelet.
The following wire is required:
Sterling silver wire 10-gauge—18 inches.

Tools
and
Working
Materials

Metal gauge
Charcoal block or asbestos pad
Gas and air blow torch
Bench vise
Hand vise
Steel surface plate
Steel hammer
File
Oval hole draw plate
Yellow beeswax
Draw tongs or draw bench
Bench pin
Jeweler's saw frame
Jeweler's saw blade #1/0
Binding wire 14-gauge flattened
Binding wire 24-gauge
Flux

Borax slate or saucer
Solder
Jeweler's shears
Camel's hair brush
Pickle
Copper pickle pan
Copper tongs
Gas plate
Bracelet mandrel
Surface plate
Scotch stone
Felt buffing wheel
Tripoli cake
Granite pan
Soda, ammonia, and water solution
Cloth buffing wheel
Rouge stick
Potassium sulphide solution
Whiting
Chamois buffing wheel

PROCESSES
Gauging
the
Wire
p. 46

Gauge the wire, sterling silver wire 10-gauge.

PROCESSES	
Annealing p. 18	Anneal the wire.
Wire Twisting p. 102	Loop the length of wire in the center. Twist the wire with the hand vise until an even tight twist has been obtained, about twenty-four full turns.
Wire Drawing p. 96	Draw the twisted wire length through the oval hole draw plate until the twist has been flattened (Fig. 29).
Annealing	Anneal the wire.
Bending	Bend the wire so the ends overlap—an 8-inch circle is the usual size.
Sawing p. 31	Saw the overlapped pieces at an angle so there is no break in the twist when the ends are connected as shown in Fig. 92.
Filing p. 25	File the ends to make a perfect fit.
Binding	Flatten about 2 inches of 14-gauge binding wire in the roller. Place a strip of 14-gauge flat binding wire in back of the joint. Bind the flattened twist to the flat binding wire with 24-gauge wire on both sides of the joint. *Note:* Be sure the wires have been held firmly and a good joint has been made.
Soldering p. 38	Solder the joint.
Pickling p. 22	Clean in pickle.
Shaping	Hammer lightly on a round bracelet mandrel with a mallet to form into a circle.

PROCESSES

Truing

Place on a surface plate.
Tap the edges lightly with a mallet to true.

Cleaning

Remove scratches or excess solder with a file and scotch stone.

Polishing
p. 71

Buff with a felt buffing wheel and tripoli.
Polish with a cloth or chamois buffing wheel and rouge.

Coloring
p. 72

Color with potassium sulphide solution.
Rub with whiting and a soft cloth.
Buff with a cloth or chamois buffing wheel.

SET OF THREE BRACELETS

Wire
Twisting

Sterling silver wire annealed 10-gauge.
Make a chevron of twisted wires as shown in Fig. 28.
Follow the directions given above.

Wire
Drawing

Sterling silver wire annealed 8-gauge.
Draw the wire through the oval hole draw plate.
Make the bracelet following directions given above.

BRACELET DESIGN

FOUNDATION

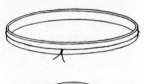

ORNAMENT

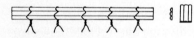

**JOINING THE ORNAMENT
AND THE FOUNDATION**

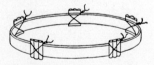

SAW

*Fig. 93.—Band bracelet with applied
units of wire*

BRACELET BAND WITH APPLIED WIRE UNITS

Foundation — Band of sheet silver.

Ornament — Wire units.

Foundation

Sterling silver sheet annealed 18-gauge 8 inches long ¼ inch wide.

Bend the strip so the two ends meet.

Bind and solder the joint.

Shape round.

File the edges.

Ornament

Sterling silver wire annealed 8-gauge.

Draw the wire half round in two sizes.

Cut the smaller wire in two.

Bind the smaller wires on each side of the larger wire.

Solder the wires together.

Saw in ½-inch units.

Joining the Ornament and the Foundation

Divide the band into five equal parts.

Bind the units to the band.

Solder in place.

Saw off the protruding wires.

Clean, polish, and color.

BRACELET BAND WITH APPLIED
WIRE UNITS
Fig. 93

Type
of
Bracelet

Straight band with applied wire units.
The following silver and wire is required:
    Sterling silver sheet 18-gauge 8 inches long
    1/4 inch wide for the foundation.
    Sterling silver wire 8-gauge drawn half
    round for the ornament.

Tools
and
Working
Materials

Metal gauge
Charcoal block
Gas and air blow torch
Snub nose pliers
Binding wire
    26-gauge
Pickle
Copper pickle pan
Copper tongs
Gas plate
Flux
Borax slate or saucer
Solder
Jeweler's shears
Camel's hair brush
Bracelet mandrel
Mallet
Surface plate
File
Scotch stone
Polishing motor
Felt buffing wheel

Tripoli cake
Soda, ammonia, and
    water solution
Granite pan
Bench vise or draw
    bench
Half round hole draw
    plate
Yellow beeswax
Draw tongs
Bench pin
Jeweler's saw frame
Jeweler's saw blades
    #1/0
Dividers
Ruler
Cloth buffing wheel
Rouge stick
Potassium sulphide so-
    lution
Whiting
Chamois buffing wheel

PROCESSES	FOUNDATION
Gauging the Metal p. 346	Gauge the metal.
Annealing p. 18	Sterling silver sheet 18-gauge 8 inches long ¼ inch wide. Anneal the strip.
Bending	Bend the strip so the two ends meet. File if necessary to make an even joint.
Binding	Bind together.
Soldering p. 38	Solder the joint.
Pickling p. 22	Clean in pickle.
Shaping	Hammer lightly on the round bracelet mandrel with a mallet to form into a circle.
Truing	Place on a surface plate. Tap the edges lightly to true.
Filing p. 25	File and rub on a flat piece of emery cloth if necessary.
Cleaning p. 70	Remove scratches and excess solder with a file and scotch stone.
Polishing p. 71	Buff with a felt buffing wheel and tripoli.

PROCESSES	ORNAMENT
Wire *Drawing* p. 96	Sterling silver wire 8-gauge. Draw the wire through the half round hole draw plate. Two sizes will be necessary; the smaller wire should be twice the length of the larger wire.
Sawing p. 33	Saw the smaller wire in two even pieces.
Binding	Bind the two smaller wires one on each side of the larger wire, as shown in Fig. 93.
Soldering	Solder the wires together.
Sawing	Saw the soldered strip of wire in five ½-inch units.

JOINING THE ORNAMENT AND THE FOUNDATION

Spacing	Divide the band into five equal parts and scratch a line across the band at right angles.
Binding	Bind the units of wire at right angles with the band so the outer edge of the small wire lies on the division line. Let the wires extend over the edges of the band ⅛ inch. The unit must touch the band at all points as shown in Fig. 93.
Soldering	Solder the wire units to the band.
Pickling	Clean in pickle.
Sawing	Saw the protruding wires even with the edge of the band.
Filing	File to smooth the edges.
Cleaning	Remove any scratches or excess solder with a file and scotch stone.

Polishing

Polish with a felt buffing wheel and tripoli.
Polish with a cloth or chamois buffing wheel
and rouge.

Coloring
p. 72

Color with potassium sulphide solution.
Rub with whiting and a soft cloth to remove
excess color.
Buff with a chamois or soft cloth buffing wheel.

SET OF BRACELETS

Take any width silver for the band and proceed
as above.
The band may be sawed in sections after the
units have been soldered and several bracelets
may thus be made.

Chains, interwoven, coiled, and linked

CHAINS

Chains are made of interlinked wire rings, called links. Chains are worn as necklaces, girdles, and bracelets. They are also used to hold ornaments such as an ear drop, a pendant, or a medal. Often they are the only means of holding some useful object such as a watch, eyeglasses, or a hand bag.

Effective chains may be made of unsoldered links as shown in Fig. 96. Most chains, however, are made of links that are soldered to insure strength and finish. Round or oval links are the forms most commonly used although many modifications of these basic forms are used singly or combined for repeats and connecting decorative units. The shape of the wire may be round, half round, oval, or square or any other shape. The wire used for the links may be smooth or twisted or a combination of the two to give a varied texture to the chain.

A chain must be flexible. In order to assure flexibility links must move freely in each other. Links and motifs combined for a more elaborate chain must adhere to this rule also.

Although a simple chain of links of equal size and shape is a simple piece of jewelry the principles of size, weight, and texture must be used consistently to produce it. When the links and motifs are combined they must be in scale and consistent in weight and design with each other and the ornament with which the chain is to be used.

Pendant and chain.
Cross of coiled sil-
ver wire and
balls.
Chain of coiled
units and oval
links.

Necklace of coiled
wire chain and
domed units.

281

CHAIN OF ROUND AND OVAL LINKS

Oval rings linked with round rings.

Construction

Sterling silver wire annealed 18-gauge.

Make a round coil of wire.

Saw the coil into rings.

Solder the joints.

Sterling silver wire 10-gauge drawn half round.

Make an oval coil of wire.

Saw the coil into rings.

Pull the ends apart to open.

Link the oval ring into the four round rings.

Bring the ends of the oval ring together.

Rouge the joints of the round rings.

Solder the joints of the oval rings.

Repeat until the desired length has been made.

Clean, polish, and color.

Fig. 94. — *Chain of round and oval rings*

CHAIN OF ROUND AND OVAL LINKS
Fig. 94

Type
of
Chain

Round and oval rings.

The following wire is required:

Sterling silver wire 18-gauge for the round rings.

Sterling silver wire 10-gauge drawn half round for the oval rings.

Twice the number of round rings as oval rings should be made.

Tools
and
Working
Materials

Metal gauge

Binding wire 26-gauge

Jeweler's shears

Charcoal block

Gas and air blow torch

Pickle

Copper pickle pan

Copper tongs

Gas plate

Steel hammer

Steel surface plate

Boards (Fig. 33)

Bench vise

C clamp

Round split mandrel (Fig. 34)

Hand drill

Round wooden core the inside diameter of the coil

Jeweler's saw frame

Jeweler's saw blade #2/0

Snub nose pliers—two pairs

Flux

Borax slate or saucer

Camel's hair brush

Solder

File

File brush

Half-round hole draw plate

Draw tongs

Yellow beeswax

Oval mandrel

Wrapping paper

Binding wire 28-gauge

Jeweler's hand vise

Scotch stone

Lead jaws for vise

Polishing motor

Tools	Bristle buffing wheel	Potassium sulphide so-
and	Tripoli cake	lution
Working	Soda, ammonia, and	Whiting
Materials	water solution	Soft cloth
	Granite pan	Soft cloth or chamois
	Chamois buffing wheel	buffing wheel
	Rouge stick	

PROCESSES	
Soldering p. 38	Place several rings on the charcoal block and solder the joints.
Wire Drawing p. 96	Sterling silver wire 10-gauge. Draw the wire half round.
Annealing	Anneal the wire.
Making Oval Rings p. 113	Make oval rings as shown in Fig. **41**.
Opening the Rings	Open the rings as shown in Fig. **40**.
Linking the Rings	Connect four round rings with an oval ring. Join the two ends of the oval ring as shown in Fig. 94.
Rouging	Rouge the joints of the round rings.
Holding the Ring	Place the joint of the oval ring on the binding wire hook as shown in Fig. 12.
Soldering	Solder the joint. Continue joining and soldering the links until the chain is the desired length.
Cleaning p. 70	Clean in pickle. Remove excess solder or scratches with a file and scotch stone.

PROCESSES

Polishing   Buff with a bristle buffing wheel and tripoli.
p. 71

Coloring   Color with potassium sulphide solution.
p. 72   Remove any excess color with whiting.
                 Polish with soft cloth or chamois buffing wheel.

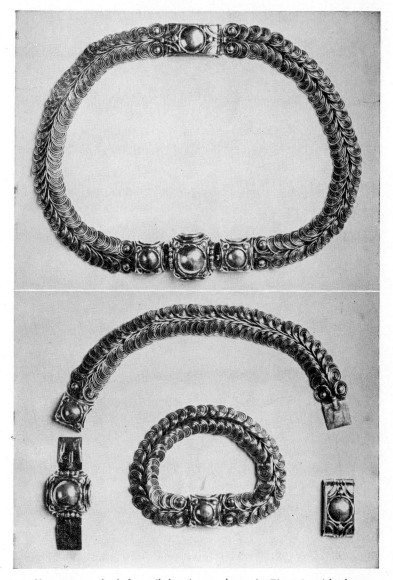

Necklace composed of flat coiled units as shown in Fig. 96, with clasps as shown in Figs. 102, 103, 104, and catch as shown in Fig. 105. It can be broken into separate units and used as bracelets.

CHAIN OF INTERWOVEN LINKS

Round rings of wire interwoven.

Construction

Sterling silver wire annealed 18-gauge.

Make a coil of wire on a steel mandrel 10-gauge.

Saw into rings.

Form a double chain with six rings of wire.

Insert a wire through rings A and B.

Turn back E to the left, F to the right.

Pull C toward the worker, D away from the worker.

Fig. 95.—Chain of interwoven round rings

Insert two rings AB of the new unit at O.

CHAIN OF INTERWOVEN LINKS
Fig. 95

Type
of
Chain

Round rings interwoven.
The following wire is required:
Sterling silver wire 18-gauge.
Sixteen inches of wire makes about 26 rings or 1 inch of finished chain.

Tools
and
Working
Materials

Metal gauge
Binding wire
  28-gauge
Jeweler's shears
Charcoal block
Gas and air blow torch
Pickle
Copper pickle pan
Copper tongs
Gas plate
Steel hammer
Steel surface plate
Boards (Fig. 33)
Bench vise
C clamp
Hand drill
Split mandrel (10-gauge steel rod or 8-penny nail)
Round wooden core the inside diameter of the coil

Jeweler's saw frame
Jeweler's saw blade
  #2/0
Snub nose pliers—two pairs
Lead jaws for vise
Scratch awl or any pointed tool
Polishing motor
Chamois buffing wheel
Rouge stick
Soda, ammonia, and water solution
Granite pan
Potassium sulphide solution
Whiting
Soft cloth buffing wheel

PROCESSES	CONSTRUCTION
Gauging the Wire p. 346	Gauge the wire. Sterling silver wire 18-gauge.
Coiling p. 20	Coil the wire and bind as shown in Fig. 4.
Annealing p. 18	Anneal the wire.
Pickling p. 22	Clean in pickle.
Making Round Rings p. 112	Coil the wire on a 10-gauge steel mandrel, Washburn and Moen Mfg. Co. gauge, or 1350 micrometer. Insert a wooden core in the coil. Saw the coil into rings.
Opening the Rings	Open the rings as shown in Fig. 40.
Linking the Rings	*Step 1* Form a double chain of six rings as shown in Fig. 95.
Closing the Joints	Close the openings in the rings.
Inserting the Holding Wire	Insert a wire through the rings AB to form a loop. (This makes the links easier to hold when starting the chain.) Hold the wire loop in the left hand.

PROCESSES
Forming   *Step 2*
the   Turn back link E to the left.
Chain   Turn back link F to the right.
                   Step 3
                   Pull link C toward the worker.
                   Push link D away from the worker.
                   This completes the first unit. Insert a large pin
                   in the opening at O to keep the unit in place
                   until the next two links are inserted.
                   Step 4
                   Insert two links AB of the new unit in the
                   opening at O as shown in Fig. 96.
                   Close the links as directed above.
                   Link the other four rings to form a double
                   chain as described above to prepare for the next
                   unit in the same way the first unit was made.
                   Repeat from Step 2.
                   Continue this repetition until the chain is the
                   desired length.
                   Inspect the chain to see that all links are closed
                   as tightly as possible and that the openings of
                   the links are on the inside of the chain.

Polishing   Polish with chamois buffing wheel and rouge.
p. 71

Coloring   Dip the chain in a potassium sulphide solution.
p. 72   Rub the chain with a soft cloth and whiting
                   until the chain is a polished silver, the oxidized
                   silver left only in the recessed parts.

Buffing   Polish with chamois or soft cloth buffing wheel.

CHAIN DESIGN

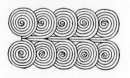

UNIT

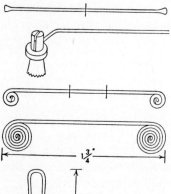

CHAIN OF FLAT COILED UNITS

Foundation and Ornament

Linked coils

Units of Chain

Sterling silver wire annealed 22-gauge.

Cut the desired number of wire lengths 7 inches long.

Make a flat coil on each end of the wires.

Tap each coil lightly on a steel surface with a steel hammer.

Loop each unit in the center.

Bend the loop back and down.

Joining the Units to Form the Chain

Insert the loop of Unit 2 from the front through the loop of Unit 1, the coils under the coils of Unit 1.

Insert the loop of Unit 3 from the front through the loops of Units 1 and 2, the coils under the coils of Unit 2.

Every new unit added must pass through the loops of two preceding linked units.

Tap the loops on the underside lightly with a narrow steel hammer.

Bend the coils at an angle.

**JOINING THE UNITS
TO FORM THE CHAIN**

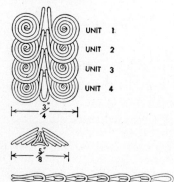

UNIT 1

UNIT 2

UNIT 3

UNIT 4

Fig. 96.—*Chain of interlinked coiled units*

CHAIN OF FLAT COILED UNITS
Fig. 96

Type *of* *Chain*	Coiled units linked.
	 The following wire is required:
	     Sterling silver wire 22-gauge.
	     Seven inches of wire required for one unit.

Tools *and* *Working* *Materials*	Metal gauge Ruler Sheet iron—two pieces about 4 inches square Iron binding wire 22-gauge Jeweler's shears Gas and air blow torch Pickle Copper pickle pan Copper tweezers Gas plate Mandrel, coiling machine, or round nose pliers Steel surface plate Flat face steel hammer Square nose pliers with smooth jaws Scratch awl or other pointed tool Polishing motor Cloth buffing wheel Rouge stick Potassium sulphide solution Whiting Cloth or chamois buffing wheel

PROCESSES

Gauging *the* *Wire* p. 346

UNIT OF CHAIN

Gauge the wire, sterling silver wire 22-gauge.

PROCESSES

Annealing   Anneal the wire between iron sheets.
pp. 18, 20

Pickling   Clean in pickle.
p. 22

Determining   Determine the number of units required to
the   make the chain.
Number
of Units

Cutting   Cut a 7-inch length of wire to be used as a
                     pattern.
                     Cut the desired number of lengths required for
                     the bracelet.

Coiling   Make a flat coil on each end of the wire as
p. 114   shown in Fig. 42 or 43.
                     About five rows of wire are required to make
                     each coil.
                     When these two coils are finished the length
                     should measure 1¾ inches.
                     Repeat the above with the other lengths of wire.
                     Keep the coils uniform.

Truing   Place the coils on a flat steel surface.
and   Hammer lightly with a steel hammer to flatten
Hardening   the coil; this process hardens the wire and helps
                     to keep the coil firm.

Looping   Loop the coiled unit in the center with the
                     round nose pliers.
                     Let the coils lie on the outside of the loop.

Measuring   Measure the unit which should be ¾ inch from
                     the base of the coil to the tip of the loop and
                     ¾ inch across the coils, as shown in Fig. 96.

PROCESSES
Bending
the
Wire
to
Form
the
Hook

Hold the coils with the long side of the snub nose pliers across the upper edge of the coils and bend the loop at right angles to the coils. Remove the snub nose pliers and complete the loop to form a hook with a pair of round nose pliers held in the bend of the loop. Press over with the fingers as shown in Fig. 96.

Repeat with the other units. Keep uniform.

JOINING THE UNITS TO FORM THE CHAIN

Connecting
the
Units

Insert the loop of Unit 2 from the front through the loop of Unit 1; the coils under the coils of Unit 1.

Insert the point of a scratch awl or any other pointed tool through the loops and pull them so the ends lie next to each other; this makes it easier to insert the loop of the next unit.

Insert the loop of Unit 3 from the right side through the loops of Units 1 and 2. The coils must lie under the coils of Unit 2, as shown in Fig. 96. Remember after the first two units have been joined every unit inserted must pass through the loops of the two preceding linked units.

Continue linking the other units to form the chain.

Adjusting
the
Coils

Adjust the coils to overlap evenly.

PROCESSES

Tightening the Loops	Place the chain of coils on a smooth surface, the looped or underside facing up. Tap the loops lightly with a narrow faced steel hammer.
Bending the Coils	Turn the chain on the right side. Bend the coils down to a slight angle to measure 5/8 inch as shown in Fig. 96. Pinch the coils close together to cover the loop.
Polishing p. 71	Polish with a cloth buffing wheel and rouge.
Coloring p. 72	Color the chain with potassium sulphide solution. Remove any excess color with whiting. Polish with a soft cloth or chamois buffing wheel.

CHAIN OF ROUND COILED UNITS AND OVAL LINKS

Fig. 97.—Chain of round coiled units linked with oval rings

Type of Unit and Chain	Unit—Wire coil. Chain—Oval links. The following wire is required: Sterling silver wire 18-gauge for the unit. Sterling silver wire 10-gauge drawn half round for the link.

Tools and Working Materials	Metal gauge	Gas plate
	Charcoal block	Bench vise
	Gas and air blow torch	Round mandrel
	Pickle	Jeweler's saw frame
	Copper pickle pan	Jeweler's saw blade
	Copper tongs	#2/0

Tools and Working Materials	Hand vise or square nose pliers	Binding wire flat 14-gauge
	Jeweler's shears	Scotch stone
	File	Polishing motor
	File brush	Felt buffing wheel
	Flux	Bristle buffing wheel
	Borax slate or saucer	Tripoli cake
	Solder	Soda, ammonia, water solution
	Camel's hair brush	Granite pan
	Half-round hole draw plate	Chamois or cloth buffing wheel
	Draw tongs	Rouge stick
	Yellow beeswax	Potassium sulphide solution
	Oval mandrel	Whiting
	Wrapping paper	Soft cloth buffing wheel
	Binding wire 28-gauge	

PROCESSES

Gauging
p. 346

Gauge the wire.

Annealing
p. 18

Sterling silver wire 18-gauge.
Anneal the wire.

Looping

Loop the end of a length of wire on a round mandrel to form a ring. Make a second loop 1 inch from the first loop.

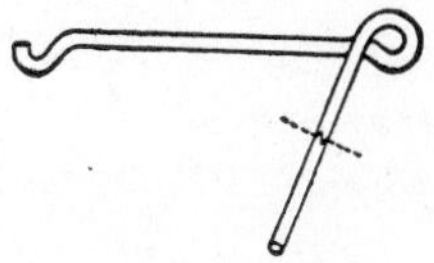

Sawing
p. 31

Saw the first loop in half.

Fig. 98.—*Looped wire ready to coil*

PROCESSES
Coiling

Hold the half ring with the pliers.

Hold the looped end in the jaws of the bench vise.

Coil the wire end which extends from the loop around the wire between the loop and the half ring, until it reaches the base of the half ring. Bring the loose end around the mandrel.

Sawing

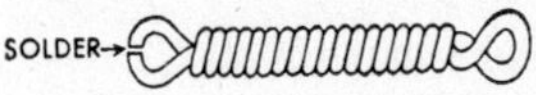

SOLDER→

Fig. 99.—*Coiled unit ready to solder*

Saw the wire loop even with the sawed ring.

Soldering
p. 38

Bring the ends of the wire together to form a ring.

Solder the joint.

Drawing
p. 96

Sterling silver wire 10-gauge.

Draw the wire half round.

Annealing

Anneal the wire.

*Making
Oval
Rings*
p. 113

Make oval rings as shown in Figs. 36, 41.

*Opening
the
Joints*

Open the joints as shown in Fig. 40 of two-thirds of the oval rings.

*Closing
the
Joints*

Close the joints of one-third of the oval rings.

Soldering

Solder the joints of the closed oval rings.

PROCESSES
Joining
the
Unit
and
Links
to form
the
Chain

Join the ring of the coiled unit to the soldered oval ring with the open oval ring.
Close the ring to make an even joint.
Continue until all the rings and units have been joined.

Soldering

Place the ring joint on the iron binding wire hook as shown in Fig. 12.
Solder the joint.
Solder the joints of all the rings in the same manner.

Cleaning
p. 70

Clean in pickle.
Remove excess solder or scratches with a file or scotch stone.

Polishing
p. 71

Buff with a felt and bristle buffing wheel and tripoli.
Polish with a cloth buffing wheel and rouge.

Coloring
p. 72

Color with potassium sulphide solution.
Remove any excess color with whiting.
Polish with a cloth or chamois buffing wheel.

CLASP DESIGN

CLASP-RING SOCKET AND SWIVEL CATCH

Socket—Ring of wire.

Catch—Swivel wire and balls.

SOCKET

Socket

    Sterling silver wire 14-gauge.

    Make one ring for the socket.

    Sterling silver wire 18-gauge.

    Make one small ring of wire.

    File side of the small ring at the joint.

    Solder the rings together at the joints.

CATCH

Catch

    Sterling silver wire 18-gauge.

    Measure the outside diameter of the socket ring.

    Saw a piece of wire to this measurement.

    Make a small ring the size of the small ring attached to the socket and flatten the side at the joint.

    Fine silver wire.

    Make two small balls.

    Solder the small ring to the center of the two balls on each end of the wire length.

    Clean and polish.

Fig. 100.—Clasp with ring socket and swivel catch

CLASP—RING SOCKET AND SWIVEL
CATCH
Fig. 100

Type
of
Clasp

Ring socket.

Swivel catch.

The following wire is required:

Sterling silver wire 14-gauge or lighter for the socket.

Sterling silver wire 18-gauge for the catch and small rings.

Fine silver wire for the balls.

Tools
and
Working
Materials

Metal gauge	Pickle
Round mandrel—two sizes	Copper pickle pan
	Copper tongs
Round nose pliers	Gas plate
Jeweler's saw frame	Scotch stone
Jeweler's saw blade #1/0	Polishing motor
	Felt buffing wheel
File	Tripoli cake
Gas and air blow torch	Soda, ammonia, and water solution
Charcoal block	
Flux	Granite pan
Borax slate or saucer	Soft cloth or chamois buffing wheel
Solder	
Jeweler's shears	Rouge stick
Camel's hair brush	

PROCESSES

Gauging
the
Wire
p. 346

SOCKET

Gauge the wire.

PROCESSES

Ring *Making* p. 112	Sterling silver wire 14-gauge. Make a large ring. Sterling silver wire 18-gauge. Make a small ring.
Filing p. 25	File one side of the small ring at the joint.
Soldering p. 38	Solder the flattened side of the small ring over the joint of the large ring.

CATCH

Sawing p. 31	Sterling silver wire 18-gauge. Saw a piece of wire to measure the outside diameter of the large ring.
Ring *Making*	Make a small ring and file joint, as above.
Ball *Making* p. 120	Fine silver wire. Make two small balls equal in size.
Soldering	Solder the flattened side of the small ring to the center of the wire length. Solder two small balls on either end of the wire. Connect the last two open rings of the chain with the two small rings. Solder the joint.
Cleaning p. 70	Clean in pickle. Remove excess solder with a file and scotch stone.
Polishing p. 71	Buff with a felt buffing wheel. Polish with a chamois buffing wheel and rouge.

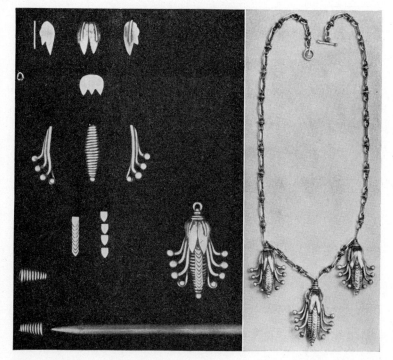

Units soldered together to form the motif—
wire coil, balls, stamped forms, repoussé leaves

Necklace of chain with three
motifs

SOCKET

CATCH

CLASP—TUBE SOCKET AND SPRING CATCH

Socket—Tube.

Catch—Spring.

Socket—Sterling silver sheet annealed 20-gauge.

Make a tube $3/16$ inch in diameter, and $5/8$ inch long.

Solder the seam and silver sheet over each end. Make sure there is an air escape.

Drill a hole in center of one end.

File the soldered ends even with the tube and the hole square.

Sterling silver wire 20-gauge.

Make a small ring. File flat at the joint.

Solder the flat side in the center of the plate opposite the drilled end.

Catch—Sterling silver wire oblong $1/16$ inch by $1/8$ inch.

Saw A $5/8$ inch and B $3/4$ inch.

Score and bend A at right angles to the $1/8$-inch face $1/8$ inch from the end.

File the end of A in a groove and file half way through the $1/16$-inch thickness, at the angle; the notch should be the width of 20-gauge metal.

Sterling silver wire 20-gauge.

Make a small ring as above.

Solder to the end of the wire B.

Bind A and B together at the end.

Solder the joint.

Hammer the end on a steel plate. File edges.

Clean, polish, and color.

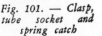

Fig. 101. — Clasp, tube socket and spring catch

CLASP—TUBE SOCKET AND SPRING CATCH
Fig. 101

*Type
of
Clasp*

Tube socket.

Spring catch.

The following sheet metal and wire are required:

Sterling silver sheet 20-gauge for the socket and for the ends of the socket.

Sterling silver wire 20-gauge for the rings.

Sterling silver wire 10-gauge drawn $\frac{1}{16}$ inch by $\frac{1}{8}$ inch for the catch.

*Tools
and
Working
Materials*

Metal gauge	Draw tongs
Gas and air blow torch	Flux
Charcoal block	Borax slate or saucer
Pickle	Solder
Copper pickle pan	Camel's hair brush
Copper tongs	Center punch
Gas plate	Hand drill
File	Twist drill #70
Ruler	Mandrel $\frac{1}{8}$ inch round
Dividers	
Jeweler's shears	Square hole draw plate
Block of hard wood with semi-circular groove	Bench pin
	Jeweler's saw frame
Raising hammer with thin neck or chasing tool	Jeweler's saw blades
	Snub nose pliers
Wax	Binding wire flattened
Bench vise	Binding wire
Round hole draw plate	Steel surface plate
Burnisher or knife	Flat-face steel hammer
	Scotch stone

Tools	Polishing motor	Soft cloth
and	Felt buffing wheel	Rouge stick
Working	Tripoli cake	Cloth buffing wheel
Materials	Soda, ammonia, water solution	Potassium sulphide solution
	Granite pan	Whiting

PROCESSES   SOCKET

Gauging
p. 346

Gauge the metal.

Annealing
p. 18

Anneal the metal.

Pickling
p. 22

Clean in pickle.

Tube
Drawing
p. 98

Sterling silver sheet 20-gauge.   Make a tube
$3/16$-inch diameter by $5/8$ inch long.

Soldering
p. 38

Solder a piece of silver to close end of the tube.
(See Special Soldering, p. 45. Soldering hollow
pieces to flat surfaces.)
Solder the seam of the tube at the same time.

Filing
p. 25

File the end pieces even with the tube.

Drilling
p. 35

Mark and drill a hole in the center of the plate
soldered at one end of the tube.

Filing

File the drilled hole $1/8$ inch square.

Ring
Making
p. 112

Sterling silver wire 20-gauge.
Make a ring, file it flat at the joint.

Soldering

Solder the flat side of the ring in the center of
the plate opposite the drilled end.

PROCESSES	CATCH
Wire *Drawing* p. 96	Sterling silver wire 10-gauge. Draw the wire $1/16$ inch by $1/8$ inch.
Annealing	Anneal the wire.
Sawing p. 31	Saw two lengths of wire A $5/8$ inch and B $3/4$ inch as shown in Fig. 101.
Scoring p. 157	Score A on the $1/8$-inch face $1/8$ inch from the end.
Bending	Bend at a right angle.
Soldering	Solder at the angle.
Filing	File A at the angle on the $1/8$-inch face half way through the $1/16$-inch thickness of the wire. Let this groove be the width of 20-gauge metal. File the end of A in a groove as shown in Fig. 101.
Ring *Making*	Sterling silver wire 20-gauge. Make a ring as above.
Soldering	Solder on the end of wire B.
Binding	Bind A and B together. Insert flat binding wire $1/4$ inch from the end between A and B.
Soldering	Solder the ends of A and B.
Pickling	Clean in pickle.
Hammering	Hammer the soldered ends of A and B on a steel plate to harden.
Filing	File to make smooth and even.
Cleaning p. 70	Remove excess solder with a file and scotch stone.
Polishing p. 71	Buff with felt buffing wheel and tripoli. Polish with a cloth buffing wheel and rouge.

SOCKET

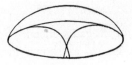

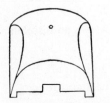

Fig. 102.—Clasp, square socket, with wire and balls

CLASP—SQUARE SOCKET

Socket—Dome on a flat foundation.

Ornament—Dome, wire units, and balls.

Socket

Sterling silver sheet annealed 24-gauge.
Inscribe a circle on the metal.
Cut out the disk.

Dome the disk.

Divide the base in four equal parts.
Draw a semi-circle from each point on the inside of the dome.
Trace the lines with a chasing tool.

Cut a V-shaped piece from each of the four points.

Bring the sides together until they meet.
Solder the joints.
File the base even.

Punch a hole in the top of the dome.

Saw one side at the base; the depth should be the thickness of 18-gauge metal and leave a border about $\frac{1}{16}$ inch at each end.

Saw or file a notch in the center of the sawed side $\frac{1}{16}$ inch in width and the depth of 18-gauge metal.

Clean and polish.

Ornament

ORNAMENT

Sterling silver sheet 26-gauge.
Cut and dome a disk.
Fine silver wire 20-gauge.
Bend four wires the same curve as the chased lines on the socket.
Bend four shorter wires the same curve.
Make a ring to fit around the dome.
Notch the ring at intervals.
Make four balls; flatten slightly.

JOINING THE ORNAMENT
AND THE SOCKET

Joining the Ornament and the Socket

Bind and solder the eight wires to the four sides of the socket.

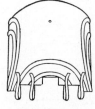

Bind and solder the dome and ring to the center top.
Solder the four balls in the corner spaces.

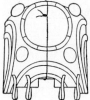

JOINING THE SOCKET
AND THE FOUNDATION

Joining the Socket and the Foundation

Sterling silver sheet 24-gauge.
Cut the sheet silver slightly larger than the base of the socket.
Bind the socket to the silver foundation.
Solder in place.
Saw and file the foundation even with the base of the socket.
File all edges smooth.
Clean and polish.

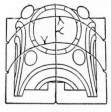

Fig. 103.—*Clasp, square socket. with wire and balls*

CLASP—OBLONG SOCKET

Socket—Curved form on a flat foundation.

Ornament—Dome, wire units, and balls.

Socket

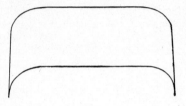

Sterling silver sheet 24-gauge.

Cut an oblong piece of silver.

Curve the silver slightly to form an arch.

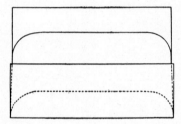

Solder sheet silver over one of the open sides of the socket.

Saw and file even with the curved outline.

Repeat with the other opening of the socket.

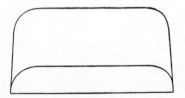

Saw an opening on the narrow end and notch the center.

Proceed as described in the square socket.

Ornament made to conform to the oblong shape.

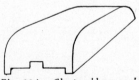

Join to the foundation as described in the square socket.

Clean and polish.

Fig. 104.—Clasp, oblong socket decorated with wire and balls

SPRING CATCH

Sterling silver sheet 24-gauge.

> Cut a strip of silver:
>
>> Length—twice the length of the socket.
>>
>> Width—the size of the sawed opening.

Sterling silver wire or sheet 18-gauge $\frac{1}{16}$ inch wide.

> Loop the end of the wire.
>
> Solder the unit of wire to the strip of silver.
>
> Divide the strip of silver.
>
> Bend over the blade of a knife.
>
> Hammer the bent end to harden.
>
> File to fit the opening.
>
> Clean and polish.

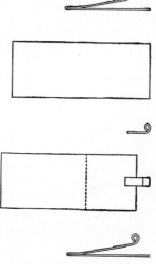

Fig. 105.—*Spring catch*

CLASP—SQUARE AND OBLONG
SOCKET AND SPRING CATCH
Figs. 102, 103, 104, 105

Type
of
Clasp

Square socket—oblong socket.

Spring catch.

The following sheet metal and wire are required:

Sterling silver sheet 24-gauge for the socket, foundation, and the catch.

Sterling silver sheet 26-gauge for the small dome.

Fine silver wire 20-gauge for the wire decoration and the balls.

Sterling silver wire or sheet 18-gauge, $\frac{1}{16}$ inch wide, for the catch.

Nickel silver 24-gauge may also be used for the catch.

Tools
and
Working
Materials

Metal gauge

Gas and air blow torch

Charcoal block

Pickle

Copper pickle pan

Copper tongs

Gas plate

Dividers

Jeweler's shears

Lead dapping block

Dapping die cutters and punches

Dapping die hammer

Chasing tool

Chasing hammer

Snub nose pliers

Flat file

Small pointed punch

Jeweler's saw frame

Jeweler's saw blade #1/0

Bench pin

Scotch stone

Polishing motor

Felt buffing wheel

Tripoli cake

Soda, ammonia, and water solution

Small stiff scrub brush

Cloth buffing wheel

Tools
and
Working
Materials
	Rouge stick
	Round nose pliers
	Round mandrel the
	    size of the small
	    dome
	Round mandrel for
	    balls
	Triangular file
	Binding wire
	    26-gauge
	Bristle buffing wheel
		Bench vise
		Oblong hole draw
		    plate
		Draw tongs
		Steel plate
		Steel hammer
		Potassium sulphide so-
		    lution
		Whiting
		Soft cloth
		Soft cloth or chamois
		    buffing wheel

PROCESSES

SQUARE SOCKET

Gauging p. 346	Gauge the metal.
Annealing p. 18	Anneal the metal.
Pickling p. 22	Clean in pickle.
Dome *Making* p. 120	Sterling silver sheet 24-gauge. Cut a disk with dapping cutters or jeweler's shears. Dome the disk.
Measuring	Divide the base of the dome in four equal parts. Draw a semicircle on the inside of the dome with the dividers from the four marked points.
Chasing p. 77	Place the dome on a lead dapping block convex side up. Trace the marked semicircle with a chasing tool.
Cutting	Cut four V-shaped pieces from each of the four corners.

PROCESSES

Shaping

Pull the sides together with the snub nose pliers until the edges of the V are brought together.

Soldering
p. 38

Solder the four corners.

Pickling

Clean in pickle.

Filing
p. 25

File the base even. This should make a square form with sloping sides, the top slightly rounded.

Punching

Punch a small hole in the center of the dome.

Sawing
p. 31

Saw one side of the base to within $\frac{1}{16}$ inch of each corner; the depth should be .040 or the thickness of 18-gauge metal.

Saw a notch in the center of the sawed side $\frac{1}{16}$ inch wide and the depth of 18-gauge metal.

Cleaning
p. 70

Clean with scotch stone.

Polish with a felt buffing wheel and tripoli.

SEPARATE PARTS OF THE ORNAMENT

*Dome
Making*

Sterling silver sheet annealed 26-gauge.

Cut and dome a disk to fit in the center of the socket dome. Leave about $\frac{1}{16}$ inch flat space from the base of the small dome to the chased lines.

Shaping

Fine silver wire 20-gauge.

Bend four wires semicircular to fit the curve of the chased line on the socket dome.

Bend four shorter wires the same curve.

*Ball
Making*
p. 122

Make four balls and flatten slightly.

PROCESSES

Ring *Making* p. 112	Make a ring to fit around the small dome.
Soldering p. 38	Solder the joint.
Filing	File notches at intervals around the ring.

JOINING THE ORNAMENT AND THE SOCKET

Binding	Bind with cotter pins the eight wires to the four sides.
Soldering	Solder in place.
Pickling	Clean in pickle.
Binding	Bind the ring and dome to the center of the socket.
Soldering	Solder the four balls on the four corners next to the wire ring.

JOINING THE SOCKET AND THE FOUNDATION

Soldering	Sterling silver sheet 24-gauge. Bind and solder the socket on the silver.
Pickling	Clean in pickle.
Sawing	Saw the edges even with the sides.
Filing	File the edges to smooth.
Cleaning	Remove any scratches or excess solder with a file and scotch stone.
Polishing p. 71	Buff with bristle buffing wheel and tripoli. Polish with cloth buffing wheel and rouge.

PROCESSES	**OBLONG SOCKET**
Gauging	Gauge the metal.
Annealing	Anneal the metal.
Pickling	Clean in pickle.
Cutting	Sterling silver sheet 24-gauge. Cut an oblong piece of silver.
Filing	File the edges even.
Shaping	Curve the silver slightly. Bend the ends at a slight angle.
Soldering p. 38	Lay the bent strip on the silver sheet so the entire opening on one of the curved sides is covered. Solder in place.
Sawing p. 31	Saw the applied piece even with the curve and straight across the base. Repeat with the other open side.
Filing p. 25	File to smooth all edges. Proceed as described in the square socket: Decoration may have to be added or changed somewhat to conform to the oblong shape. Cut opening. Decorate. Mount on a foundation.

PROCESSES	**CATCH**
Gauging	Gauge the metal. Sterling silver 24-gauge.
Measuring	Measure twice the length of the socket, the width the size of the opening in the socket.

PROCESSES

Drawing or Rolling Wire p. 96	Draw a piece of wire through the rectangular draw plate to measure 18-gauge in thickness and $\frac{1}{16}$ inch in width. The wire may also be rolled in the rolling mill to this measurement.
Annealing	Anneal the wire and sheet.
Bending	Loop the end of the wire.
Soldering	Solder the bent wire in the center of one end of the measured length with the curved end of the wire up.
Measuring	Divide the strip in two parts, the section holding the unit the shorter.
Bending	Fold over a thin piece of steel such as a steel knife blade on the line so the soldered unit is on top.
Hammering	Hammer the folded end on a steel plate to harden the metal.
Filing	File the edges to fit the opening.
Cleaning p. 70	Remove any scratches or excess solder with a file or scotch stone.
Polishing p. 71	Buff with a felt buffing wheel and tripoli. Polish with a cloth buffing wheel and rouge.
Coloring p. 72	Color the socket and catch with potassium sulphide solution. Remove any excess color with whiting. Polish with cotton buffing wheel.

OPENWORK BEAD DESIGN

OPEN-WORK BEAD OF WIRE UNITS AND BALLS

Foundation and Ornament—Round bead of
  wire units and balls.

CONSTRUCTION

Construction.

Sterling silver wire annealed 18-gauge.

Saw eight pieces of wire the measured length.

Bend to form curved units.

Bind and solder four units together to form
a motif.

Repeat with the other four units.

Dome the two motifs.

Bind and solder the two domes together to
form a bead.

Fine silver wire.

Make four balls.

Make two rings to fit the openings on each
end of the bead.

Solder the rings and the four balls in the center of the four circles formed by the motifs.

Bind and solder the two rings on each end of
the bead.

Clean, polish, and color.

*Fig. 106.—Open work
bead of wire*

OPEN-WORK BEAD OF WIRE UNITS
AND BALLS
Fig. 106

Type
of
Bead

Foundation and Ornament—Round bead of wire units and balls.

The following silver wire is required:

Sterling silver wire 18-gauge for the bead.

Fine silver wire for the balls and rings.

Tools
and
Working
Materials

Metal gauge	Wooden dapping
Gas and air blow torch	punch
Charcoal block	Mallet
Pickle	Binding wire
Copper pickle pan	26-gauge
Copper tongs	Small round mandrel
Gas plate	Riffle file
Jeweler's saw frame	Scotch stone
Jeweler's saw blade	Polishing motor
#1/0	Bristle buffing wheel
Round nose pliers	Tripoli cake
Steel tweezers	Soda, ammonia, and
Staples of binding wire	water solution
Flux	Granite pan
Borax slate or saucer	Cloth buffing wheel
Jeweler's shears	Potassium sulphide so-
Solder	lution
Camel's hair brush	Whiting
Dapping die block	Chamois buffing wheel

PROCESSES

Gauging

p. 346

Annealing

p. 18

Construction

Gauge the wire.

Sterling silver wire 18-gauge.

Anneal the wire.

PROCESSES

Pickling p. 22	Clean in pickle.
Sawing p. 31	Saw one piece of wire the desired length. Saw seven pieces the length of the measured piece.
Shaping *the* *Units*	Form a circle on both ends of the wire with the round nose pliers. Repeat the above with the other seven pieces of wire. Bring the ends together with the circles on the inside to form units as shown in Fig. 106.
Joining *the* *Wire* *Units*	Place the four curved units on the charcoal block to form a motif as shown in Fig. 106. Each unit must touch the unit on the right and left and the spacing must be even. Pin to the charcoal block as shown in Fig. 12. Repeat the above with the other four units.
Soldering p. 38	Solder the wires where they touch.
Doming p. 120	Place the motif in a hole in the dapping die slightly larger than the diameter of the motif. Dap the motif until it fits the curve of the hole. Remove and place in the next smaller hole. Repeat until the motif is in the shape of a half sphere. Repeat the above with the second motif; it must be the same size and shape as the first motif.
Binding p. 46	Bind the two motifs together.
Soldering	Solder the motifs.

PROCESSES	
Ball *Making* p. 122	Fine silver wire. Make four balls.
Ring *Making* p. 112	Make two rings to fit the opening on each end of the bead.
Soldering	Bind and solder the two rings and the four balls in place.
Cleaning p. 70	Clean in pickle, remove any scratches or excess solder with a file or scotch stone.
Polishing p. 71	Buff with a bristle buffing wheel and tripoli. Polish with a cloth buffing wheel.
Coloring p. 72	Color with potassium sulphide solution. Remove any excess color with whiting. Polish with a soft cloth or chamois buffing wheel.

ROUND BEAD DESIGN

FOUNDATION

ORNAMENT

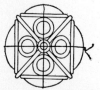

Fig. 107.— *Round bead decorated with wires and domes*

ROUND BEAD DECORATED WITH WIRE AND DOMES

Foundation—Round bead.

Ornament—Wire and domes.

> Foundation
>> Silver sheet annealed 26-gauge.
>> Cut and dome two disks.
>> Drill holes in the center of each dome.
>> Bind and solder.

> Ornament
>> Fine silver wire 18-gauge.
>> Cut four wires $\frac{1}{16}$ inch longer than half the circumference of the bead foundation.
>> Shape the wires the contour of the bead.
>> Insert the wire ends in the drilled holes.
>> Divide the bead into four equal parts with the wire.
>> Drill a hole in the foundation in each of four sections formed by the wires.
>> Make four rings to fit between these sections.
>> Fine silver wire 20-gauge.
>> Make eight rings to fit the spaces at each end.
>> Fine silver wire 22-gauge.
>> Make two rings to fit around the holes in the ends of the bead.
>> Fine silver sheet 26-gauge.
>> Cut and dome four disks the inside diameter of the largest ring.
>> Bind and solder the wires and domes to the foundation.
>> Clean, polish, and color.

ROUND BEAD DECORATED WITH
WIRE AND DOMES
Fig. 107

Type
of
Bead

Foundation—Round bead.
Ornament—Wire and domes.
The following silver sheet and wire are required:

Sterling silver sheet 26-gauge for the foundation and domes of the ornament. A commercial bead may be used for the foundation if desired.

Fine silver wire 18-gauge for the four half circles and large rings.

Fine silver wire 20-gauge for the eight medium rings.

Fine silver wire 22-gauge for the two small rings.

Tools
and
Working
Materials

Metal gauge
Charcoal block
Gas and air blow torch
Pickle
Copper pickle pan
Copper tongs
Gas plate
Lead dapping block
Dapping cutters and
   punches
Dapping die
File
Dividers
Hammer
Center punch
Hand drill

Twist drill
Binding wire
   26-gauge
Ruler
Jeweler's shears
Flux
Borax slate or saucer
Solder
Camel's hair brush
Square nose pliers
Round mandrels—
   three sizes
Scotch stone
Polishing motor
Tripoli cake

*Tools
and
Working
Materials*

Bristle buffing wheel
Soda, ammonia, and
    water solution
Cloth buffing wheel
Rouge stick

Potassium sulphide so-
    lution
Whiting
Soft cloth or chamois
    polishing wheel.

FOUNDATION

PROCESSES

Gauging
p. 346

Gauge the metal.

Annealing
p. 18

Sterling silver sheet 26-gauge.
Anneal the metal.

Pickling
p. 22

Clean in pickle.

*Dome
Making*
p. 120

Cut and dome two disks of equal size. Each
dome must be a half sphere if the bead is to be
round.

Filing
p. 25

File the base of the domes even.

Drilling
p. 35

Make a depression with the center punch in
the center of each dome.
Drill holes as marked with the center punch.

Soldering
p. 38

Bind and solder the two domes together.

ORNAMENT

Cutting

Fine silver wire 18-gauge.
Cut four wires $\frac{1}{16}$ inch longer than half the
circumference of the bead.
Shape the wire the contour of the bead foundation.

PROCESSES *Placing the Wires*	Insert the wire ends in the holes of the bead. Make sure the bead is divided by the wires into four equal parts and the wires must touch the bead at all points.
Drilling	Drill a hole in the foundation in the center of each of the four sections formed by the wires.
Ring Making p. 112	Make four rings to fit these sections.
Ring Making	Fine silver wire 20-gauge. Make eight rings to fit the triangular sections formed by the wires. Fine silver wire 22-gauge. Make two rings to fit around the holes in each end of the bead.
Dome Making	Sterling silver sheet 26-gauge. Cut and dome four disks the inside diameter of the four rings.

JOINING THE ORNAMENT AND THE FOUNDATION

Soldering	Bind and solder the rings and domes in place.
Cleaning p. 70	Remove scratches and excess solder with a file and scotch stone.
Polishing p. 71	Buff with a bristle buffing wheel and tripoli. Polish with a cloth buffing wheel and rouge.
Coloring p. 72	Color with potassium sulphide solution. Remove any excess solder with whiting. Polish with a chamois buffing wheel.

OVAL BEAD DESIGN

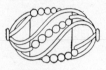

OVAL BEAD DECORATED WITH WIRE AND BALLS

FOUNDATION

Foundation—Oval bead.

Ornament—Wire and balls.

Foundation

    Silver sheet 26-gauge.

    Cut and bend an oblong strip of silver.

    Bind and solder the seam.

    Form into a cylinder.

    Cut and dome two disks the diameter of the cylinder.

    Drill a small hole in the center of each dome.

    File the edges.

    Solder the domes one on each end of the cylinder to form a bead.

    Clean and polish.

ORNAMENT

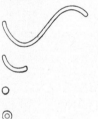

Ornament

    Fine silver wire 18-gauge.

    Cut four wires ½ inch longer than the bead and eight wires one-third as long as the bead.

    Shape the wires to fit the foundation.

JOINING THE ORNAMENT AND THE FOUNDATION

    Make 24 graduated silver balls to fit between the ends of the small wires.

    Make two rings to fit around the holes of the bead.

Joining the ornament and the foundation.

Bind and solder the wires to the foundation.

Solder the balls and rings in place.

Clean, polish, and color.

Fig. 108.—Oval bead decorated with wire and balls

OVAL BEAD DECORATED WITH
WIRE AND BALLS
Fig. 108

Type
of
Bead

Foundation—Oval bead.

Ornament—Wire and balls.

The following sheet silver and wire are required:

Sterling silver sheet 26-gauge for the foundation.

Fine silver wire 18-gauge for the wire bands and balls.

Tools
and
Working
Materials

Metal gauge
Ruler
Charcoal block
Gas and air blow torch
Pickle
Copper pickle pan
Copper tongs
Gas plate
Flat file
Dividers
Jeweler's shears
Flat nose pliers
Iron binding wire 26-gauge
Flux
Borax slate or saucer
Solder
Camel's hair brush
Round mandrel
Mallet
Lead dapping block

Dapping cutters and punches
Dapping die block
Center punch
Hand drill
Twist drill #60
Scotch stone
Polishing motor
Felt buffing wheel
Tripoli cake
Soda, ammonia, and water solution
Granite pan
Cloth buffing wheel
Rouge stick
Potassium sulphide solution
Whiting
Chamois polishing wheel

PROCESSES	FOUNDATION
Gauging p. 346	Gauge the metal.
Annealing p. 18	Sterling silver sheet 26-gauge. Anneal the metal.
Laying out the Pattern	Determine the diameter and length of the bead.
Cutting	Cut an oblong strip of silver. The length should be three and one-seventh times the diameter of the collar which forms the center part of the bead as shown in Fig. 108. The width of the strip plus the two domes determines the length of the bead.
Bending	Bend so the two edges meet.
Binding	Bind to make an even joint.
Soldering p. 38	Solder the seam.
Shaping	Tap lightly over a round mandrel with a raw-hide or wooden mallet to form a cylinder.
Filing p. 25	File the edges even.
Dome Making p. 120	Cut and dome two disks. The base of the domes should be the diameter of the cylinder.
Drilling p. 35	Drill holes in the center of each dome.
Filing	File the base of each dome even.

PROCESSES

Soldering   Bind and solder the domes on each end of the cylinder to form a bead.

Cleaning   Clean in pickle.

p. 70   Remove any scratches or excess solder with file and scotch stone.

Polishing   Buff with a felt buffing wheel and tripoli.

p. 71.

ORNAMENT

Cutting   Fine silver wire 18-gauge.

Cut four pieces of wire ½ inch longer than the length of the bead.

Cut eight pieces of wire one-third as long as the bead.

Forming   Curve the four wires to fit the foundation as shown in Fig. 108.

Curve the short wires slightly.

Ball Making   Make enough small balls to fit between the ends of the small wires.

Ring Making   Make two rings to fit around the holes in the end of the bead.

JOINING THE ORNAMENT AND THE FOUNDATION

Placing the Wires   Insert the ends of the long wires in the holes of the bead.

Make sure the bead is divided into four equal parts.

Soldering   Bind and solder the wires to the foundation.

Solder the eight short wires between the four long wires and the rings and balls in place as shown in Fig. 108.

PROCESSES

Cleaning
p. 70

Clean in pickle; remove any scratches or excess solder with a file and scotch stone.

Polishing
p. 71

Buff with a bristle buffing wheel and tripoli. Polish with a cloth buffing wheel.

Coloring
p. 72

Color in a potassium sulphide solution.
Remove excess color with whiting.
Polish with a soft cloth or chamois buffing wheel.

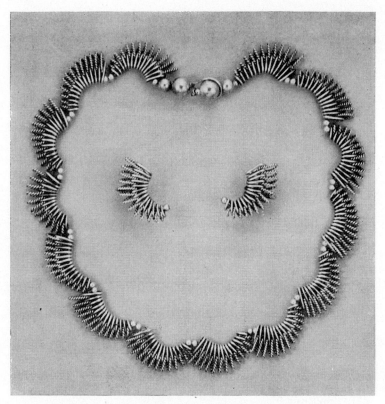

Necklace of crescent wire beads

CRESCENT BEAD OF MESHED WIRE COILS

Foundation and ornament—Crescent bead of smooth and twisted wire, coiled tapered and meshed.

Construction

    Sheet steel 17 gauge.

    Saw a mandrel to pattern.

    Drill a $\frac{1}{16}$ inch hole in the mandrel as shown.

    Sterling silver wire 18 gauge.

    Cut a 10 inch length of wire.

    Insert one end in the hole of the mandrel.

    Turn the end to form a hook.

    Coil the wire 14 times on the mandrel as shown.

BEAD DESIGN

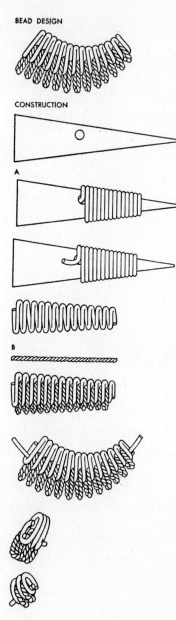

CONSTRUCTION

A

B

Crescent bead of wire coils

Anneal the coil.

Remove the coil from the mandrel.

Pull the two ends of the wire to spread.

Cut the wire ends as shown. Sterling silver wire 22 gauge.

Cut a 23 inch length of wire.

Twist the double length 100 full turns.

Anneal the twisted length. Coil the wire 13 times around the mandrel.

Anneal the coil.

Remove the coil from the mandrel.

Pull the two ends of the wire to spread.

Cut the wire ends as shown. Mesh A and B coils.

Sterling silver wire 18 gauge.

Cut a 1½ inch length of wire.

Thread the wire length through the meshed unit AB.

Shape the unit as shown.

Saw the ends of the threading wire even with AB unit. Solder both ends of the AB unit to the threading wire.

Clean, polish and color.

CRESCENT BEAD OF MESHED WIRE COILS

Type of
Bead

Foundation and Ornament—Crescent bead of smooth and twisted wire, coiled tapered and meshed.

The following silver wire is required:

Sterling silver wire 18 gauge

Sterling silver wire 22 gauge

Tools
and
Working
Materials

Metal gauge B&S

Sheet steel mandrel 17 gauge

Jeweler's saw frame

Jeweler's saw blades 1/0

File

Emery cloth	Copper tongs
Center punch	Hot plate
Hand drill	Jeweler's shears
Twist drill $\frac{1}{16}$ inch	Round nose pliers
Ruler	Square nose pliers
Blow torch	Soldering tweezers
Charcoal block	Soldering flux
Pickle	Solder—easy—
Pickle pan	Camel's hair brush

PROCESSES

CONSTRUCTION

Gauging
the
Metal
p. 364

Gauge the metal sheet.

Steel sheet 17 gauge.

Transferring
the
Pattern
pp. 33-36

Transfer the pattern to the steel as shown in Fig. 109.

Sawing
p. 25

Saw the metal following the scratched line of the pattern.

Filing
p. 25

File to smooth the edges.

Finish with emery cloth.

CRESCENT BEAD

Center punch the mandrel as shown in Fig. 109.

Drill a $\frac{1}{16}$ hole as marked with the center punch.

Gauge the wire.

Sterling silver wire 18 gauge.

Anneal the wire.

Cut a 10 inch length of wire.

Insert one end of the wire through the hole in the mandrel and hook as shown in Fig. 109.

Coil 14 times around the mandrel toward the tapered end.

Anneal the coil.

Remove the coil from the mandrel.

Clean in pickle.

Pull both ends simultaneously to spread.

The space between the coils should measure about 18 gauge, a flat tool may be inserted between each wire to space evenly, if necessary.

Cut the ends of the wire even with the last rings on each end of the coil, as shown in Fig. 109. The ends should be cut on the same side.

Gauge the wire.

Sterling silver wire 22 gauge.

Anneal the wire.

Cut a 23 inch length of wire.

Double the length and twist 100 full turns as shown in Fig. 109 at B.

Anneal the twist.

Insert one end of the wire through the hole in the mandrel and hook as shown in Fig. 109 at A.

Coil 13 times around the mandrel toward the tapered end.

PROCESSES	CRESCENT BEAD
Annealing	Anneal the coil.
	Remove from the mandrel.
Pickling	Clean in pickle.
Spreading the Coil	Spread the coil as described above.
Cutting	Cut the ends as shown.
Meshing the Coils	Mesh A and B coils as shown in Fig. 109.
Gauging	Gauge the wire.
	Sterling silver wire 18 gauge.
Annealing	Anneal the wire.
Cutting	Cut a 1½ inch length, to be used as a threading wire and spine.
Threading	Thread the wire through the opening formed by the coils A and B.
Shaping	Shape the coils as shown in Fig. 109.
Sawing	Saw the protruding ends of the threading wire.
Filing p. 25	File the ends even with the ends of the coils AB.
Soldering	Paint flux on both ends of the AB coil.
	Dry the flux with the flame of the blow torch.
	Place the solder to touch the threading wire and AB coils on both ends.
	Solder together.
Pickling	Clean in pickle.
Cleaning p. 70	Remove any excess solder with a file and scotch-stone.
Polishing p. 71	Buff with a bristle buffing wheel and tripoli.
	Wash in ammonia solution.
	Polish with a chamois buffing wheel.
Coloring p. 72	Color in potassium sulphide solution.
	Remove any excess coloring with whiting.
	Polish with a soft cloth or chamois buffing wheel.

SOURCES OF SUPPLY

Jeweler's Tools and Supplies

Anchor Tool and Supply Company
12 John Street, New York 7, New York
Metal Crafts Supply Company
Providence, Rhode Island
William Dixon Incorporated
32 East Kinney Street, Newark, New Jersey

Gold and Silver, Sheet and Wire, Solder and Flux

Handy and Harman
82 Fulton Street, New York 7, New York
1900 West Kinzie Street, Chicago 22, Illinois
3625 Medford Street, Los Angeles 33, California
T. B. Hagstoz & Son
709 Sansom Street
Philadelphia 6, Pennsylvania
Wildberg Brothers Smelting and Refining Company
635 South Hill Street, Los Angeles 14, California
742 Market Street, San Francisco 2, California

Stones

Ernest Beissinger
417 Clark Building, Pittsburgh 22, Pennsylvania
Paul Dreher
717 Sansom Street, Philadelphia, Pennsylvania
Francis J. Sperisen
166 Geary Street, San Francisco, California
International Gem Corporation
15 Maiden Lane, New York 7, New York

SOURCES OF SUPPLY (cont.)

Enamels

Carpenter and Wood Inc.
Providence, Rhode Island
B. K. Drakenfield and Company
45 Park Place, New York 7, New York
Metal Crafts Supply Company
Providence, Rhode Island
Thomas C. Thompson
1205 Deerfield Road, Highland Park, Illinois

Furnaces

Anchor Tool and Supply Company
12 John Street, New York 7, New York
Electric Hotpack Company
Coltman Avenue and Melrose Street
Philadelphia, Pennsylvania
Hevi-Duty Electrical Company
Milwaukee 1, Wisconsin
Hoskins Mfg. Company
4445 Lawton Avenue, Detroit, Michigan

Metal Foils

Hastings and Company
2314 Market Street
Philadelphia 3, Pennsylvania

Metallic Lustres

D. M. Campana Art Company
442 North Wells Street, Chicago 10, Illinois

Casting Supplies

Dental Supplies—see the telephone book (yellow pages)
for—Dental wax for patterns, mold material, casting machines
burn out furnaces and tools.

APPENDICES

SOLDERS AND FLUXES—TYPES AND USES

METALS	FLUX	SOLDER
Silver to Silver Fine or Sterling	Anti borax flux and water 1 tablespoon 2 oz. water—dissolved Borax—prepared in sticks or cones Rubbed on slate with water Other fluxes for hard solder are available	Medium-flowing silver solder for a general use Hard-flowing silver solder for (a) Built-up pieces which are heated many times (b) Pieces made of metal heavy enough to withstand much heat Easy-flowing silver solder for (a) Final soldering on certain types of built-up pieces (b) Delicate and light-weight pieces
Silver soldered to Gold	Fluxes as indicated	Silver solder as above
Gold soldered to Gold	Fluxes as indicated above	Gold solder the color of the gold
Silver soldered to Copper	Borax in any form used thick	Silver solder as above
Copper soldered to Copper	Borax in any form used thick	Silver solder as above
Tin to Tin	Zinc chloride one part, water one part Other fluxes for soft solder are available	Lead and tin solder

CLEANING MATERIALS AND SOLUTIONS—TYPES AND USES

CLEANING METHODS	FORMULA	TO REMOVE
Pickle	Sulphuric acid (Immerse) 1 part acid 10 parts water	Oxide from silver, gold, and copper
	Nitric acid (Immerse) 1 part acid 8 parts water	Oxide from gold over 14-K
	Nitric acid (Dip) 50 parts acid 50 parts water	Fire coat from silver
	Hydrofluoric acid (Dip)	Pickle from metal Residue left by abrasives on an enameled surface

338

CLEANING METHODS	FORMULA	TO REMOVE
Water	Cold water (Rinse)	Pickle from metal
		Powdered rouge from metal
	Heat (Immerse)	Burned pitch from metal
	Repeat if necessary	
	Hot water (Rinse)	Remaining pickle following cold water rinse
	Hot water and strong soap powder (Rub with soft brush)	Oil and loose particles of wax from wax pattern
	Hot water (Immerse)	Oil left on metal from tripoli cake or rouge stick
	Washing soda, small amount of ammonia	
	As above (Scrub with stiff brush)	Oil in recessed parts
Kerosene	Any grade of kerosene (Rub with cloth or stiff brush)	Pitch from warm metal
Alcohol	Pure or denatured alcohol (Rub or soak if necessary)	Dry shellac from metal
		Shellac, alcohol, dye solution from metal
		Oil from metal before transferring design with carbon paper
Paraffin	Melted paraffin (Brush with stiff brush)	Pitch or jeweler's cement from warm metal

CLEANING METHODS	TOOLS	TO REMOVE
Filing	File	Burrs, scratches, tool marks, and solder
Scraping	Scraper	
Burnishing	Burnisher (Rub)	Tool marks, and dullness from the metal

CLEANING METHODS	ABRASIVES	TO REMOVE
Buffing	Felt buffing wheel (Buff)	Scratches or irregularities on flat or rounded surfaces
Polishing	Tripoli cake	
	Bristle buffing wheel charged with tripoli cake (Buff)	For recessed parts
	Soft cloth or chamois buffing wheel charged with rouge (Buff)	For high polish
	Corundum stone and water (Rub)	Discoloration at the edge of an enameled surface
	Scotch stone and water (Rub)	Scratches on metal
	Emery cloth (Rub)	Scratches and tool marks
		Fire scale, lead particles which adhere to a surface hammered on lead
	Pumice powder (Rub)	Scratches and tool marks
		Oil from metal surface
	Ink eraser (Rub)	Tool marks and scratches during the carving process
	Whiting powder (Rub)	Oxidation after coloring

PREPARATION AND CARE OF TOOLS AND MATERIALS

Tools often have to be mounted in handles, ground, tempered, and sharpened, before they are ready for use. Many have to be cleaned and oiled during the working processes. It is also necessary to keep them from scratching and chipping one another when put away. Some tools and materials are affected by dust and certain material deteriorates in light and air. Acids must be handled and stored with special care.

THE GRAVER

The graver and the handle come separately. The graver has to be made shorter and inserted in the handle, ground, and sharpened before it is ready for use.

Tools	Bench vise
and	Mallet
Working	Polishing motor
Materials	Emery wheel
	Ruler
	Scratch awl
	Oil stone—hard
	Light oil
	Cloth dampened with kerosene

PROCESSES

Breaking	Place the graver in the bench vise with the un-
off the	tempered or pointed end extending above the
End	jaws of the vise about one inch.
	Break this end off with a mallet.
	Remove from the vise.

PROCESSES

Pointing and Tempering the End

Grind the end to a tapered point; dip in water at intervals. During the final grinding let the end become hot enough to turn a straw color.

Dip immediately in water to harden. This prevents the end just ground from bending when forced into the wooden handle.

Joining the Handle to the Graver

Place the blade in the vise with the pointed end one inch above the jaws of the vise.

Drive the wooden handle on the pointed end with the mallet. The blade must fit firmly in the center of the handle.

Remove from the vise.

Holding the Tool for Measuring

Hold the tool in the right hand.

Let the handle rest in the palm of the hand on the joints of the second and third fingers.

Close the hand so the blade rests on the second joint of the first finger and the fingers curve around the handle in toward the palm.

Place the ball of the thumb on the blade in the carving position as shown in Fig. 21.

Scratch a line on the blade about 3/4 inch beyond the end of the thumb.

Shortening the Graver

Place the blade in the jaws of the bench vise with the scratched line even with the upper edge of the jaw.

Break off the end which extends above the vise with a mallet.

Place the emery wheel on the motor.

Holding the Tool While Grinding

Hold the tool in the right hand.

Press the further end of the tool against the emery wheel with the first two fingers of the left hand.

Grinding
the
Blade

Grind the end of the blade on the emery wheel to a 45° angle. This is the cutting angle for gold, silver, and copper and other materials of the same hardness. This angle is cut greater if the material is harder and less if the material to be cut is softer.

Move the tool from side to side to prevent grooving the wheel.

Grinding discolors the end of the blade if the tool becomes too hot during the grinding. If this occurs grind off the discolored portion as the temper has been destroyed.

Sharpening
the
Blade
p. 88

Sharpen the blade on the oil stone.

Regrind the tool when the 45° angle is worn off.

THE OIL STONE

During the sharpening process not only the center of the stone but the whole surface should be used. After the gravers have been sharpened repeatedly grooves will be worn into the stone. When the grooves become too deep the stone can be ground smooth.

Tools
and
Working
Materials

Sheet of heavy glass
Emery powder 8/0
Ammonia
Hot water
Soft cloth

GRINDING THE OIL STONE

Grinding   Place 8/0 emery powder on the glass sheet.
Place the oil stone with the grooved side on
the emery and glass.
Grind the stone on the emery until the grooves
have been removed.

Washing   Wash in ammonia and water.
Rinse in hot water.
Dry with a soft cloth.
Always remove the oil from the stone before
putting away. Keep it in a covered container.

FILES

The file and handle come separately. Only the smaller files,
such as needle files, have the handle as part of the file.

A rack should be used to hold the large files when they are
put away as shown in Fig. 114. A small holder or partitioned
box can be used for the smaller files. The teeth of the files will
become dull if allowed to rub on each other or other steel tools.

Tools   Bench vise
and   Brace and bit
Working   Wooden mallet
Materials   Chalk
File brush

PROCESSES

Holding   Select the proper size handle for the file.
Place the wooden handle in the jaws of the
bench vise with the flat side up.

PROCESSES

Drilling   Drill a hole in the center of the handle.

Mounting   Place the point of the tang into the hole drilled
                          for it.
                          Drive the tang into the handle with a mallet
                          until it reaches the shoulder of the file.

Chalking   Rub the teeth of the file with chalk. This helps
                          to keep the teeth clean.

Cleaning   Clean files with a file brush if the teeth become
                          clogged with metal filings. Files should be put
                          away clean.

STEEL HAMMERS AND STEEL STAKES

All working surfaces of the hammer and stake should be free from dents, scratches, and grit. A rack as shown in Fig. 114 should be used to hold them and protect their polished surfaces from scratches. To remove scratches or dents use coarse to fine abrasives depending upon the depth of the mark. Deep scratches or dents should be removed as follows: Place the stake or hammer in the vise. File in the lengthwise direction of the scratch or dent until the depth has been reached. Follow with corundum wheel, emery cloth, coarse to fine, felt buffing wheel and tripoli cake, and cloth buffing wheel and rouge.

STEEL BURNISHER

Keep the burnisher well polished with chamois cloth and rouge. Wrap in a chamois cloth when not in use.

DRAW PLATES

Dip draw plates in kerosene occasionally and keep in a clean drawer

POLISHING MOTOR

Keep the motor clean and well oiled.

BLOW TORCH

The blow torch becomes clogged with carbon if the yellow flame is left on for any length of time.

ENAMELS

Enamels may be kept in chunks in covered boxes.

Powdered enamel should be kept in well-corked and labeled bottles. If dry, it can be kept for a long time. Enamel kept under water deteriorates in a short time.

BUFFS

Buffs which are used for different abrasives should be kept in separate containers and away from dust and dirt.

POTASSIUM SULPHIDE

Potassium sulphide is purchased in lump form and is yellow. It must be kept in a tightly covered can or dark bottle as it deteriorates in contact with air and somewhat in light. A quart or more of the solution may be kept ready for use. Keep in a covered jar.

CUTTLE-BONE

Keep in a covered container to prevent them from becoming brittle and dry.

SOLDERING NEST

Coil and twist light iron binding wire together to form a nest. Hammer slightly in the center. Bend four heavy wires over the nest and twist them together under the nest to form a handle as shown in Fig. 11.

PICKLE PAN

Keep the pickle pan free of pickle when not in use.

PICKLE

A quart or more of pickle may be mixed in a porcelain or earthenware pitcher ready for use (1 part acid, 10 parts water). *Acid must be poured into the water.*

GAUGES

Gauges are tools used to measure the thickness of metal and wire. The one commonly used by American gold and silversmiths is the Brown and Sharpe gauge. For steel wire and drill stock the American Steel Wire gauge is used. Gauges are made of metal carefully scaled to measure to .1, .01, .001 of an inch. The number designating the gauge appears on one side of the scale, as 18-gauge, and the decimal equivalent on the opposite side.

To measure the thickness of metal sheet or the diameter of wire, slip the slot in the gauge nearest the thickness over the metal and read the gauge number, as 18-gauge, or the decimal equivalent, if desired. Transposing from one standard to another can be done by use of the figures given in the comparative table (p. 347). Closer measurements, when required, can be obtained by using the micrometer.

The gauge numbers referred to in this book for various metals are measured by: The Brown and Sharpe gauge for gold and silver, American Steel Wire or Washburn and Moen gauge for drill stock.

COMPARATIVE TABLE OF DIFFERENT STANDARDS FOR SHEET-METAL AND WIRE GAUGES

NUMBER OF GAUGE	AMERICAN OR BROWN & SHARPE	AMERICAN STEEL AND WIRE COMPANY OR WASHBURN & MOEN MFG. CO.	BIRMINGHAM METAL GAUGE	BIRMINGHAM OR STUBS WIRE GAUGE
1	.2893	.2830	.0085	.300
2	.25763	.2625	.0095	.284
3	.22942	.2437	.0105	.259
4	.20431	.2253	.0120	.238
5	.18194	.2070	.0140	.220
6	.16202	.1920	.016	.203
7	.14428	.1770	.019	.180
8	.12849	.1620	.0215	.165
9	.11443	.1483	.024	.148
10	.10189	.1350	.028	.134
11	.090742	.1205	.032	.120
12	.080808	.1055	.035	.109
13	.071961	.0915	.038	.095
14	.064084	.0800	.043	.083
15	.057068	.0720	.048	.072
16	.05082	.0625	.051	.065
17	.045257	.0540	.055	.058
18	.040303	.0475	.059	.049
19	.03589	.0410	.062	.042
20	.031961	.0348	.065	.035
21	.028462	.0317	.069	.032
22	.025347	.0286	.073	.028
23	.022571	.0258	.077	.025
24	.0201	.0230	.082	.022
25	.0179	.0204	...	.020
26	.01594	.0181	...	.018
27	.014195	.0173	...	.016
28	.012641	.0162	...	.014
29	.011257	.0150	...	.013
30	.010025	.0140	...	.012

Example of use of table: Given gauge No. 20 on the Brown & Sharpe Gauge, which measures .031961, find the nearest decimal equivalent to .031961 on the Washburn & Moen Gauge which is found to be .0317 for which the corresponding gauge No. is 21.

Courtesy of Camp Hanoum, Thetford, Vt.

Fig. 109.—Camp Workshop

THE WORKSHOP

Jewelry can be made in a comparatively small shop simply equipped. It is better to start with minimum essential tools than to expose the beginner to a lot of tools which will not be used for the simpler problems.

For classes of sixteen people eight benches which will accommodate two persons are required. For general work purposes a work bench, table sink, buffing machine, enameling oven, draw bench, book case, table, storage cupboards are necessary. Work space may be enlarged by adding individual benches, or reduced in size, but the general equipment should remain the same. An electric motor can be substituted for the buffing machine. The aisles

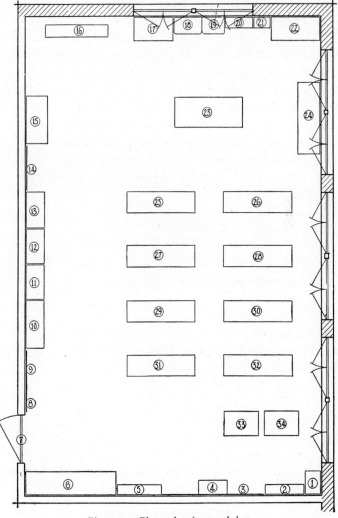

Fig. 110.—Floor plan for workshop

Scale: ⅛ inch = 1 foot

between the benches must be at least two and a half feet to allow for easy passing, an open area near the door. The light should come from the left of the worker if possible.

The benches in a camp shop may seat several workers and may be built parallel to the side openings if the shop is surrounded with trees or shrubs to soften the glare of the summer sun. The side walls of the shop may open up to form an awning for protection as shown in Fig. 109. Shadow boxes of asbestos can be used to shelter the flame of the torches when necessary.

Work bench and storage cupboards and a floor plan for a shop to accommodate sixteen persons are illustrated in Figs. 110, 111, 112, 113, and 114. Groups may use this shop alternately.

1. File case.
2. Book shelves.
3. Corkboard.
4. Glass show case.
5. Cupboard with shelves.
6. Closet with rod for coat hangers.
7. Entrance door.
8. Cork bulletin board.
9. Blackboard.
10. Drawer closet (See Fig. 111).
11. Tool closet (See Fig. 114).
12. Storage closet (See Fig. 113).
13. Storage closet (See Fig. 113).
14. Blackboard.
15. Enameling muffler.
16. Draw bench.
17. Cupboard the height of the sink with acid- and heat-resistant top.
18. Sink.
19. Drainboard, cupboard, and shelves below.
20. Shelf.
21. Cupboard with shelves.

22. Polishing motor.
23. Stationary bench.
24. Table.
25-32. Work benches (See Fig. 112).
33. Table.
34. Desk.

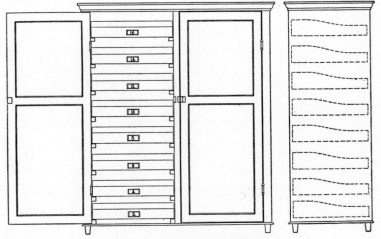

Fig. 111.—Individual tool drawers

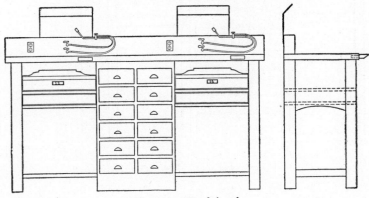

Fig. 112.—Work bench

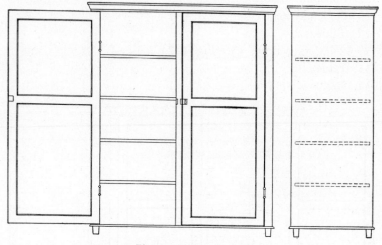

Fig. 113.—Storage closet

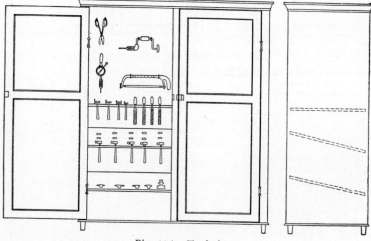

Fig. 114.—Tool closet

GLOSSARY

ABRASIVE—A substance used to rub or wear away a surface.

ADJUST—To arrange, to fit, or to place in a position for operation.

ANNEAL—To make metal soft and pliable by heating.

APPLIQUÉ—The process of cutting out a piece or pattern from one material and laying it upon and attaching it to another.

ASSEMBLE—To fit and join together into usable form.

BANGLE—An ornamental circlet of metal or other material.

BASSETAILLE—A method of applying enamel, similar to champlevé.

BEARING—The edge of the flange inside the bezel which supports or bears the setting.

BEZEL—The collar of metal that holds the stone or gem.

BENCH PIN—A wedge-shaped block of wood affixed to a bench to support work during sawing or filing.

BINDING WIRE—Annealed iron wire used to hold parts together during the soldering process.

BORAX SLATE—A slab of slate containing a saucer-like hollow in which prepared borax or borum junk is rubbed in water to form flux.

BOX—A bezel formed by a separate strip shaped and soldered on the piece of jewelry to frame and hold the setting.

BRACELET—A band of metal or interwoven links of wire made to fit the arm or wrist.

BROOCH—An ornamental clasp provided with a pin or other means of fastening.

BUFF—To polish by light friction.

BURNISH—To make smooth and bright.

BURNISHER—A pointed steel tool with oval section used for burnishing.

353

CABOCHON—A term used to describe a stone curved in contour, polished, but not faceted.

CASTING—Shaping objects by pouring or forcing molten metal into a form or mold.

CHAMOIS—A soft leather made from the skin of the chamois.

CHAMPLEVÉ—A method of fusing enamel into sunken surfaces in the metal.

CHARCOAL BLOCK—A block of chemically prepared charcoal, used to hold metal for soldering, annealing, and melting.

CHASING TOOLS—Steel implements with rounded ends similar to dull chisels, used to trace lines on surfaces of metal.

CLASP—A catch or a hook used as a fastener.

CLOISONNÉ—A process of enameling by laying out boundaries of flat wire and then filling between with the paste colors.

COIL—To twist or form wire and similar material spirally, cylindrically, or in a series of rings.

COLLAR—A metal band used for various construction purposes.

CONTOUR—The sectional form or outline of a figure or object.

CONVENTIONAL—A formalized or geometric representation of a natural or other object.

COSTUME JEWELRY—Necklaces, bracelets, buttons, clips, buckles, chains, earrings made to be used as accessories for costumes in the prevailing mode.

COTTER PIN—A small strip of iron formed into a clamp to hold parts together for soldering.

CRADLE—A sheet iron or nickel form bent and perforated to hold the enameled article in the furnace during the firing process. See Fig. 50.

CUTTERS—Dapping die cutters, tools for stamping out thin disks of metal on a lead block.

CUTTLE-BONE—A material used to make molds in which rings and other articles can be cast.

CRUCIBLE—A clay pot used for melting metals.

DAPPING—A soft tapping or pounding.

DAPPING BLOCKS—Solid lead blocks used for various cutting and stamping processes.

DAPPING DIES—Metal blocks containing convex depressions of various curves and sizes, into which thin pieces of metal can be dapped into rounded contours.

DAPPING DIE CUTTERS—Metal tools with tube-like cutting ends used to stamp out disks of thin metal on a lead or wooden block.

DAPPING PUNCHES—Domed steel tools used to dap hemispherical forms.

DENTIMETRE—A small handle in which wire can be held when measuring the circumference or girdle of a stone. See Fig. 57.

DIVIDERS—A steel instrument like a compass used to inscribe circles and divide lines.

DRAW PLATE—A flat piece of hardened steel pierced with holes in graduated sizes used to reduce the size or change the shape of wire.

DRAW TONGS—Pliers having one handle hook-shaped to permit a firmer grasp.

ENAMEL—A vitreous material applied by fusion to metals such as gold and copper, usually for purposes of decoration.

FILE—A flat steel tool with rough faces used to smooth surfaces or to wear them down by rubbing away with friction. *Riffle file*—A bar with file at either end with or without curved points, the center portion serving as a handle.

FILIGREE—Delicate jewelry with lace-like qualities.

FLANGE—A rib or rim for re-enforcement set inside a bezel to form a bearing for the setting.

FLUX—Any substance which is used to aid the fusion of metals.

FUNNEL—A small cone-shaped passage through which molten metal is carried to the mold.

FINE SILVER—Pure silver free of alloy which melts at a higher temperature than sterling silver.

GAUGE—A term used to denote the thickness of plate or wire.

GIRDLE—The greatest circumference of a stone.

GRAVERS—Tools for carving or making fine lines and engraving.

HAND DRILL—A holder for the drill shank, often equipped with gears and shank to operate by hand.

HOTTEST FLAME—The point of the flame of the blow torch just above the tip of the oxygen cone, where the flame is the hottest.

INLAY—To lay or insert one piece of material in another, the finished surfaces of the parts being flush.

INTERLINKED—United together as are units of a chain.

INTERWOVEN—Woven together, or intermingled.

INVESTMENT—A plastic substance in which a pattern is placed to form a mold to be used for casting.

INVESTMENT FLASK—A brass cylinder fitting around the collar of the sprue former and encasing the investment.

K.—Abbreviation for the word karat.

KARAT—A unit of weight for gems or a standard measuring purity of metals as gold.

LIMOGE—The process used for pictorial work of painting on metal without a retaining wall.

LIVER OF SULPHUR—See potassium sulphide.

MANDREL—An axis or spindle of metal, sometimes slightly tapered to a point, used for shaping rings, links of a chain, or other bands of metal.

MELTING FLAME—The part of the flame of the blow torch just above the tip of the oxygen cone.

MOTIF—The theme or dominant feature of a design.

MUFFLE—An oven, ordinarily of clay and of half cylindrical form, used in operations that do not require direct heat.

OIL STONE—A smooth stone on which, when moistened with oil, tools are sharpened.

ONGLETTE—A point graver, sharply pointed.

OPAQUE—Permitting no passage of light.

OXIDIZE—To unite chemically with oxygen for the purpose of coloring.

PAVED—A term used to describe a setting sunken flush with the surface of the design. See Fig. 62.

PICKLE—A specified mixture of water and a given acid used to clean metal.

PIERCING—Cutting out portions of a solid background, leaving the design in the metal.

PITCH—A prepared pitch in which articles are embedded during the processes of embossing, chasing, hammering, etc.

PITCH BOWL—A cast iron bowl into which pre-pared pitch is poured when ready for use.

PLIERS—Steel tools with snub, round, or pointed jaws used to hold or to shape parts.

PLIQUE À JOUR—A system of applying enamel by placing the colored paste in the cells of fretwork, as of filigree or pierced metal, and then fusing it.

POLISHING MOTOR—A machine or hand tool fashioned for light friction or buffing.

POTASSIUM SULPHIDE—Commercially known as liver of sul-phur, a substance used to color metals.

PRIMITIVE ORNAMENT—Decoration that has the simplicity, crudity, rudeness, or other characteristics of primitive and aboriginal peoples.

PUMICE—A volcanic stone in powdered form used for cleaning and buffing.

PUSHER—A stone-setting tool consisting of a small steel rod of square section, inserted in a round-shaped handle, used to push bezels or the points of crown settings around a stone.

RAISE—To raise is to fashion a piece of metal into shape by beating or pounding.

RAWHIDE—Untanned skin of cattle.

REAMER—A tool with a cutting edge which is employed to enlarge holes.

RECESS—An indentation in a line, surface, or mass.

REDUCING FLAME—The point of the flame of a blow torch lying about one-half inch from the tip of the oxygen cone, a trifle farther than the melting flame, at which point the heat is not so intense although hot enough to keep the metal molten.

REPOUSSÉ—The process of beating from the back to raise the design.

RING CLAMP—A device composed of two semi-conical members held together by a metal band.

RING SIZES—A series of graduated rings, clustered on a band and marked with standard ring sizes to measure fingers.

ROUGE—A red mineral powder mixed into a paste with water used to protect solder or metal from excessive heat during the soldering process.

ROUGE STICK—A buffing composition used for polishing.

SAMPLER—A project to demonstrate the employment of various tools, processes, methods, techniques, etc.

SCORING—Indenting or incising the surface.

SCOTCH STONE—Bars of prepared stone, used with water as an abrasive.

SCRATCH AWL—An awl made with a sharp, tapered point used for laying out work.

SHELLAC—An orange resinous flake substance used, as a rule, to hold articles in place for carving and setting of stones.

SHELLAC MOUNTING STICK—A tool consisting of a wooden disk with a handle on the flat surface of which shellac is melted.

SHANK—The band of a ring which fits around the finger.

SOCKET—A ring or hollow tube used to receive the catch of a clasp or fastener.

SPINDLE—A tapered and threaded shaft or axle attached to a motor to hold buffing and grinding wheels.

SPLIT MANDREL—A mandrel with a sawed slit in which wire may be inserted.

SPRUE HOLE—A hole through which metal is poured into the mold.

SPRUE PIN—The pin which holds the wax pattern in position in the investment.

SPRUE FORMER—A metal base to which the sprue pin is attached.

STAKE—A steel rod with highly polished surface upon which metal is hammered into shape.

STERLING—A standard of silver requiring 925 parts of silver to 75 of alloy.

STONE LIFTER—A prepared wax used to raise or lift a setting from its collar while fitting it to its bezel.

STONING—A process of rubbing with scotch stone.

TEMPLATE—A gauge, mold, or pattern, frequently formed of cardboard or thin plate, used as a guide in mechanical work.

TRAGACANTH—A flake gum mixed with warm water to form a paste.

TRANSFERRING—To carry from one thing to another.

TRANSLUCENT—Transmitting light imperfectly.

TRANSPARENT—Allowing light to be presented almost perfectly.

TRIPOLI CAKE—A commercially prepared form of an abrasive stone known as tripoli.

TWIST DRILL—A cutting tool used for boring in a hard substance as metal. The tool is driven by machine or hand.

VENTS—A small flue or air passage to release air or gases.

VIBRATE—To move to and fro rather rapidly.

WHITING—A white powdered chalk used for polishing.

WOODEN CORE—A solid block or cylinder of wood used to hold a coil of wire for sawing.

BIBLIOGRAPHY

METALWORK AND ENAMELLING, by Herbert Maryon, 317 pp. London: Chapman and Hall, Ltd., 1912.

Three hundred and thirty-three line drawings by Cyril Pearce together with many plates contribute to the presentation of the constructional and technical elements of design as well as of the artistic and aesthetic details. Various chapters treat of tools, materials, soldering, stone setting, repoussé, spinning, enameling, and wire work. Enameling together with alloys of various kinds is discussed as are processes and tools. A generous number of tables on gauges, composition of alloys, standards of weights, etc., is supplied.

This is, as the author states, a practical treatise on the craft of the gold and silversmith, and an excellent one.

SILVERWORK AND JEWELRY, by H. Wilson, illustrated with diagrams by the author. New York: D. Appleton and Company. New enlarged and revised.

This book is for the craftsman and the person who is learning to create in metal. It discusses operations, processes, and tools. Many cuts illustrate designs, tools, and methods. The second edition has new sections written in collaboration with Prof. Unno Biser of the Fine Arts College, Tokyo; among these are descriptions of Egyptian and Oriental methods of work.

JEWELRY MAKING AND DESIGN, by Augustus F. Rose and Antonio Cirino, B.S. Providence, R. I.: Metal Crafts Publishing Co., 1917.

The first section of this book presents twenty chapters on jewelry making, stone cutting, gold, silver, weights and processes involved in jewelry making, and articles of jewelry including methods of ornamentation.

The second section is devoted to analysis of jewelry design, rendering, and the application of design to various types of jewelry.

METALCRAFT AND JEWELRY, by Emil F. Kronquest, 180 pp. Peoria, Ill.: Manual Arts Press, 1926.

The eleven chapters are devoted to discussions and classifications of processes, tools, and materials and are illustrated with 175 line drawings and photographs.

THE STORY OF THE GEMS, by Herbert P. Whitlock, 200 pp. New York: Lee Furman, Inc., 1936.

In these sixteen chapters there are authoritatively presented discussion of stones, gems, and semi-precious stones as well as organic products used as gems. The weighing of stones and antique uses of gems are interestingly discussed and the numerous plates, two in color, add to the volume's attractiveness.

JEWELRY, GEM CUTTING, AND METALCRAFT, by W. T. Baxter, 212 pp. New York and London: Whittlesey House, McGraw-Hill Book Co., Inc., 1938. Revised and enlarged, 1950.

Primarily for the craftsman at home and for the student, it is arranged in two main divisions; the first containing discussions of various metals, soldering, etching, tools, etc.; the second part deals with jewelry making, soldering, blow torches; it lists the operations required in ring making and includes photos and diagrams of stone setting, necklaces, pendants, earrings, etc. Methods of identifying and classifying stones and material on gem cutting as well as a list of dealers arranged according to their particular line are also given.

THE CURIOUS LORE OF PRECIOUS STONES, by George Frederick Kunz. New York: Halcyon House. Seventh printing, 1938.

A delightful book for those who enjoy color and beauty in gems and are intrigued by the poetry and tradition of them.

Together with 86 illustrations in line, halftone, and color, the eleven chapters present traditions and superstitions of stones, birth stones, crystal balls, talismans, etc.

NAVAJO SILVER; A Brief History of Navajo Silversmithing, by Arthur Woodward. Field Notes by Richard Van Valkenburgh. . . . 76 pp. Bulletin No. 14. Museum of Northern Arizona, Flagstaff, Arizona. 1938. Northern Arizona Society of Science and Art.

Fifty-six pages of this small volume are given to six chapters of varied length. Twenty more pages contain miscellaneous data, from various sources, concerning Navajo smithing; list of Navajo smiths, 1850-1900; Navajo words referring to metal crafts, etc.

The six chapters present a history of the silver craft; its probable origin and introduction, about 1830, to the tribe; a discussion of the metal workers whose ability influenced the red men; the various ornaments including pendants, buttons, bracelets; the source of turquoise and silver, as well as later day tendencies to sham and imitation.

There are fourteen illustrations of Navajo silver, chiefly photographic. It is an interesting book for any reader of American history, arts, crafts or folk-lore, and particularly valuable for students of design.

THE NAVAJO AND PUEBLO SILVERSMITHING, by John Adair, 220 pp. Norman University of Oklahoma Press, 1944.

A fascinating story of the somewhat modern art of silvercraft among the aborigines of our southwest. Not only is it generous in historical data but it contains many suggestions for both the design and process of silvercraft. Numerous and excellent photographic illustrations give added value.

The appendix contains a list of Hopi, Navajo and Zuni silversmiths, an interesting tribute to these little known artists. A volume that is both good reading and good study.

RINGS THROUGH THE AGES. An Informal History, by James
Remington McCarthy, 202 pp. New York and London: Harper
and Bros., 1945.

> *An entertaining volume in many places humorous yet valuable
> to the artist and designer as well as to the craftsman especially
> if he is interested in jewelry.*
> *There are countless vignettes of legend and history as seen
> through the finger ring.*

HAND MADE JEWELRY, by Louis Wiener, 200 pp. Toronto,
New York, London: D. Van Nostrand Company, Inc., 1948.

> *A manual of techniques. In addition to the Introduction and
> seventeen chapters, there is an Appendix containing sugges-
> tions for a practical shop both in plan and essential equip-
> ment; tests and tables; 110 or 115 illustrations and figures,
> both line and photographic, showing jewelry designs as well
> as tools and processes. The volume is attractive and is a simple
> and practical reference book for craftsmen.*

CHAINS AND BEADS, by Greta Pack, 200 pp. New York,
London, Toronto: D. Van Nostrand Company, Inc., 1951.

> *A work manual of chains and beads, along the line of the
> same author's JEWELRY AND ENAMELING. The work-
> ing drawings and descriptive text can be followed easily by the
> person who understands the basic processes of jewelry work.
> The book contains twenty-eight plates of line drawings and
> six photographs showing the combination of chains, units and
> beads. The appendices include a table of wire gauge standards
> and sources of supplies.*

ENAMELING ON METAL, by Louis-Elie Millenet, 112 pp.
New York and Toronto: D. Van Nostrand Company, Inc., 1951.

> *This is a compact little volume confined to discussion of sub-
> ject matter indicated by its title. Its reading necessitates a
> concentration usually required by translations. H. de Koningh,
> the translator from its original French and the author of "The*

Preparation of Precious and other Metal Work for Enameling," has included many brief or sentence explanations which clarify terms and phrases.

The author is one of a long line of artists and authorities in the art of enameling and a feeling of definite authority pervades his descriptions, rules, directions. At the time of translation, the author was devoting his entire time to the manufacture of enamels and colors.

ENAMELING, PRINCIPLES AND PRACTICE, by Kenneth F. Bates, 208 pp. Cleveland and New York: World Publishing Co., 1951.

The author, instructor in design at Cleveland School of Art since 1927, in this volume presents ten chapters as well as the Appendix which includes Glossary, Bibliography, Index and more than 125 illustrations, line and photographic, four being in color. The context includes history, materials, processes of enameling and national types. Descriptions of old designs and often their uses and development are given as well as tables, lists of supply houses, glossary, bibliography.

THE PREPARATION OF PRECIOUS AND OTHER METAL WORK FOR ENAMELLING, by H. de Koningh, 76 pp. New York: D. Van Nostrand Company, Inc. Undated.

Having stated that processes employed by enamellers when men first began to decorate metal with glass have changed little throughout the ages, the author describes how best to prepare various choice metals for different types of enameling and he also discusses, briefly, current soldering, casting, their designs, constructions, as well as their faults and failures. It is a valuable little manual for the specialist in preparing metal as for those who adorn the metal with enameling. Several illustrations from photographs are rather too small to be of great use.

THE ART OF THE LAPIDARY, by Francis J. Sperisen, 382 pp.
The Bruce Publishing Company, Milwaukee, Wisconsin, 1953.

These twelve chapters contain a discussion and illustrations in the art of classifying gems, through physical and optical characteristics. Two chapters are devoted to cutting and polishing stones and the various steps in doing the actual work. The entire book is well illustrated with drawings of tools and equipment and operations in preforming lapidary work, carefully written and not difficult to follow.

Reference lists and tables, Vocabulary and glossary, bibliography and index are included.

INDEX

367